# UP THE CREEK

A lifetime spent trying to be a sailor

*For Vivienne, Tim and Sophie*

*with my love*

# UP THE CREEK

A lifetime spent trying to be a sailor

Tony James

SEAFARER BOOKS
SHERIDAN HOUSE

© Tony James 2006

*First published in the UK by*
Seafarer Books
102 Redwald Road
Rendlesham
Woodbridge
Suffolk IP12 2TE
www.seafarerbooks.com

*And in the USA by*
Sheridan House Inc.
145 Palisade Street
Dobbs Ferry
NY 10522
www.sheridanhouse.com

UK ISBN   0 9547062 7 7
USA ISBN 1 57409 222 7

British Library Cataloguing in Publication Data
James, Tony
  Up the Creek : a lifetime spent trying to be a sailor
  1.James, Tony 2.Sailors – Great Britain – Biography
  3.Sailing – Anecdotes
  I.Title
  797 .1 '24 '092

  ISBN-10: 0954706277

A CIP catalog record for this book is available from the Library of
Congress, Washington, DC

Edited by Hugh Brazier
Typesetting and design by Julie Rainford
Cover design by Louis Mackay
Drawings by Trevor Ridley
Front-cover photo by George Ody Photography, Minehead
Photographs from the author's private collection, except where
otherwise credited

Printed in Finland by WS Bookwell OY

# CONTENTS

# FOREWORD

The first time I met Tony James it could have ended in a punch-up. We had arranged to meet in a pub in a village on the edge of the Quantocks – as you do. Although we had spoken on the telephone often enough about the great series of articles that he was writing for my magazine, *Traditional Boats and Tall Ships*, this was to be our first meeting.

I had told Tony that I would be sitting in the bar with my wife and that he should look out for a chap in his fifties with a beard and wearing glasses. My wife and I had been sitting in the pub for about ten minutes when a cove came over and said that he hoped that I was Stephen Swann because he had just gone up to a man who fitted the description, slapped him on the back, and uttered the words: 'You are Stephen Swann and I claim my £5.' The chap had apologised for not being Stephen Swann, and after he too had apologised Tony beat a hasty retreat.

As I got to know Tony as a friend I came to regard that first meeting as somehow typical of the man. You see, Tony is, it seems to me, ever so slightly out of sync with the world – in the nicest possible way, you understand. He is a man who finds life both amusing and bemusing, often at the same time: it is a combination that results in an individual whose company is always a delight and whose writing is a joy.

Tony is a writer by trade. During the course of a long career that has taken him from local to national newspapers and now sees him working freelance, he has written on just about every subject under the sun. He has enough nom de plumes to fill a telephone directory and has ghosted more books than you could shake a boathook at. Yet aside from a £1.25 book called *Boating on a Budget* published some thirty years ago, this is the first 'proper' book under his own name. Don't ask me why. If I could write only half as well as Tony, Waterstone's shelves would be groaning under the weight of books by yours truly. Still, my contribution to the literature of sailing will be that I 'discovered' Tony James, the book author.

It happened like this. One day Tony rang up to ask me if I would mind reading 'half a book' that he had written. I said only on condition that it contained a lot of sex and violence. He replied that it didn't but that it did contain a lot of gratuitous sailing. I couldn't refuse. Well, that half a book turned out to be very good indeed. I told Tony that if he had any sense he would find a publisher and if he didn't I would find one for him. Well, as it turned out that is just what I finished up doing. I sent Tony's half-a-book to Seafarer, they liked it and took it on – the only trouble was they insisted on having the other half. Tony duly obliged.

He had written a kind of sailing memoir. Now, sailing memoirs, with one or two exceptions, fade from the memory quicker than the wake behind an Essex smack. Not to put too fine a point on it, most of them bore me rigid. In fact, given the option of reading your average memoir or, say, a three-volume tome on the evolution of the double sister-block, 1756–1762, I would unhesitatingly opt for the latter – it would be more enthralling. I say that Tony had written 'a kind of sailing memoir'. That phrase needs explaining. Of course, there are lots of boats and sailing a-plenty, and a host of great, not to say slightly barking, characters, but there is also a more personal strand running through the book as well. It is subtitled 'a lifetime spent trying to be a sailor', the inference being that the author has not yet managed it. Tony is a sailor, make no mistake about that. Not that you would ever get him to admit it: being good at something is just not funny. And, above all, *Up the Creek* is laugh-out-loud funny. That humour derives from any number of sources, but if I had to pick out a couple, one would be the author's ability to laugh at himself – he has taken self-mockery to new depths

– and another would be his highly tuned antennae for the absurdities of everyday speech and the banalities of life – especially the sailing life.

In short, *Up the Creek* is unlike any other sailing memoir that you have read. It is a modern, one is tempted to say post-modern, take on the genre and is destined to become a classic. Enjoy.

STEPHEN SWANN
*Dorchester*
*September 2005*

# ACKNOWLEDGEMENTS

All the events described in this book are true and I have only changed the names of one or two characters to save any slight embarrassment.

My grateful thanks, for all their help, to Patricia Eve of Seafarer Books and to her colleagues Hugh Brazier, Louis Mackay, Julie Rainford and Trevor Ridley. Sincere thanks also, for their support, to Sarah Broadhurst, Don Sutherland and Martin Hesp.

Special thanks are due to my good friend, and East Coast icon, Stephen Swann, to the utterly indispensable John Nash, and to Vivienne for her relentless editing and loving support.

I am indebted to all the sailing folk whose stories bring the book to life and, in particular, to the lads – nothing would have been the same without them. Thanks, finally, to everyone who gave me their views and advice on the book, but I went ahead and wrote it anyway.

CHAPTER 1

# Around the world with Captain Lumbers

When I went home and said I was sailing round the world, my mother said I should remember I had a rupture and my father reminded me I couldn't do geometry and had been sick in a rowing boat on a boating lake in Nottingham. I heard him walking around the house singing 'Barnacle Bill the Sailor' but then, as he was doing a Masonic exam in Leicester, he had more important things to think about.

You couldn't blame them. I was eighteen and had never shown the remotest interest in the sea; indeed I had only seen it once during a family holiday in Skegness. Four sports masters had failed to teach me to swim (my mother gave me a note saying I had heavy bones), I had read Conrad and W.W. Jacobs and remained unimpressed and Hornblower seemed a twerp. Like New Orleans jazz, pigeon-breeding, church architecture and unattainable married typists at work, this sudden nautical preoccupation seemed to my parents to be yet another ephemeral fad intended to disturb them. 'The sooner that lad goes in the army the better,' my father said to my mother. 'I'm fed up with him upsetting you.'

There had never been any seafaring in my family. My father, the manager of a sawmill in Derbyshire, came from a long line of hosiery-workers and greengrocers and my mother's father was a country stationmaster on a London North Eastern Railway branch-line. He played the organ in a local church and believed, without any apparent justification, that he was the heir to a long-extinct Derbyshire peerage.

My father's name was Albert but he was always known as Jimmy or Jamie. Outside the house he was popular, with a wide circle of friends and much admired as a raconteur. He spoke slowly and deliberately with long pauses before speaking and, like Doctor Johnson, whom he slightly resembled, prefaced most of his sentences with a drawn-out 'Why...' But inside the house he seldom spoke except to ask the times of meals, which he usually ate separately from my mother, whose name was Phyllis, my sister Geraldine, and me. His solitary meals seemed to consist largely of cold meats and tomatoes sprayed with vinegar, and when we had roast dinners he preferred the fat and red meat while the rest of us ate the lean. We had the radio on to counteract the silence of family meals. On Sundays it was the *Billy Cotton Band Show* and *Family Favourites*.

We lived in a house with a walled garden next to the timber yard in the middle of a small country town. A door in the garden wall gave access to the sawmill with its lethally unguarded circular saws and planing machines among which I wandered as a small boy, blissfully unaware of the danger, amid clouds of sawdust and flying chippings. Trees were brought into the timber yard by tractors and trailers and craned off into huge piles, on which I played with my friends, unaware that the trunks could slip and we could be killed. We pretended they were ships and castles and that the spaces between the trees were caves or the inside of whales. Industrial safety was unknown in those sunlit days and drama was everywhere in the sawmill. Pieces flew off machinery and sliced holes in the roof. Men cut themselves with axes, became trapped under heavy planks and were knocked unconscious by the flailing handles of hand-wound cranes. But the silver blurs of the saw-blades were the biggest and ever-present menace.

One day when I was about nine I was sitting in the corner of my father's office when a sawyer from the lower mill came in, his hand wrapped in a piece of sacking. 'I've cut me thumb off in the circular saw,' he told my father. 'Could you take me up the infirmary?' My father shut a ledger and reached for his trilby. 'Have you got the thumb?' he asked. 'They can sometimes sew it on again.' Apparently it had been left where it fell, under the saw, and as we poked about in the sawdust another workman asked what we were looking for. 'You wunner find it,' he told us, 'I gen it the ferret.' When he came home for his tea my father never mentioned the incident and when my mother recounted my version he said I had made it up. Later I heard him tell the story many times to an appreciative circle of friends.

There was no doubt I was a disappointment to my father. I was poor at sport and mathematics, in which he excelled, and I had outspoken views on things l knew little about like religion and politics. Once when I raised my voice above the *Billy Cotton Band Show* to denounce the existence of God, there was a long pause before my father said, 'Why … a lot more important people than you believe in God, including the King and General Montgomery.' I held a grudge against General Montgomery from then on and greatly enjoyed the wartime newspaper headline:

'Monty Flies Back To Front.'

My father had lost interest in school when, in an art lesson, he was asked to draw a freehand straight line and drew it so straight that he was accused of cheating. A lifelong holder of grudges, he swore that in future he would never again subject himself to such indignity and in future would teach himself anything he wanted to know. At ten he was sent for a piano lesson, returned home saying 'I think I've got the hang of it now', and never went again. He taught himself to read sheet music well enough to play the accompaniments of Victorian ballads he sang at Masonic evenings and at military camps in a strong baritone. His singing was greatly admired but he seldom sang at home.

He also taught himself wood-carving and cabinet-making and restored furniture in a workshop in the garden. He favoured bulky dark sixteenth-century country furniture – chairs, chests and wardrobes which he found rotting in farm sheds and painstakingly rebuilt, concealing new wood with a mixture of creosote and brown boot polish. His prize find was an Elizabethan double wardrobe which had been cut down the middle and one half used as a rabbit hutch. The other half was found several years later by my father in a farm ten miles away. Joined together and lovingly restored, the wardrobe was sold by my mother on my father's death for a high price at auction. She said she had never liked it because it was 'too heavy'.

My father made things other than furniture, often staying in the workshop until late. A friend asked him to make a dog kennel but was unable to give a precise size.'How big's your dog?' asked my father. 'You've seen it running around,' said the man. 'It's a brown 'un.'

My father also bought an old van and converted it into what he called 'a bit of a shooting-brake', building on a beautifully jointed wooden body, lethally glazed with ordinary window glass. 'You can't do that, Jim,' said his friend John Mackay, a coal merchant. 'What if you had an accident?' 'Why, I'm not going to have one,' my father said.

Almost from my birth, my mother had been convinced that I was a sickly child, despite the assertions of the family doctor that although small and thin, there wasn't much wrong with me. From a book, inherited from her mother, called the *Medical Inquire Within,* she deduced that I had a rupture, weak lungs, and something called sunlight deficiency. As a result, she bought a small second-hand truss from a Methodist bring-and-buy sale, borrowed a primitive sunray lamp which blasted a sinister purple light onto my white bony back, and took me to the local gasworks to breathe the corrosive fumes of a heap of tar claimed to be good for respiratory troubles. Eventually noticing I had developed the complexion of a Bedouin, the doctor had the lamp sent back, forbade visits to the gasworks and threw the truss into his wastepaper basket.

From an early age I was aware that my parents were uneasy in my company. I was not the child they had wanted or expected and, taking advice from my father's friend John Mackay, they sent me at ten to a fourth-rate private boarding school some eight miles away, in the belief that I would learn to 'stand up for myself' and become what my father called 'a normal sort of youth'. It was a forlorn hope. My only interest at school was crossing off each day of term on a large calendar kept under the bed. The near-starvation diet gave me eczema, I created a school record by being beaten four times in one day, got a solitary O-level for English, and left two days after my sixteenth birthday. I vowed never to set foot in the place again and never have.

Back home my father didn't speak to me for several days, instead sending messages via my mother asking what I intended to do with my life as there was no place in the timber trade for someone who couldn't calculate a square root or even subtract two numbers. I sent a message back thanking him for his interest but as it happened I had a job already. I was starting the following week as a junior reporter on the *Derby Evening Telegraph*.

\*\*\*\*\*\*

Two years later, in the summer of 1953, still a junior reporter and finding most of the work unutterably dreary, something rather curious happened. I met a bad-tempered man repairing a rotting boat in a field alongside a canal and from then on things were never quite the same again. A man signing himself Derek Arthur George Lumbers had complained to the paper about an article I had written on a boat club he had started on the banks of the Trent and Mersey Canal on a piece of blighted Midlands landscape known as Swarkestone Bubble. He was twenty-six, an invoice clerk at the Derby Rolls Royce factory on the rare occasions he turned up, and was regularly threatened with the sack.

Derek Lumbers looked like a young and emaciated Dustin Hoffman and had recently destroyed his hearing in an explosion in the garden shed while making bullets for an illegal revolver a relative had stolen in the war. The club he had founded in a muddy creek consisted of a few shabby plywood cabin-cruisers, a leaking barge done out in Fablon, and former War Department bridge pontoons, converted by wiry pensioners into floating summer houses with French windows and silver-painted anchors. There was a lot of pipe-smoking, tying of bowlines and boiling water for tea, but no one seemed over-anxious to go anywhere.

I rode cautiously along the canal-side on my New Hudson autocycle one wet Wednesday afternoon to present the then-unknown complainant with a copy of a correction to my article, to be published the following day. It had been written to the news editor's dictation, and contained the mitigation: 'We trust the mistake has caused no personal inconvenience.' Even so, I was not looking forward to delivering it. The creek was deserted, apart from a man in wellingtons standing by a sad-looking yacht which was lying ashore in a nettle-filled ditch. He was cooking a pork chop on a piece of galvanised sheet heated by a blowlamp and I remember saying to myself, 'I don't like the look of you, you bugger,' which turned out to be one of my better character assessments.

When I introduced myself, Derek Lumbers seemed to have forgotten about his complaint and was more interested in talking about his yacht and his plans for sailing single-handed around the world, financed, he hoped, by possible compensation for a motorcycle accident. But even to someone knowing nothing of ships and the sea, this seemed not a very good idea. The boat was a 28-foot pre-war gaff-rigged Norfolk Broads yacht, built for sheltered waters and in such an advanced state of neglect that, climbing aboard, I put my foot through a plank in the hull. Though this was later repaired with a patch made from a baked bean tin, Derek never tired of reminding me of the incident and twenty years later would still be attributing many of his subsequent misfortunes to that moment of supreme clumsiness. During that afternoon aboard the boat, grandiosely named *Arcturus*, after the brightest star in the constellation Bootes, a curious metamorphosis apparently occurred. I had embarked as a third-rate trombonist in an amateur jazz band and confirmed landlubber, and disembarked, for reasons that still escape me, two hours later an aspiring Francis Chichester.

At the time I made my family announcement about going round the world, Derek hadn't actually asked me to join him, but I presumed, if I showed enough interest, it would only be a matter of time. The Lumbers family lived in the next village in a dark cottage reeking of dogs and the subterranean smell of stew. At weekends, when I called, they would be drinking tea in their night clothes at midday.

Coming from a family always washed and dressed by 8 am, I found this interesting and mildly disturbing.

The father, Jim, a thin sad man, employed at Derby locomotive works, known as 'up the loco', had a history of kidney trouble and drank warm water. He called Derek 'Cap'n' and had hoped that one day he would settle down and marry and join the British Legion so that they could play billiards together in the evenings. But he had long realised there was little chance of this. Derek spent little time at home. Usually he was on the boat, which was two miles away, or, dressed in greasy slacks and a pullover with a collar, and smelling of Brylcreem, out on assignations in his untaxed Standard Ten car. These usually involved picking up girls in coffee bars in Derby, falling out with them and sitting alone in his car by the river near the cattle market listening to Radio Luxembourg.

Occasionally we went out together to bleak country inns where men sat in silence over halves of mild and dogs stood by the door. One night our discussion on the existence or otherwise of God continued while we were standing side by side in the open-air gents in the car park. When Derek decided that the matter could be neatly settled by inviting the Almighty to strike him dead on the spot, I prudently retreated to the water-closet. The matter was resolved to Derek's satisfaction, but when we were stopped by the police on the way home and later both heavily fined for not having tax and insurance, I was not so sure.

Meanwhile, I borrowed every maritime book in Derby public library – volumes by deep-sea sailors like Clark Russell, Richard Dana, Morley Roberts, Alan Villiers, and long-forgotten Edwardian yachtsmen like R.T. McMullen, Claud Worth and Alec Glanville. From outdated editions of Nicholl's *Seamanship*, Norie's *Navigation* and Kipping's *Sails and Sailmaking*, I learned a mass of archaic information from making out a bill of lading to flaking out a rope in a Flemish coil and doing a harbour stow. None of it ultimately proved to be much use.

In retrospect, what I seemed to be doing was inventing a romantic and macho image without inconveniencing myself – after all, you can't come to much harm sailing in a field a hundred miles from the sea. Nor was I to know that, at that time, Cap'n Lumbers had never been to sea either, but had invented a fictitious CV from books, sailing magazines and other people's experiences. Later I discovered that one of his most fruitful sources was a man known as 'Uncle Billy', who kept a small transport café with his wife Joyce on the A38 a few miles from Burton-on-Trent.

Uncle Billy, whether he liked it or not, also became my mentor and inspiration. A small man with a haunted expression, he was in his late sixties and a victim of asthma and rheumatism. His favourite phrase, when the café was busy and his wife was desperately trying to serve a growing queue of impatient lorry-drivers, was 'I think it's time for a little lie-down.' As a lad, Uncle Billy had apparently served his apprenticeship in the last of the four-masted barques of Liverpool's William Thomas Line and the back room of the café was a shrine to a distant nautical age, with photographs and half-models on the walls and a sea chest in the corner.

It became a routine to ride my autocyle the ten miles to the café on Sunday afternoons to hear Uncle Billy's stories of life in the great steel Cape Horners: fires, strandings and shipwrecks, tyrannous skippers, brutal mates and riding the easting down to Valparaiso. There were riotous times ashore: confrontations with villainous mulattoes in the bars of Kuching and Kota Baharu, ending inevitably with 'Then I chinned him and down he went.' There were the hardships and dangers of the South American nitrate runs, the agonies of a pal frozen to death on the dog-watch off Bergen and the sadness of seeing fine ships go to the breaker's yard.

Uncle Billy's sea chest was an unending source of fascination. An apprentice's cap and brass-bound uniform lay on top of a set of oilskins, leather sea-boots and a bag containing an assortment of fids, knives, palm, sail-hooks, marlin-spikes, a variety of needles, hanks of sail twine and lumps of beeswax. In a drawer at the bottom of the chest were Uncle Billy's tarnished sextant, parallel rules, dividers, a 1928 copy of the Admiralty *Navigation Manual*, some shark's teeth, an ornamental Turk's-head and a faded neatly folded Red Ensign. I tried to persuade Uncle Billy to teach me how to use the sextant but he said his eyes weren't what they were and the instrument remained in its case.

Years later, when Uncle Billy was dead, the café replaced by a Little Chef and Joyce in a residential home, I discovered by chance a possible reason for Billy's reluctance. He had bought the marine artefacts at a War Department auction in Market Harborough and gradually constructed a life history around them. He had never been to sea, not even on a cross-Channel ferry, and had spent his working life as a plasterer's mate and a gardener in Derby Borough Parks Department before buying the café with his wife. 'It didn't bother Joyce,' said my informant. 'She couldn't see any harm in it, and it gave him an interest.' Whether Cap'n Lumbers knew about Uncle Billy's fictitious history, I couldn't say. He never mentioned it. But by then he had taken most of the stories of Billy's nautical life and artfully woven them into his own.

In the meantime, I needed a boat, not necessarily to use or even to repair, but to talk about to my new friends, and I asked my father if he knew anyone who sold boats. 'Why,' he said after a pause so long that I wondered if he had fallen asleep or even died, 'we'll have to ask Archie.' Archie was a friend with whom my father took mid-morning coffee in the café in the Derby branch of Boots, which my father always called 'Boots Cash Chemists'. He was a self-employed grocer whose shop made the place in the TV comedy *Open All Hours* look like Fortnum and Mason. The shop was filthy and the stock largely uneatable.

One of my first jobs, when I once worked there for a week in the school holidays, was to polish the mildew off the black puddings with a rag soaked in Vaseline. But it was always crowded, mainly with people wanting to borrow money, seeking advice on personal problems or complaining about toothache – Archie did a bit of amateur dentistry in the back room.

Sadly, Archie couldn't help with a boat but suggested George, a rakish figure in an archery club blazer, who described himself as a 'retail consultant' but in fact lurked around milk bars doing dodgy deals. Like my father, he was a Freemason. His finest moment came when he bought a thousand left-footed shoes, wrapped them up in pairs and sold the lot in an hour at Leicester market during a virtuoso performance worthy of Max Miller. Only one customer complained – a man with only a right leg. 'We're out of your size, I'm afraid,' said George, returning his money.

George recounted with pride a visit he made to the doctor after damaging his back lifting a stolen washing machine up a spiral staircase. 'Doctor, I've twisted myself,' he reported. 'I have to say this, George,' replied the GP, 'you're the only bugger who could.'

George knew of a boat laid up in a builder's yard, twenty miles away, a nondescript cabin-cruiser which my father swapped for a load of firewood and a fur coat my mother wouldn't wear, saying it had the moth. My father had the boat transported to our back garden one night on a lorry driven by a man with one eye who apparently owed my father a favour – but then, most people did. The boat stayed next to the broad-bean bed for seven years, rotting in the sun, until my father dismantled it and used the remaining sound timber to make a bird house for the lawn. The important thing was that I now technically owned a boat, and Cap'n Lumbers doodled some plans for turning it into a gunter-rigged barge-yacht. I carried them in my wallet: they were my membership of the marine fraternity. In fact it never occurred to me to return the boat to the water, which in any event would have been a job far beyond my capabilities, but that was now unnecessary. I was having too much fun sailing in my mind, where there was no need to frighten yourself or even learn to swim.

Meanwhile, at Swarkestone Bubble, a disturbing reality was looming. *Arcturus* was back in the canal, reasonably watertight, and Cap'n Lumbers was readying her for sea. He had his brother-in-law, a hair-stylist with his own salon, as crew but wanted someone else as well. One sunny Saturday afternoon in May 1954, we were fitting some saucepan racks in the galley and listening to Stockhausen on a suitcase-sized Pye portable radio when Cap'n Lumbers formally asked me to join his crew. It was the proudest moment of my life so far. With absurd formality we shook hands and slapped each other on the back. Only as I rode home on the autocycle that evening through the hawthorn-decked lanes did the euphoria begin to be replaced by what Claud Worth had succinctly described as 'morbid apprehension'. I had, some weeks earlier, asked Uncle Billy for some guidance on coping with the psychological perils of the ocean and he had merely replied, 'Don't let yourself be worried by the noise.'

In the meantime, I had other problems. It took me two days to summon the courage to tell my parents that I had actually given in my notice at the newspaper and was leaving home in six weeks' time to sail around the world. The reaction wasn't quite what I imagined. My father said he thought he was getting a stye, and went into the greenhouse, while my mother reacted like a character in a BBC radio *Play For Today*, by first weeping and then shouting.

She was very cross, she said – not particularly with me, because I'd always been easily led, and that was an inherited weakness from my father's side – but with Cap'n

Lumbers, who had seriously unsettled me and would wreck my life if I wasn't very careful. 'I've been making inquiries in Barrow-on-Trent [the Captain's home village] and there have been a lot of problems with that family,' my mother said. 'And that's only the half of it. I hope, by Jove, that this will be a warning to you. You've got a real career ahead of you, particularly if you can master shorthand.' Upset by her ferocity, I took Conrad's *Typhoon* to bed and became thoroughly depressed. Drake, Nelson and Joshua Slocum, I decided, had not had to contend with a family as unsupportive as mine. Years later, I discovered I indeed hadn't known the half of it. My mother had apparently visited Elsie Lumbers and threatened to put an injunction on her son if he insisted on taking me to sea, but nothing came of it.

On the first Sunday in June, *Arcturus*, with Cap'n Lumbers and his brother-in-law on board, left Swarkestone on passage to Great Yarmouth via the River Trent and a convoluted series of canals. I stood with Mr and Mrs Lumbers on the canal bank in the rain to wave them goodbye. 'Well,' said Jim Lumbers, to no one in particular, 'there we are.' He died a few weeks later.

I was to join *Arcturus* at Yarmouth in a fortnight's time after working out my notice. The brother-in-law would return to his salon in Derby and the vessel would sail for Ostend in Belgium and thence to what Cap'n Lumbers vaguely referred to as 'other destinations'. At least that's what was supposed to happen. It took ten hours to reach Great Yarmouth from Derby by rail. As my mother had heard that it was always twice as cold at sea as on land, I carried two suitcases of heavy clothing including a belted raincoat, Hush Puppies and trilby hat.

I also had several Derby Co-operative Society carrier bags containing food my mother had provided, including pork pies and sticks of celery, my trombone, carried in my sister's hockey bag, and the Edwin H. Morris book of *100*

*Authentic Arrangements for Dixieland Bands*, wrapped in cellophane, for when we dropped anchor in New Orleans. I settled uneasily into my new home, now tied to a rusty freighter opposite Yarmouth fish market and overlooking the Nelson memorial. Never having slept on a boat before, I was continually woken by the wash of trawlers leaving at dawn for the North Sea. I suffered panic attacks in the tiny, damp forward cabin, crammed with suitcases and already mildewing clothes. The brass valves and sluices of the lavatory were a worrying mystery and I was frightened by the primus stove. This was certainly not how it was in the books or when riding the easting down to Valparaiso.

Four days later, early on a rose-pink morning, nothing else was moving on the river as I untied the mooring lines from the freighter, shoved off and jumped aboard. What happened next was quick and spectacular. *Arcturus*, driven by a small silver-painted Seagull outboard motor, swung out into the fast-flowing ebb, hit some lethal underwater obstacle, leaned heavily to starboard and sank. We had travelled less than 100 yards around the world. There was just time to load our suitcases, trilby hats, raincoats and Hush Puppies into the dinghy before the boat disappeared, leaving only the cabin-top and the mast with its bedraggled Jolly Roger. I couldn't reach my trombone, stowed in the forepeak, and as the instrument filled with water it gave a low and heart-rending moan of reproach that I can hear to this day.

An hour later, I was in a telephone box outside the Alhambra Theatre, wet through, and asking for my job back. Luckily they hadn't yet advertised the vacancy and the following week I was back home, covering Derby Borough Magistrates' court, pensioners' meetings and swimming galas, as though nothing had happened. The time I had taken off was subtracted from the following year's holidays and there was a small deduction for extra national insurance. I sat and failed a shorthand exam for the third time. Safe normality had returned. Cap'n Lumbers wrote to say that *Arcturus* had reappeared at low tide. He had managed to salvage and repair her and wanted to know when I was returning to continue the voyage. I didn't reply. I couldn't bring myself to tell him that the reality of seafaring was not a patch on my maritime fantasies and that I would stick with them for the time being.

We lost touch for nearly four years, but mutual friends told me of Cap'n Lumbers' activities. While sailing *Arcturus* single-handed to London he had gone aground on a sandbank and was towed by lifeboat into Walton-on-the-Naze, where for three months he took up with an Irishwoman who kept bees, and was provided with clothes and pocket money by the Shipwrecked Mariners' Society. Eventually he sailed up the Thames. After numerous mishaps, including hitting a dredger off Canvey Island, *Arcturus* moored illegally at a jetty adjoining Battersea Funfair, demolishing an ornate Chinese pagoda and doing serious damage. Sailing undetected up-river, Cap'n Lumbers hid the boat in a canal at Staines, near London Airport, where it was later set on fire by teddy boys.

In subsequent years he would reappear spasmodically to disrupt my life and his aura of seedy swashbuckling made me feel restless and dissatisfied with whatever I happened to be doing at the time. Once, when I had settled journalistic employment in London and was beginning to build something of a social life, Cap'n Lumbers arrived unexpectedly at my flat to try to persuade me to join the crew of a yacht sailing to the West Indies. It was captained by a villainous-looking man with one eye who had apparently been exposed by the *Sunday Mirror* for organising a black mass coven and had convictions for piracy in Puerto Rico. Both were penniless and slept uninvited on my floor for a week. My mother, visiting me in London for the day, viewed the pirate with distaste and remarked, 'He's very common, isn't he?'

I declined the transatlantic berth and once again Captain Lumbers left me in no doubt that I had let myself down and had once more taken the coward's way out. 'I can't go on giving you these chances just because you come from Derby,' he said as he ate the last of my cornflakes. 'One day you'll look back and regret you didn't make something of yourself.' I later heard that hours after the yacht left Southampton, the pirate succumbed to migraine and was not seen on deck for the rest of the trip, leaving Cap'n Lumbers in charge of a crew of two terrified air-hostesses and a Chinese acupuncturist, none of whom had previously been to sea. It was then, like a character in a Jack Hawkins war movie, that the shambling Lumbers metamorphosed into a steely-eyed hero, bringing the yacht safely through a north-westerly gale and into English Harbour, Barbados. The carefully crafted fiction of his life had finally and magically become fact.

Several years later, when working as a reporter and education correspondent on the *Daily Gleaner* newspaper in Jamaica, I returned one evening to my flat overlooking Kingston harbour, to find two men asleep there. Inevitably, one was Cap'n Lumbers, who had flown in from Miami to deliver a tugboat from Jamaica to Trinidad. The other was a local limbo dancer named Captain Fish, who Cap'n Lumbers had met in a bar. Both were drunk. When Cap'n Lumbers left the island, Captain Fish stayed on for several days before I could finally persuade him to leave. I later discovered that he had stolen my Parker fountain pen presented to me by my mother for passing the Eleven Plus examination, and a pair of cricket trousers.

I never saw Cap'n Lumbers again. Some years later, still, so far as I knew, without any recognised qualifications, he was inexplicably given command of a 100-foot replica of a nineteenth-century tea-clipper owned by a Los Angeles charter syndicate. With thirty middle-aged Americans aboard, the ship sailed for New Zealand and Australia on a six-month cruise. A month later it mysteriously went aground on a well-charted reef in the Cook Islands in the South Pacific. The disgruntled passengers were flown home and while insurers haggled over liability and a tug was sent from Port Moresby, Cap'n Lumbers was seen to disembark with his dunnage and motor to a nearby island in the ship's launch. He refused any further involvement in the stranded ship's plight, and disappeared.

I wrote several times to a sketchy address provided by his sister, but heard nothing, and eventually the letters were returned undelivered. Years later my mother sent me a report from the *Derby Evening Telegraph* that Derek Arthur George Lumbers was dead. He was sixty-two. He had been managing a cinema and skippering a small inter-islands freighter. He had married a woman believed to be the niece of the prime minister of the Cook Islands, and the family moved to New Zealand and had three daughters, one named Elsie after his mother, but the circumstances and details of his death remained a mystery. Years afterwards, on a fleeting visit to Derbyshire, I visited Barrow-on-Trent on a bleak autumn afternoon hoping to discover what had actually happened to my friend. I found that none of the Lumbers family remained and their cottage had been sold and gentrified with coach-lamps.

# CHAPTER 2

# All at sea

For several years I was too occupied with other things to think about boats. It wasn't until the mid-seventies, when I was married with two young children and living in a converted convent on the Devon coast, that I actually began to sail rather than merely talk about it. I pottered on the creeks of the Exe estuary with my son and daughter in an old wooden Enterprise sailing dinghy as an escape from an unworkable marriage. When we arrived home wet and mud-caked, with small crabs wrapped in our hankies, we would find ourselves locked out and would climb through a window to find notes saying things like 'Gone to Buddhist meditation in Honiton.'

Sometimes, after my wife had perhaps threatened me with the breadknife or was searching the countryside with a torch for a lost goat, I would take the dinghy out alone on moonlit nights from the silent villages of Lympstone or Topsham and sail the silver channels between the dark mud. I often had the vast estuary to myself. Far from shore, where the tide hit the hull with a strange chopping sound and the wind funnelled up from the unseen sea, the boat danced a mad marine ballet, gybing and tacking, freeing off and hardening sheets, running and reaching, heaving-to and wearing ship – finally giving clumsy reality to the terms I had read about so often in books and used knowingly in conversation, but with little practical idea of their purpose.

Once I got the tide wrong and had to drag the boat back to shore through half a mile of mud. It was a wonderful practical demonstration of the tidal rule of twelfths. When I failed to tighten the rigging screws, the mast fell down. These simple inflexible rules of cause and effect gave a strange sense of security. Sailing, I decided, worked on some pretty basic formulae and maybe wasn't beyond my capabilities after all. Heartened by this discovery, I bought a small two-berth sailing cruiser in which we made timid forays to sheltered beaches and cooked beans on a primus stove. My children brought friends and they played cards in the tiny cabin. I did a navigation course and learned Morse code, semaphore and the etiquette of flags. I had the boat for two years and my wife, who was learning the flute, never asked to see it, or inquired why her family returned home soaked to the skin on Saturday afternoons.

I joined a sailing club, proposed by my navigation tutor and seconded by a chandler who sensed he was onto a good thing. I was humble and eager to learn. I bought people drinks in exchange for advice on compass deviation and sacrificial anodes, and began to smoke a pipe. Too timid to take my own tiny craft any further than the estuary fairway buoy, I begged rides with people who took their boats to sea. My first invitation, to help crew a Dutch steel ketch owned by a dentist on passage for a heavy weekend in Torquay, was a disaster. We fell out as we hauled up the anchor and didn't speak a civil word until we dropped it again two days later. In the interim I broke my glasses, lost my watch over the side, was poisoned by a tin of prawns a year beyond their sell-by date and had my reef knots criticised for being inside out. To cap it all, the dentist wrote a humorous piece for a yachting magazine on our nightmare cruise and so actually made a profit out of giving me a hard time.

Undiscouraged, I turned my attention to a grubby converted fishing boat on a nearby mooring, sailed by two elderly men who always smiled as they rowed past. Eventually, after weeks of cajolery, they gave in and offered me a trip to Salcombe. It was a revelation. Joe and Jim had sailed together around the West Country for twenty years without having a good word to say for, or to, each other. Jim would tell anyone who'd buy him a drink that Joe was the most useless skipper who ever failed his Yachtmaster's practical and Joe complained that Jim couldn't be trusted to steer a course from the back door to the coal shed and, worse, still hadn't paid his share of the bag of groceries they bought in Swanage in 1964.

From our own boat we had noticed that Joe and Jim's Sunday evening routine rarely varied. They would return from a weekend cruise not speaking. They would tidy the boat in silence. Then, like Laurel and Hardy, they would climb ponderously into the dinghy, each desperate not to lose dignity, and Jim would row ashore. On the slipway, as they parted, Jim would break the silence with his ritual farewell: 'And don't think I'm coming with you next weekend, pal.' Come Friday night, he'd be there as usual. On passage to Salcombe it soon became apparent that everything on the boat centred around food. Jim was a compulsive cook and Joe a compulsive eater. In a nasty sea when rounding Start Point that Saturday afternoon, a plank sprang at waterline level and water quickly ruined a quid's worth of teabags. In search of something to put over the leak, they opened a tin of beans and flattened out the can into a patch. This was a long job because the beans, once opened, had to be cooked and eaten with bacon and several slices of fried bread. Finally, after bananas and custard, we attacked the leak. Joe put the boat hard on the port tack and Jim dangled head-first over the side to hammer the tin over the hole. I held his legs. The job was done and no further mention was made of it. Joe and Jim were more concerned about getting into Salcombe before the cafés closed. Joe died a year later, the boat was sold and no one was able to tempt Jim back onto the water. Were twenty years of acrimonious crewing enough for anyone? 'It's not that,' said Jim. 'It just wouldn't be much fun without Joe.'

My notice on the 'crew available' board in the sailing club bore strange fruit. I sailed briefly with Dennis, the owner of a pre-war Nicholson sloop who had a thing about anchors. We had five on board and when he sailed on other boats he had been known to take his own anchor with him. Anchoring once in Helford River he gave his crew, anxious to get ashore to the pub, a lecture on the relative efficacy of the Bruce, Danforth, stockless and CQR anchors before settling for a trusty fisherman. Ten minutes later, ashore and busy with the mandatory lighting of our pipes, we were rewarded by the sight of the Nicholson dragging serenely down the river and onto the mud. Dennis had somehow managed to drop the anchor into a submerged biscuit tin.

That first season I also made several trips with a lugubrious local figure known as Uncle Ronald in his converted former Walmer lifeboat. Uncle Ronald never made plans, on the premise that the more you made, the more there was to go wrong. I experienced the theory in practice when sailing with him in Brittany off the Ile Brehat in thick fog and Uncle Ronald cheerfully admitted he was lost. 'Not to worry,' he said, 'I think I'll need a Guinness for this one.' A bottle was brought on deck. 'I think we'll go that way. It's as good as any,' said Uncle Ronald and took the helm. Minutes later the fog lifted to reveal that he had piloted us unerringly through a tight circle of rocks.

That autumn, when it was becoming too cold to get your feet wet, the season's last trip was with a husband and wife who wanted to winter their elderly 30-foot gaff-rigged Falmouth quay punt in Brighton marina. 'Patsy's fine on day trips,' said the skipper over a pint, 'but she tends to get rattled when things start to get lumpy. I always feel happier with another chap on board.'

Patsy was a quiet little woman in a blue cardigan who sat in the forward cabin with the *Telegraph* crossword while manly things like tidal drift were being discussed at the chart table. The only time she spoke was to ask if I had sugar in coffee. Just before we left Exmouth on the afternoon tide, the skipper decided to further augment his crew with a worried-looking young chap who had done a bit of dinghy sailing and wanted a cheap trip to see his mother in Hove. The wind, from the south-west, increased at nightfall. The Dinghy Sailor and I put a couple of reefs in the mainsail, but the boat was still rolling heavily and the skipper had gone to bed with toothache. At 8 pm we were ten miles east of Portland and it was blowing harder than ever. I was wishing I was at home watching the end of *Coronation Street* when, without warning, the mast fell down. It had snapped off ten feet from the top and sails and rigging cascaded into the sea. A horrified face appeared at the hatch and quickly vanished. The toothache, it seemed, was no better. Then, amid the confusion, a small voice said 'I'll start the engine and then we'll get things tidy.' Patsy was in command and of course, looking back, she always had been.

When we anchored safely in Swanage Bay shortly after

midnight, Patsy went below to put the kettle on and the skipper finally emerged, pale and heroic, to survey the damage. In the strange game they played, the roles had once again reverted to normal. The yacht stayed in Swanage for repairs and the Dinghy Sailor and I went home on the train. The skipper saw us off. 'I can't thank you enough for taking care of Patsy when I was laid up,' he said. 'Women are useless in a crisis.' Some time later, in a marina where they were something of a legend, I heard more about Patsy and Bob. 'It's her boat,' said my informant. 'She's got an Ocean Yachtmaster's. Poor old Bob gets seasick in the bath!' I saw the boat again years later in Dieppe and went over to say hello. Bob clearly didn't recognise me but couldn't wait to tell someone who could speak English what a hell of a trip they'd had from Portsmouth. Patsy came out of the doghouse and was solemnly introduced. She had brought me a cup of coffee. It had exactly the right amount of sugar.

I would like to report that the next sailing season found me still learning the seaman's art and modestly venturing further from the fairway buoy as my skill and competence increased, but that wasn't what happened at all. Such responsibility soon went out of the window when I took up with the Rodneys. For some time I had searched for the word to describe an increasingly familiar nautical phenomenon and my friend Willie unwittingly supplied it one lunchtime when we were sitting on the wall outside the Pier Hotel on Exmouth dock with a bag of crisps and two middle-aged bearded men walked past and into the private bar. They were almost identically dressed in faded salmon trousers, dirty blue smocks, caps sporting tarnished badges, and, strangely for a warm spring day, thigh-length waders. One wore a lanyard with a hand-bearing compass and from the other's belt dangled an extensive array of knives, shackle-keys, marlin-spikes and prongs. As they disappeared inside, Willie helpfully defined the species: 'A brace of

Rodneys, eh?' he said. I would have followed them inside for further sociological research but the money had run out so we returned to my boat to open a can of beans and listen to the lunchtime shipping forecast. I soon realised that once you started looking, *Homo sapiens roddus* were everywhere, but like other exotic species they were easier to identify than define. They were male, bearded, calculatingly scruffy, and rich. Their boats were big and ethnic, usually gaff-rigged converted Victorian workboats or gentlemen's yachts with no expense spared to maintain a casual perfection. I was fascinated and envious. My ambition from then on was to be a Rodney.

One of my first role models was a man who lived in a Georgian country house and contrived to look like the out-of-work second mate of a Victorian dredger. Generally known as Captain McWhirr, after the heroic unimaginative skipper in Conrad's short story *Typhoon*, he could be seen, in obligatory greasy cap and threadbare pea-jacket, in grim pubs along the south-west coast talking about woman and the price of fish to monosyllabic companions. He hated yacht clubs and would never speak to anyone he suspected of having a university degree. Captain McWhirr was proud of his working-class Liverpool background. After the financial collapse of a smallholding on the Wirral, his redoubtable mother had loaded a van with children and poultry and driven to the West Country, where she rented a small farm and the family eventually prospered. By the time I met him, Captain McWhirr had all but retired and owned a beautiful 50-foot ketch, in which he cruised every summer in search of sexual adventures, which mainly consisted of preventing confrontations between his wife and mistresses who were half his age. One evening there was a scene reminiscent of a Jacques Tati movie, during which a girlfriend rowed a dinghy vigorously away from the bow of the moored ketch as the vengeful wife, in a similar boat, approached the stern.

Later he remarried and sailed to the West Indies with his new young wife and a crew of quarrelling relations. The boat was subsequently wrecked in a hurricane and became the instant target of thieves with chainsaws who stripped it of everything except, inexplicably, the fine teak wheel, which was returned to Captain McWhirr and hung over his fireplace. Undiscouraged, he replaced the lost boat with an expensive steel sloop and sailed abroad with his new family of small children and we lost touch. Years later, walking through a crowded marina in La Rochelle, I heard, above the screeching of a small child, a Liverpudlian voice shout, 'If you do that again, I'll hang you up by the foreskin.' Captain McWhirr was sitting on his boat under an awning surrounded by arguing children and eating a lobster. He did not seem surprised to see me and we had a nice chat.

Not all the Rodneys I met at that time were as rich as Captain McWhirr. Some, like Les, a well-known marine artist, had a bizarre charisma which I envied perhaps more. Les was to me the human embodiment of Rat in *Wind in the Willows*: small, laconic, sandy-haired and with a twinkling eye. I liked him very much. Continual financial crises stimulated a relentless flow of ersatz eighteenth-century seascapes which were made into prints, tablemats and revolving lampshades and sold in department stores and other national outlets, including Boots Cash Chemists. But however hard he worked, Les never seemed any better off. He complained that he was permanently in danger of losing his rented riverside farmhouse and his sailing boat, a prettily converted 70-year-old Looe hooker. However, nothing seemed to perturb him and Les appeared to live in a strangely two-dimensional world in which disasters were greeted with a mild 'Blood and sand!' and good news with 'It's getting better!'

He affected to despise the facility he had acquired as a sign-writer in Harrogate – referring to it mockingly as 'mastery of the fine line' – which allowed him to work so rapidly that pictures loomed out of the canvas while you watched, as though emerging from a thick fog. Sometimes Les would paint several pictures at a time, walking along a line of canvases to put in a succession of identical wave patterns, cloud formations or men in neckerchiefs heaving at capstans. The vast bulk of pictures were of the same basic scene – one or two galleons at anchor at sunset under vertiginous cliffs in a twilight resembling translucent tomato sauce. Pigtailed men in striped smocks were usually rowing purposefully towards a distant jetty. 'They're going to the Spar shop for some fags,' the artist explained.

The galleons were always seen from the stern, not for any aesthetic reason, but because it cut down the time spent on the rigging and superstructure, which were drawn with the aid of a sign-writer's stick and many cups of tea. Occasionally Les would vary the subject, once producing several dozen paintings on the wrecking theme in which men with lanterns lured ships onto needle-sharp rocks amid a frenzy of foam and spray. Viewed, as usual, from behind, the vessels sped towards destruction like darts entering a dart-board. I once asked if we could see the rocks so clearly, why couldn't the doomed mariners? He replied, 'That sort of talk could put me out of business.' Les's detachment from his pictures never ceased to surprised me. I once caught him examining with a lens one of his wrecking scenes in which a tiny figure was waving a lantern at the bottom of a precipitous cliff. 'How did the bugger get down there?' he asked in genuine perplexity. 'He's only got one leg.'

In an attempt to get income-tax relief on his boat, Les decided to make it into a floating studio, which involved painting 'Marine Artist' in huge letters on the mainsail and putting an easel in the cockpit. Two days later the boat was booked to appear in a Swedish television version of Count Dracula, using a cove in Torbay as the place where the Count first set foot in England. The money was good and

Les and his regular crew, Sid, a man with a liking for pink scarves and recruited mainly for his skill with the chip pan, spent a day washing the letters off the sail. On the way to Torbay, in thick fog, Les rehearsed his five-word part – 'We have arrived, Count Dracula' – but sadly never had the chance to perform it. He had got the date wrong. They were two days late and Count Dracula had returned to Sweden. Les was outraged that he never got his money.

A gifted technician, Les seriously believed his pictures were aesthetically worthless. On one occasion, painting a seascape on a Cornish beach, he was watched by a holiday-maker who remarked that such a gift was God-given. 'It's bloody rubbish,' Les said mildly. 'I just do them for the money.' When the man remained unconvinced, Les, realising words were not going to be enough, drew out a large brush, dipped it in black paint, and destroyed the picture with a few scything strokes. 'That's my personal opinion of it,' he said, opening a thermos of tea. 'I'm sorry you did that,' the man said. 'I was going to buy it.' 'I think that's probably cured me of the grand gesture,' said Les, relating the story. Les prided himself on selling everything he painted, even if it meant drastic modification. 'I did a picture once of this cockerel with these bloody great wattles hanging either side of its beak. I couldn't sell the bugger. So I turned it upside down and made it into a horse and cart. I sold it to a vicar the next day.' He smiled a gentle smile at the memory of a job well done.

Many years afterwards, when crewing a friend's boat up the Bristol Channel, we put into the Cornish port of Padstow the weekend of the hobby-horse celebrations, and found Les running a posh tourist gallery selling things like Scandinavian glass and tiny abstracts of silver wire and yak wool. He was obviously doing well. He had a nice car and was wearing a smart jumper and there were none of his pictures on the walls of the busy and crowded gallery. When I asked for details of the transformation and how he had come by his good fortune, he smiled a gentle smile which was full of secrets. 'Let's just say,' he said, 'that it's getting better.'

\*\*\*\*\*\*\*

I had never been much of a drinker, a condition largely inherited from my mother who suffered 'liverishness' after more than one small sherry, but I knew this would have to change once I aspired to Rodney status. A pint of mild was enough to make me sick and cause a violent hangover the following day, but I persevered, and eventually learned to vomit unobtrusively in pub gardens and over the sides of boats without destroying the bonhomie of the occasion. I disliked the taste and effect of strong drink, and still do, but it was soon apparent that drinking at sea was an essential part of being accepted as a man in a man's world, and so I did the best I could.

One day someone will doubtless write an EU-funded treatise on the correlation between alcohol and the seafaring life, but things seem to have changed little from the days of the cartoon in a Victorian copy of *Punch* in which the mate of a fishing smack stands on the quay looking down to where the skipper lounges on the rail.

Skipper: 'Did you get the provisions?'

Mate: 'Yes, half a loaf and four bottles of whisky.'

Skipper: 'What are we going to do with all that bread?'

My first major encounter with Rodneys apparently intent on drowning themselves in drink was in the summer 1974 when I was invited to make up a crew of three to sail a yacht to France. We met at a pub in Emsworth on Friday evening to 'take ale' and work out the itinerary. At closing time we walked along the quay to encounter our first problem. Not only could the skipper not find his boat but he couldn't remember its name. Finally we climbed aboard a rather smart motor-sailer, only to be confronted by a

woman in pyjamas and hairnet who threatened us with a
fire extinguisher. We were on the wrong boat. When we
finally found the skipper's rather tatty Macwester 28, he fell
headlong down the saloon steps and lay apparently dead
until morning. The rest of us considered the situation over
a case of Newquay Steam Beer but came to no firm
conclusion. We awoke at lunchtime the following day,
found the boat aground and returned to the pub to take ale
and consider the situation again. At 4 pm, we left the
mooring, motored somewhat erratically towards the
entrance to Chichester Harbour, went aground on the edge
of Thorney Island, threw out an anchor and went to sleep.

When we awoke it was dark so we had another drink
and returned to bed. On Sunday morning the sun was out,
the boat was floating and someone suggested a gentle sail
towards a pub at Wittering. That moment the wind
dropped and the engine wouldn't start. All that bouncing
about on the mud had split the fuel tank. We hitched a tow
with a fishing boat back to Emsworth in time for a
lunchtime drink and toasted the completion of an
interesting cruise. I did intend to write to my erstwhile
companions pointing out that such behaviour was both
dangerous and irresponsible, but for some reason could
not recall any of their names.

For years, it never ceased to surprise me how liquor
could transform the characters of even the most
introverted yachtsmen. For instance, at a rally of traditional
boat owners in Plymouth, we were resigned to the usual
earnest discussions about the power–weight ratio of triced
loose-footed mainsails and the efficacy of the Matthew
Walker knot, when it was discovered that a Thames barge
chartered by a whisky company was serving unlimited
amounts of 20-year-old malt free for half an hour. As a
result, men whose usual evening quota was a pint of
shandy and a bag of pork scratchings were to be seen in
their underpants dangling upside down in the rigging. A

man returning to his boat climbed steadily down the dockside ladder, apparently unaware that he was actually descending beneath the water. I was sitting minding my own business when a military-looking gentleman later identified as a retired surgeon-commander approached and said, 'Give us a kiss, Spider.' I apparently declined on the grounds that we hadn't been introduced.

During my integration into the yachting scene, I found that drink came in many guises and currencies but it soon became apparent that bottles obtained from 'the other side' after some dashing cross-Channel jaunt were the ultimate badge of courage. 'Have a taste of this, old lad,' invited the owner of a smart little yacht, tied to the buoys in Newton Ferrers creek on one golden evening. 'Someone had told me about this place in Tréguier. Nothing under ten years old, all chateau-bottled. We bought six bottles back in a seven gusting eight. It seems to have travelled OK.' It was certainly a nice claret and he was very generous with it, so it would have been pretty curmudgeonly to have let on that I'd seen his wife peeling off the Sainsbury's sticker as I pulled alongside in the dinghy.

*******

Looking back, drink was probably the least of my troubles during that summer. To a marriage which for years had been a ritual of confrontations, rows and silent sulks was now added a cold-eyed ferocity which sent me fleeing into my double-locked office in the room which was once the convent chapel, with a camp-bed and my mother's old Baby Belling cooker. I gave the children, Tim and Sophie, a key so that they could come in for bedtime stories and give me the lowdown on what was happening in the rest of the house. My wife, it seemed, had engaged a solicitor named Mr Horsey, who at that moment was belying his Beatrix-Potter-like name by preparing a divorce petition which would give his client the house and all its contents.

Besieged in the corner of the gloomy old house, sleep was rare and fitful. Thunderous hammering at dawn made me wonder how much the stout Victorian doors would stand and I usually went to bed fully dressed, ready for a quick getaway. During the day there was silent glaring through the stained-glass window and notes held up by unseen hands. Not surprisingly, it was sometimes difficult in such conditions to concentrate on freelance writing and so earn the money for the alimony I would have been delighted to pay if only my wife would agree to a divorce settlement which did not insist on my having the custody of the family goats, one of which was mentally disturbed after an accident with a car and now wore a black beret. Like Uncle Ronald steering through the rocks, I had rarely made plans but instead responded hurriedly to situations, and now it seemed that one possible solution to the current intolerable situation would be to become a full-time Rodney and sail away to Valparaiso or somewhere similar. At least I might get a good night's sleep.

When the children were at school and my wife in conference with Mr Horsey or milking the goats I spent time on the telephone to yacht brokers looking for some maritime refuge. But I was soon rumbled. When my son made a paper glider from a page of details of a boat once owned by the late lamented pianist Semprini on the Essex marshes, my wife turned off the electricity to the chapel and cut the phone wires with her secateurs. It was, I decided, high time I ran away to sea. True, my horizons – in those pre-mobile-phone and pre-email days – were limited by the need to be reasonably near a public phone and post-box for my job, but would it actually be feasible to live and work on a boat, and could I possibly afford it?

A talk with a kindly yacht broker in Plymouth gave me the impression that it probably was, and maybe I could – so long as I was sensible, and picked the right boat.

Captain Jack Flowerdew, who had come ashore after twenty years on deep-sea salvage tugs to start a one-man brokerage in a former sweetshop next to a brothel in Union Street, was happy to provide the logistics of live-aboard survival in exchange for the price of a 4 pm all-day breakfast. Apparently I should look for something big and strong, of steel or even concrete, that could be covered in thick cheap paint once every ten years, contained no wood that needed varnishing, had full headroom throughout the boat, a double bed, a modern lavatory, a fridge and if possible a washing machine. The perfect boat, according to Captain Flowerdew, should move as little as possible but, when it did, should have the largest possible engine. If it had sails they must be small and inconsequential. The craft should be able to be manned by one person or at the most two.

'Otherwise you'll be on the phone all the time looking for crew and when they let you down you won't be able to go anywhere. They'll also eat and drink a lot and expect you to pay for it. They'll also probably block up the lavatory.' A sensible boat, he continued, should have large windows to accommodate tomato plants and other salad crops, wide decks with high and sturdy rails, and be moored near a video shop, a bookie's, a supermarket and a decent pub. 'Keep away from the sea as much as you can,' Captain Flowerdew said, obviously remembering his days in the salvage trade. 'It causes nothing but trouble. Avoid old boats with tall masts, long bowsprits, miles of rope and fancy sails. And don't have any animals. You'll forever be taking them ashore at night to piss and that will bugger up your love-life something rotten. Are you going to eat that sausage?' It was obviously very sound advice. I thanked him for it, and two months later bought a boat. Inevitably, I ignored, down to the very last detail, all of Captain Flowerdew's recommendations.

CHAPTER 3

# The lads come aboard

The young man sitting in the dinghy which had been pulled up the slipway on West Mersea beach reminded me of a figure in a minor painting of the Newlyn school. His clothes, a ragged blue guernsey, serge trousers and heavy boots were, I was later to learn, the costume of people pretending to be nineteenth-century Essex oystermen. In fact he was a public schoolboy of about fifteen who was waiting to row me out to view his father's boat on an autumn afternoon in 1974 and reckoned he knew a phoney when he saw one.

I had driven from Devon to the then remote Essex fishing village of West Mersea at the mouth of the Blackwater River after seeing a for-sale advertisement for a Colchester sailing smack in a yachting magazine. The boat in question was 62 feet long with bowsprit, of 16 tons displacement, with six berths, a solid fuel stove, and a full-sized gas cooker. She was built by Aldous of Brightlingsea as an oyster dredger in 1900 and had been extensively refitted and restored by the present owner. She was named *Shamrock* and her price was £6,500. Later I discovered that this was, at that time, the highest price ever asked for an Essex smack. At the time of reading the advertisement I did not know exactly what an oyster smack was, and had no available money. Nevertheless I decided that come what may, I would buy *Shamrock* and sail her away in search of adventure.

Meanwhile, even West Mersea was a mystery. According to the AA Handbook, it was an oval island five miles long, separated from the Blackwater by mudflats and marshes and reached from Colchester by a causeway which flooded at high tide. Half-closing day was Wednesday. My Devon house, as predicted by Mr Horsey, had been awarded to my wife in the divorce settlement and was being sold to a harmless-enough man who sent me into an unwarranted fury by endlessly referring to building societies as beesocks. My wife had by now dispersed most of my belongings to Oxfam or thrown them in a shed in the garden, but I had most of my boating books in the car and spent an hour in a lay-by outside Colchester with *Traditional Working Sail of the British Isles*, boning up on Essex smacks, ready to bluff my way through the most searching examination. Uncle Billy, I reasoned, would expect nothing less.

Both men and ships seemed a hardy and illustrious breed. In the 1860s, 400 cutter-rigged smacks from 30 to 50 feet had worked the Essex oyster beds under sail and fished for sprats in the winter. Not surprisingly there were far more smacks than the local waters could support and they roamed as far as Scotland and the Channel Islands in search of deep-water oysters. Smacksmen, obviously with the approval of the author of *Traditional Working Sail*, had made things pretty hard for themselves. There was an inflexible system of sail-handling and a curious etiquette that no one spoke while sailing. Smacks, with their big heavy rigs, long bowsprits and low exposed decks, were apparently heroic sea-boats, but difficult and often dangerous to handle, and the work was miserably rewarded. In 1880 the average smack crew's wage was £10 a year. Diseased beds and overfishing had largely scuppered the Essex oyster trade by the outbreak of World War I and most of the smacks were sold away, converted into yachts or left to rot on the saltings. The oldest smack still sailing, I learned from the book, was *Boadicea*, built in 1808, and owned for the past thirty years by a local dentist, Michael Frost, who had over the years devotedly replaced timber, metal and canvas to the point where nothing original remained. So how could it be the oldest smack? It was a point worth keeping for later when lighting my pipe over a pint.

'Don't sit in the stern,' the boy said. His eyes were blue and hard. 'I'm going to scull from there. Have you ever sailed a smack?' 'I've done a little bit,' I said, 'with Mickey Frost on the old *Boadicea*.' As we rowed out towards the lines of boats moored in Mersea Deeps, some quarter-mile from shore, he told me that *Shamrock* was one of the biggest of the Colchester smacks. Before his father bought her, she had sunk in the ice, was sold as a wreck to a local boat-builder and converted into a motorboat. It had taken three years to rebuild her and put her back into her original sailing condition and now his father wanted a new challenge and intended to build a Polynesian catamaran. 'We had hoped she would stay locally,' the boy said, 'but now Dad says we're going to have to find someone with more money than sense.'

We passed yachts and fishing boats and skirted the stern of a huge piratical craft thick with ropes. A mast I estimated at 60 feet high was festooned with archaic rigging and uncountable clusters of wooden pulley-blocks. A 20-foot wooden bowsprit stuck rudely out of the front and the hull was painted an unpleasant deep green-brown reminiscent of overcooked spinach. 'You could kill yourself on a thing like that,' I remarked to the boy, tamping down my pipe. 'Or put yourself into bankruptcy. What a bloody liability.' At that moment a small bearded man appeared above the spinach. 'Welcome aboard *Shamrock*,' he said.

Scrambling up the side, I looked across the wide decks to where a row of small beautiful children stared unblinkingly and a large dog leaped maniacally up and down the companionway steps. The bearded owner, an architect, introduced his young wife and two friends, and suggested a short sail up the Blackwater towards Maldon. I stood in a pose intended to suggest some sort of expert approval as the men threw themselves into superhuman tasks. It took two to haul up the vast canvas mainsail and two to hand-crank the reluctant diesel engine. Everything was heavy and noisy, greasy and inconvenient, then suddenly we were sailing in strangely ominous silence, the huge sails and spars subduing and utilising some enormous force as the smack slipped fast and cleanly through the water, leaving virtually no turbulence behind.

Off Shinglehead Point, a couple of miles upstream, I took the tiller as a further mass of canvas was hoisted – apparently a topsail, jib topsail and a reaching staysail – to make the boat lean awesomely away from the wind and bury itself in white foam, showing off, bullying the water but solely dependent on me for its direction and safety. It was a profoundly enjoyable thought. I suddenly realised I was singing 'Barnacle Bill the Sailor', and was probably as happy as I had ever been. When the owner came up to tactfully adjust the course in order to miss a large red buoy I said, 'I'll have her. Will you take a cheque?' To his credit, the owner tried to curb my folly by suggesting that at least

I should have a survey, take a few days to consider, and be on the boat more than twenty-five minutes, but I would have none of it. *Shamrock* was my passport to the big league. With a greasy cap and the current issue of Reed's *Nautical Almanac*, who would doubt my credentials now?

But that night, staying at the owner's pine and hessian residence in Colchester, I was unable to sleep. What had I done? I had no money to buy the boat, no crew to man it, no experience to sail it, insufficient knowledge to even start the engine, nowhere to moor it, no way of getting it to Devon, and huge and ungainly though it was, insufficient room to comfortably live and work. Then, as light began to seep through the hand-woven curtains, the problems were magically resolved. Uncle Billy would know what to do. And anything he didn't know, I could always look up in books. Abashed and reassured in equal quantities, I fell asleep and slept peacefully until long after breakfast.

Back in Devon with the deal done, things fell surprisingly into place. To the chagrin of my ex-wife, who had immediately instructed Mr Horsey to try to seize my new acquisition, I was able to borrow money from the business in which I was a partner and *Shamrock* became, in name at least, a company boat and safe from predators. My business partner, Tony Sharrock, went on board the company asset only once during my tenure. He said he had seldom felt so depressed and uncomfortable, and complained about the lack of ashtrays. When the weather deteriorated I arranged for the boat to be moved from Mersea Deeps and laid up for the winter in a mud-berth at a small boatyard in Peldon Creek to which I occasionally made the six-hour drive to sit for a few hours in the damp cold cabin and wonder once again exactly what I had done. Once I took a girlfriend to Peldon for the weekend, lighting the coal stove in an attempt to make things cheery, but she was not impressed by the tarpaulin-shrouded hulk in the muddy creek and I never saw her again. 'I thought you said you had a yacht,' she said. In spring I moved on board *Shamrock* for a month, leaning the boat against the river bank so that the hull could be scraped and painted at low tide. From then on, most of my life was spent at an angle of about twenty degrees. Nothing would stay on tables or shelves, food fell from plates and cups could only be half filled.

I wrote newspaper articles on my portable typewriter in the morning, posting them in a box near a pub, and working on the boat for the rest of the day. I was permanently wet, cold and had backache and lived on tinned food mostly eaten cold. However, one morning I heard larks singing high above the boat and for a moment had an almost evangelical belief that everything would eventually be all right. One evening the boat remained almost upright at low tide and I found I could sit comfortably for the first time for weeks. Almost immediately there was a hammering on the hatch and a man, wet through and naked except for a towel, shouted that the boat was about to fall over. John Millgate, owner of the boatyard, had noticed the angle of the mast from his window as he took a bath and realised *Shamrock* was lying away from the bank and would topple over at any moment. Ropes from the masthead tied to stakes driven into an adjoining field averted a certain disaster but I was in disgrace for days.

I fixed a date in April for the voyage to Devon which, in the general view, was too early, and spent the time changing the boat's colour to a light green and trying to work out what all the ropes did with the aid of arrowed diagrams kept secretly in my wallet. There was general disapproval of *Shamrock* being sold away and few people gave me any help. A notable exception was David Green, a kindly carpenter and owner of the smack *Gracie*, who spoke in an Essex accent so broad I mistook it for Australian. He pulled me to the top of the mast in a bosun's chair so that I could examine the rigging, and took me to his house, where his wife Carol provided my first cooked meal for a fortnight. When I asked him for any advice he could give me about the sailing and management of smacks, he replied, 'Keep things well bowsed down and sweated up. Don't pinch her to windward and don't put a hitch on your cleats.' Thanking him warmly, I wrote down his words and put them in my wallet with the rope diagrams without the remotest idea of what they meant.

He also said, 'Get Navvy Mussett to caulk your butts', which resulted in a very old man in waders descending into the mud and stuffing oakum and putty into some alarming cracks between the planks. In his younger days Navvy Mussett had been a legendary duck-shooter, taking his 15-foot duck punt onto the marshes, using hand paddles to move stealthily up to flocks of feeding wildfowl and firing into the midst of them with a nine-foot punt gun mounted like a cannon on the bow. 'One Christmas I went out when it was dark and was lying in the reeds when the birds started to come down. I was there for hours, just keeping the boat in place with the paddles and more and more come down until you couldn't get a fag paper between them. There was thousands. I never seen nothing like it. Then, when they was close enough, I just tapped my toe on the floorboards and as they rose off the water I let them have seven ounces of shot. But bugger me, I fired just too low and what did I get? Ten bushel of legs and feet after six hours of freezing my bollocks off.' Finishing his tale, Navvy Mussett also had some advice to give. 'The best thing you can do,' he said, accepting a tenner for his morning's work, 'is to leave the old boat here and bugger off back where you come from.'

However, there was little chance of that. John Millgate was due to help me take the smack back to the mooring in Mersea Deeps the following week, to await the arrival of the crew for the voyage home. It was a somewhat idiosyncratic selection, based largely on who could spare the time, and consisted of the former owner and his son, David Green, Dick and Liz Brown and George Robbins. David had seldom been away from Mersea. He brought his own anchor, not trusting mine, and a camera to photograph buoys and navigational marks and so prove to his mates back home that we had actually got further than Southend. Dick, the bearded curator of the Port of London Authority art collection, had been geologist on the first British post-war expedition to South Georgia. His maritime experience was largely limited to trying to cycle across the Thames from Putney to Fulham one night after the pubs had closed. He was also a part-time exponent of the Indian rope-trick.

Liz, his wife, a former policewoman and security officer at Harrods, had been allowed to steer the Argentinian supply ship in which she was travelling to South Georgia to see her husband. The captain said she was the best natural helmsperson he had ever known, although he saw little of her prowess. Suffering a nervous disorder, he was largely confined to his cabin, tying countless bowlines and sheet bends in pieces of string. George Robbins was a former tanker captain and now proprietor of a picture-framing business. He was our navigator but refused to lay anything but the sketchiest of courses, on the premise that he then couldn't be blamed if anything went wrong. 'The one thing I dreaded on the tanker was hitting a yacht,' he said. 'You had to do so much paperwork.'

If I had expected practical sailing and navigation experience during the 300-mile voyage to Devon, I was disappointed. For three days we motored in thick fog on a flat windless sea. I learned nothing of sweating up, bowsing down and putting hitches on cleats because there was little point in hoisting the sails. Off Brighton we found a dead dog tied to a floating deckchair. The chair was bought aboard and David Green slept in it for most of the voyage.

There was nothing to photograph but the fog. For nearly two days we saw no land, navigational marks or other shipping. With no radar, VHF or radio-direction finder (and this was long before satellite navigation in yachts) we chugged at five knots westwards under engine, relying on George's dead reckoning and a compass course steered unerringly by Mrs Brown. By lunchtime on the third day the cheerful George had become thoughtful, peering through the fog that hung like muslin over the boat, but seeing and hearing nothing. David was asleep in the deckchair and the rest of us were eating sausages when George suggested dropping the anchor. 'According to my reckoning,' he said, 'we're on Dartmoor just west of Newton Abbot.'

As it happened, he was not far wrong. We had been anchored for an hour when the fog suddenly lifted, revealing that another twenty minutes' steaming would have taken us up the beach at Paignton. After 200 miles sailing blind, George had brought us within ten miles of our destination, a feat he dismissed modestly as 'just drawing a line and sailing along it'. When we finally arrived, David took our picture and George later put it in one of his frames.

When the smack was secure on a mooring lent by a local fisherman and the crew had returned home, there remained the problem of appearing to be a charismatic and capable owner of the impressive new arrival. The only solution I could think of – to grow a long black beard – didn't have quite the effect I'd hoped. My Auntie Edna, on first seeing it, remarked, 'It does make you look like your sister,' and a child seeing me buying a newspaper, asked 'Mummy, is that a pirate?' only to be told 'No dear, it's just a man.'

As usual, serendipity was the main contributor to a successful outcome. Ron Lavis, the owner of a local boatyard, mentioned he had two young shipwrights who had wondered if there was any chance of sailing on *Shamrock*. 'They're rough young buggers and they've not done much sailing but you'll get your repairs done cheap. I'll kick their arses if they steal my wood or use my electricity. You'd better tell them that.' Tom and Phil appeared the following Sunday and stood silently on the deck weighing me up. Phil was seventeen and came from Bermondsey. He looked like Marc Bolan and wore several medallions and lilac-coloured platform shoes. His father worked for the little-known London Hydraulic Company, servicing the Victorian network of compressed-air pipes that still ran beneath the streets and powered the lifts of posh hotels. 'He can always tell when it's one of his pipes that's burst,' Phil said. 'It throws the paving stones 20 feet in the air.' As a child Phil was fascinated by ships in the Surrey Docks and had left his family and friends to take up a boat-building apprenticeship in Devon but was still not sure if he had made the right decision. 'I miss me mum and I'm living on bleeding parsties.'

Tom was twenty with a moustache and something of a swagger and had a girlfriend who had been married. He had done a navigation course and hoped to have a boat of his own some day. They climbed the mast to disentangle some blocks and started the engine. By the time they left an hour later we had all realised they had already become indispensable. The following weekend they brought two friends who would complete the *Shamrock* crew for the next five years. Martin was a clerk in the Exeter dole office and wore a rope bracelet around his ankle. Paddy was a builder. He had a girlfriend, Steph, whose father kept a pub in Exeter. This quartet, who would be known as the lads, soon became devoted to the boat and held themselves entirely accountable for its safety and wellbeing. If any member of the crew was unavailable, the others would select a suitable replacement. If he didn't come up to scratch he would not be invited again. I was rarely consulted about these changes in personnel. In fact, looking back, I was rarely consulted about anything.

On their first half-day sail along the coast, the lads found any excuse to climb the mast or crawl out along the bowsprit. They were fearless but responsible and instinctively understood the boat and its ways. They approved of its power and steadiness, its artisan pedigree and the functional grace of its lines. 'It's a working man's boat built to do a job,' Phil said. 'I wouldn't come out with you if you had a yacht. I hate yachts and the tossers who sail them.'

The arrival of the ship's cook was another fortuitous accident. Penelope was introduced to me in a pub by a mutual acquaintance. It was, she said, her first time out in the evening after several months of dieting and mourning the end of a long relationship with an artist known mainly for his violent temper. I liked her woollen hat and long red hair. The acquaintance explained my situation in a flatteringly inaccurate précis: 'He's a Fleet Street journalist with an ocean-going yacht,' and added, 'He's just got divorced and needs cheering up.' Penelope told me she also needed cheering up. She was in her late twenties, head of English at a local high school and lived alone in a nearby village. She told several jokes but her heart obviously wasn't in them, and when I returned from the gents she had disappeared. I discovered that she drove a powder-blue Hillman saloon and the next day found it parked in a thicket by a tiny 1920s-style Tudor cottage. I left a note under the windscreen suggesting an Indian meal the following evening. Egged on by a school colleague, she accepted. Afterwards I stayed the night and we were together for eight years.

Penelope's father had captained tramp steamers for Commons Brothers of Newcastle before becoming a pilot in the Iraq port of Basra. He had died some years earlier but she remembered how uneasy he was on leave and how he counted the days to his return to sea. He was to be found mornings and evenings in the nearby pub rejecting company in the bar and snug and preferring to sit alone on a chair in the corridor. 'The truth was, he couldn't stand people,' Penelope said. He died at sea and was buried in Iraq. Despite such nautical antecedents, Penelope was frightened of the sea. Any sign of bad weather sent her with a drink and the *Telegraph* crossword into a space behind the cooker which became known as coward's corner, and from which she emerged only to cook. The first night of a cruise was always celebrated with a sumptuous meal and the lads remember that their first experience of continental cooking was on *Shamrock*. Curiously, for a career teacher, and one who became a deputy headmistress, Penelope disliked children, especially mine. Later, when we moved to Cornwall, she left me for our next-door neighbour, a stooping submariner, whom she briefly married. I missed the red hair and the woollen hat, but I got over it, and we turned coward's corner into a wardrobe. Certainly my children were glad to see her go. They never understood what they had done to incur her displeasure.

When we started making cruises it didn't take me long to realise that the lads regarded them as heaven-sent opportunities to conduct a class war and to upset the very people I had been trying to impress. They carried aboard shiny Italian suits on hangers which they wore with flat caps in yacht clubs and picked fights with men in blazers. They were up for anything which would distress or inconvenience the enemy. When we were asked to leave a yacht club for being offensively drunk, someone returned with adjustable spanners and dismantled the urinals in the gents. We then bought chips in the town and ate them in a Victorian bandstand after Martin had found a switch which turned on strings of coloured lights and set off a fire alarm. We were moved on by police and Royal Marines. In the

Scillies, they got drunk with the crew of a visiting Royal Navy minesweeper and tried to persuade the sailors to jump ship. Two did and were arrested. In Guernsey, they stole bags of charcoal from a dock warehouse and made a bonfire on the beach. When we left Guernsey for St Malo after being told that we would never be allowed in the St Peter Port marina again, I finally lost my temper and declared it would be the last time the lads sailed on *Shamrock*. There followed a two-day silent mutiny during which the cook and I sailed the boat and the lads sat in the stern and threw beer cans into the sea. When the wind increased off the Pointe du Roc and we needed to shorten sail, their loyalty to the smack got the better of them and they set to work as though nothing had happened. That night, ordered out of St Malo after a fight in a bar, we motored the short distance to the more tolerant town of Dinard and tied up to a large mooring buoy in the river, where, in the early hours, all sleep was banished by lights, commotion and a heavy blow on the bulwarks as a large motor yacht, flying what appeared to be the House of Lords burgee, loomed alongside. The lads watched with interest but with no obvious intention of helping, as ladies and gentlemen in whites and reefer jackets made half-hearted efforts to throw ropes and fend off with mops. Finally someone managed to get a line onto the buoy and the owner called a grizzled retainer in a jersey, and said, 'George, would you be so good as to go to the front and tie one of your beautiful knots?' On the trip home, frequent requests for 'beautiful knots' put everyone in a good humour.

Why anyone would tolerate such a crew was a mystery to the yachting fraternity and a talking-point in the clubs and bars. Becoming an interesting enigma with no effort on my part was an unexpected bonus. I bought a larger longer pipe, and developed the hint of an Essex accent. The lads seemed to approve, although I discovered that they called me Captain Custard or, on a good day, Smartie Smacksman.

*******

Our first major voyage was in the summer of 1976, when Dick Brown was approached by a friend at the BBC to provide a camera platform for the start of the Tall Ships Race on the Thames and asked if we would take *Shamrock* to London for a substantial fee and a free berth in West India Dock. The lads decided we would do it and Tom was appointed navigator and sent to buy charts for the 500-mile round trip. None of them had previously been further from Exmouth on a small boat than Torquay. When my son asked if he could come with us and celebrate his tenth birthday at sea, my ex-wife took out a court injunction to prevent it. The hearing, the day before the voyage, was in chambers at Exeter Crown Court, presided over by a judge wearing what I later discovered was a Royal Thames Yacht Club tie. Briskly dismissing the application, the judge remarked that he could hardly think of a better way for a ten-year-old to spend his birthday. 'Buy him a decent knife and get him to practise his knots. You might advise your client to reach the North Foreland at least an hour before low water,' he said to my solicitor.

Mr Horsey did manage to limit the extent of the permission to four days and my ex-wife then disappeared with both children. I found them in the cinema an hour before we were due to leave and arrived in Exmouth to see *Shamrock* in full sail on the estuary. The lads, anticipating problems, had got everything ready. Phil rowed the dinghy ashore to pick us up from the beach and we caught the first of the down-channel ebb in textbook style. Anticipating a non-stop passage, we had augmented the crew with Chris Tottle, a young timber merchant who had his own binoculars and welcomed every opportunity to prove his courage. But the real reason the lads had insisted on his inclusion was so that he could tell them of the time when he appeared on the television show *The Generation Game* with his elderly mother and was warned by the host Bruce Forsyth, 'We don't want any tittle-tattle, Tottle.' We lost count of the number of times he was persuaded to tell the story during the voyage but the lads' laughter increased with each telling.

The weather was cold and wet, more like October than June, and a south-westerly gale was forecast for the evening. Around noon on the second day we were double-reefed in a grey tumbling sea off St Catherine's Point on the Isle of Wight when the smack gybed and snapped the 30-foot boom in half. We gathered up the bits and motored an uncomfortable forty miles to Chichester Harbour, arriving in late evening. The lads immediately opened their impressive toolboxes and sharpened the broken ends of the boom so that they looked like giant pencils and could be jammed into a large iron stovepipe we carried on deck. At first light next morning, with a reef in the mainsail, we continued the trip, arriving a day late but with a good tale to tell.

West India Dock, in terminal decline, was empty of ships, but staffed with a full quota of stevedores who spent their days playing cards in a shed or disappearing, once they had clocked in, to pursue second careers as decorators or carpet-layers. The vast weedy quays and rusty cranes were depressing reminders of past commercial glory. The only tiny vessel in a dock designed for twenty square-riggers, *Shamrock* was immediately an object of undivided attention. During the first day three teams of customs officers, desperate for something to do, searched the boat for drugs, finding a bottle of aspirin and some corn plasters. When they demanded our papers, the best we could provide was my driving licence and Tom's RYA Coastal Skipper certificate.

Men in caps came to check our mooring ropes and inquire about stowage of explosives. A man on a bike said he had cycled from Whitechapel to check our bills of lading and was disappointed to be sent away empty-handed. The foreman, who had observed us with suspicion, eventually came on board for a cup of tea and told us of the days when he had walked across the dock on the decks of moored ships and a docker could take home £50 a week when his neighbours were lucky to earn £5. 'We're all on borrowed time now,' he said. There were still 100 dockers on the West India payroll and there hadn't been a ship for a month. When the union's agreement with the Port of London Authority expired at Christmas, he expected pretty well all the workforce would go. But there would be bright moments to remember. He told us of a time when a cask had been damaged while unloading a ship from West Africa, spilling a potent liqueur-like liquid. 'We took it round the back and poured the stuff out into our mugs,' the foreman said. 'I've never tasted anything so strong and some of a blokes nearly passed out, although they came back for more. When it was nearly all gone we shook the barrel and heard something rattling. We broke the top off, and there was a pickled monkey inside.' Strangely, the lads didn't think that was funny.

For the start of the race, we had two BBC cameramen, a director and an electrician on board and accompanied some twenty massive square-riggers down the river to Greenwich. It was an impressive sight, but not to the electrician, there only because of a union agreement – there was no electricity on the boat – who sat in the cabin and read the *Daily Mirror*. As we came alongside the vast Russian four-master *Tovarisch*, the skipper leaned down and conversed in Russian with the redoubtable Mrs Brown, once again at our helm. Apparently he said that he liked a woman with strong arms.

The delay in Chichester meant we had exceeded the

court time-limit. I took Tim to see Max Wall, my favourite comedian, making a farewell appearance at the Greenwich Theatre as a birthday treat, but he fell asleep five minutes into the show and I laughed alone. Next day, Tim had his birthday party as we drifted back up-river past the *Cutty Sark*. We had hardly blown out the candles when a river police launch roared alongside, and he was hauled aboard with his presents and luggage by constables in lifejackets as my ex-wife, who had travelled to London to give him a rival birthday party, watched silently from the stern. Happily, he mistook the totally unnecessary confrontation for yet another adventure and waved cheerily as the launch sped away. The rest of the trip back to our berth in West India dock was subdued. Even the lads realised that a doleful domestic drama was only just under the surface and bobbed up from time to time like a drowned dog tied to a deckchair.

We were at sea, returning to Devon, when BBC television broadcast less than a minute of the race footage which had taken a day to shoot and must have cost about £10 a second in the hire of the boat alone. It was shown only on a London regional news programme so no one saw it in Devon, much to the chagrin of the lads, who had hoped to become local heroes. My sole mementoes of the voyage were a Max Wall programme and a letter containing a terse rebuke from the Metropolitan Police for wasting river police time.

The lads cheered themselves up by organising an insurance scam which enabled them to collect several hundred pounds for a new boom by setting up a fictitious boat-building firm on one specially created piece of notepaper and undercutting three local boatyards who had tendered for the job. They acquired a spruce spar from a trading schooner long abandoned up-river, floated it home one night and fashioned an immaculate boom in their employer's workshop one weekend when they knew he was away sailing.

That summer we sailed over 2,000 miles and became cocky and sunburned. After several weeks in the Scillies we were persuaded by Les, who lived nearby, to visit the former copper port of Morwellham Quay, in a deep wooded valley twenty-five miles up the River Tamar from Plymouth, which was stirring into heritage activity after decades of dereliction. On a hazy Saturday morning *Shamrock* anchored off the Royal Western Yacht Club in Plymouth and I rowed to the club looking for a chart of the Tamar but was unsuccessful. 'You'll be all right so long as you go up on the flood and keep to the middle, or is it the left?' said a man at the bar who made the Ancient Mariner look like David Beckham. 'I'll draw you a map. Pass me that fag packet. Returning with a drawing which looked remarkably like a spider-crab's intestines, we sailed north from Plymouth Sound past moored and mothballed dreadnoughts and into the Tamar on a flood tide of curiously tinged yellow water which looked like high-speed custard.

When we reached the village of Cargreen and obeyed the first of our chart's instructions we immediately went aground for fifteen minutes, time enough for someone to dinghy across to the Spaniard's pub for crisps. The next hour steadily got worse. We went aground another four times, got the topmast caught in a tree, went through someone's salmon nets and put the bowsprit over a garden wall, dislodging a small statue of Aphrodite. By now the mast was garlanded with twigs. We had seen no boats apart from a few hauled-up salmon skiffs. It was hard to believe that within living memory this had been Britain's busiest inland waterway, serving the richest copper mines in Europe and carrying more shipping traffic than Liverpool and the Mersey.

Except on the biggest of spring tides, Morwellham Quay was now literally high and dry. What had once been a lordly granite dock berthing 900 vessels a year, flanked by Victorian warehouses, was now a brown blancmange-like spread of mud and silt in which alders, willows and Indian balsam flourished undisturbed. But it was navigable – just – and traditional sailing craft were being encouraged to visit and provide a realistic backdrop for retired bank managers from Tavistock to dress up as Victorian stevedores and keep draconian order in the gift shop and car park.

Our invitation to Morwellham, arranged by Les, contained the inevitable catch: would we stop at the village of Calstock, ten miles from the port, and pick up some members of the Launceston town band who were giving a concert on the quay? 'I would do it myself,' Les said, 'but I've got a bad foot.' Three other traditional boats scheduled to make an up-river procession had wisely cried off because of the weather and the lack of pilotage information, so we took the whole band, all twenty of them. When they gathered on the foredeck to play 'The Entry of the Gladiators' the rudder came out of the water.

After some redistribution of the deck cargo we set some sail and charged off up the river in what must have been a gusting force six. The bandsmen were sensibly apprehensive. 'We thought 'twould be a motorboat,' said the conductor, 'not a galleon. I don't know what the committee will say about this.' When we abruptly went aground ten minutes later, pitching the tuba player over the side, I didn't know what they would say about that either. By now we had the engine on so we just went astern and scooped him up. The tuba, now full of water, was heavier than he was, and we hoisted it out with the topsail halyard amid mutterings about compensation. When we reached the last bend before Morwellham the bandsmen were in better spirits, and with the sun glinting on the instruments and the music echoing up the valley it was quite a stirring occasion, so ending up in a hedge had to be something of an anticlimax.

Following the instructions of man on the riverbank who pointed to an apparently impenetrable thicket and shouted

'Turn in there', we crashed through undergrowth to find ourselves in a water-filled country lane hung with enough blackberries to make a creditable blackberry and apple crumble. As the bandsmen scrambled ashore the tuba player said that he would have to ask his wife whether or not he should contact his solicitor, but there was little time for discussion: by now the tide had turned and we needed every minute of the ebb to return to Plymouth. As it was we went aground but as it was outside a pub no one complained. Les was supposed to hand on £50 for our afternoon's work but never did. Then again, we never heard from the tuba player, either.

CHAPTER 4

# A matter of convenience

When *Shamrock* was laid up that autumn in the canal basin at Exeter I knew there were several things I must do before spring. One was to get some qualifications in order to rebut the growing belief on the waterfront that the lads were in effect the skippers of the boat, and another was to sort out the lavatory.

Andrew Archer, who ran an RYA Yachtmaster's evening course in a local school, was a small mercurial figure with white hair and a neatly clipped beard, but there all similarity to an orthodox maritime instructor abruptly ended. I had first heard about him when a charter yacht he was skippering caught fire and exploded in the Channel Islands. No one was hurt, but the incident resulted in years of litigation which was never properly resolved because

Andrew denied any responsibility, claiming the fire was due to supernatural causes. No one knew quite what to make of Andrew. He spoke frequently of his days at Cambridge and his friendship with the philosopher Alfred Ayer ('Freddie still owes me £20, the bastard') and the poets W.H. Auden and Dylan Thomas, but his own qualifications and sources of income were largely a mystery; they included teaching yoga to pensioners and growing organic vegetables when the practice was still comparatively rare. He was a vegan who managed to combine a spartan lifestyle with drinking large amounts of beer and driving an Alfa Romeo car, but mainly he regarded himself as a teacher and spirit guide and could be found in pubs surrounded by admiring young women discussing the influence of Kant and Spinoza on absolute free will, and whether eating organic cabbage made you randy.

His main interest was writing plays, which were performed just before Christmas in his house, a dank Victorian villa by the river, encroached on, inexorably, by caravans, mainly because Andrew kept selling bits of his garden to a caravan park. The plays were very long and allegoric, usually based on something out of the Old Testament, and consisted mainly of Andrew dressed in tea-towels, discussing ethical dilemmas, in a voice reminiscent of the Grand Vizier at the pantomime. At half-time his large blonde wife, dressed as a fairy queen, sold biscuits and coffee.

The plays were attended mainly by silent youths in crew-neck pullovers who went to Andrew's classes on comparative religions, girls who unaccountably fancied him, and people like me, who went to snigger. Most people went only once. The performance room, panelled in tea-coloured plywood, was always bitterly cold, despite several paraffin stoves, and hung with Andrew's paintings and drawings, usually depicting small men in suits and apparitions with hen's beaks. These works of art were for sale, but remained largely unsold. Penelope found Andrew boring and self-obsessed, but I quite liked him. He had the seedy charisma which invariably seemed to impress me, and he also admired the boat.

During navigation classes he never spoke of any nautical qualifications, preferring to reminisce about his war service, spent mainly on torpedo boats in the Mediterranean, and his appreciation of Italian food and women. One lesson, I remember, was devoted entirely to the drowning of the poet Shelley in a suicidally over-canvassed yacht off the Italian coast in 1822 and ended with Andrew reciting Shelley's 'Ode to the West Wind' and advising us to have a look at 'Prometheus Unbound' for our homework. When a serious man, who owned a large plastic yacht, asked when we were going to do compass deviation, and the rule of twelfths, Andrew told him to sod off. The man never came to the classes again.

Andrew had an impressive delivery and some good phrases. One, 'obvious soon as stated', I still use whenever possible. But what made his classes popular and often oversubscribed was his uncanny ability to forecast the questions on the RYA exam papers, and so have probably the highest pass rate of any classes in the south-west. To be party to this information you needed to buy Andrew drinks and packets of nuts in the pub after class and laugh at his stories, and eventually you might be rewarded by 'I think it might pay you to have a squint at the collision regulations and the interpolation of soundings', said in a whisper behind the hand like Leslie Phillips in a *Carry On* film.

I was not the only one to notice that Andrew was distinctly uneasy at sea. Forced to take students on a practical course on a hired yacht, he would make a nest in the forward cabin with a supply of alcohol, dried fruit and nuts and Wagner on a cassette player, and give instructions that he was only to be called in what he regarded as an emergency. This did not include the distinct possibility of hitting the Channel Light Vessel in thick fog. Turning up the cassette volume and opening a bottle of Cripplecock cider, he said, 'If I get you out of every footling little scrape, you'll never learn anything.'

In the middle of the course, Andrew left his wife and family. The caravan park bought the riverside house and knocked it down. Within weeks the ground was covered by caravans and it was hard to believe the house had ever been there. A month before the Yachtmaster's exam Andrew gathered a dozen students in the pub and made some informed guesses about the contents of the forthcoming paper. Three students, Jim, Joe and Basil, were ambitious to do well, but Joe counselled caution. Their coursework, he pointed out, was barely average and spectacular marks in the exam would be noticed. They had to be sensible and aim for the pass mark of 60 per cent, which hopefully would be accepted without suspicion.

The plan was agreed, the exam taken and all three got through: Basil with 61 per cent and Jim with 63 per cent. Joe, with 94 per cent, was awarded a prize for student of the year. I got a modest pass and considered myself lucky not to be arrested. I never understood why Andrew, his life deeply influenced by a variety of religions, behaved as he did, nor will I ever know. Andrew is dead now. If he had problems navigating to heaven, I hope someone returned one of his many favours and let him have a squint at the chart.

A solution to the second pressing problem – *Shamrock*'s lavatory – was less apparent. No fault could be found with the plumbing, adapted from a cast-iron Victorian central-heating system. It was its situation that was the problem. Why someone with an Essex sense of humour had put the lavatory in what looked like a plywood telephone box in the middle of the saloon we never discovered, but it meant that nothing that went on in there could be left to the imagination. The lads found this a constant source of enjoyment but no one else did. I had long since discovered that the sanitary arrangements on small boats are a continual preoccupation and can be distressing to those of delicate sensibilities, as in the case of a retired science teacher we had met earlier that season on his gaff cutter in the Scillies as we were both preparing to leave for Newlyn. We had too much crew whereas George, as usual, was single-handed, and I offered to lend him someone for the night passage. The offer was courteously refused and I asked why. 'To tell the truth,' George replied, 'I just can't bear the thought of sharing the lavatory.'

At the other extreme there seemed to be no shortage of people who regarded the marine toilet as an outstanding example of industrial design. 'Have a look at the old thunderbox. None of your modern plastic rubbish,' cried the skipper of a converted Bristol Channel pilot cutter the lads and I visited in Alderney. He threw open the lavatory door to reveal his wife reading the cookery pages of *Woman's Own*. She managed a glassy smile and invited us for tea. At least she could get off. Not so an acquaintance whose pressurised lavatory would occasionally form a vacuum-tight bond between skin and plastic. As he sat there in agony, his wife and son crouched at his feet anxiously trying to release the pressure valve with a rusty mole-wrench and a bent spoon. Finally freed, the man spent a day in Dartmouth hospital lying on his stomach.

The urgent replacement of a plank in the hull took the money we had reserved for altering the lavatory and things remained as they were, the lads greeting every muffled fart with undisguised pleasure, and the rest of us talking loudly or suddenly finding things to do on deck. The lads took to collecting boat lavatory stories and telling them at carefully chosen inappropriate times. One concerned a man who sailed with a yachtsman of the bucket-and-chuck-it school who had a green bucket for the lavatory and a blue bucket for washing up. It was only when the skipper misread the traffic lights at the entrance to a marina that it was realised he was colour-blind.

There was also the tale of a man from Torquay whose wife agreed to his buying a sailing boat only if it had excellent toilet facilities, but when she saw the one he had chosen – a 22-foot dayboat – she was deeply displeased. Certainly it had a large and efficient lavatory, but to use it you had to crawl under the foredeck, open the hatch and sit with your head and shoulders exposed to the elements. 'No one can possibly know you're on the loo,' said the husband. 'They'll just think you're sitting looking out of the hatch.' They bought the boat and during their first afternoon sail in Torbay a large yacht sailed close and the entire crew waved and smiled. The wife waved back from her seat in the forehatch.

'What nice people,' she said. 'Do you know them?'

'Oh yes,' the husband replied, 'they sold us the boat.'

*******

The next season was dogged to a large extent by my physical incapacity. A stubborn determination to literally pull my weight on a boat which was sailed largely by brute force aggravated a musculoskeletal disorder, in other words, a bad back, which meant that despite my crisp new Yachtmaster's certificate, the lads, as usual, ran the boat while I lay on the deck and bleated orders which were largely ignored. Wherever we went, I was told that sailing, with everything coming at you at the wrong angle, is one of the worst things imaginable for dodgy backs. 'Give it up and stick to crosswords and looking at women,' was the considered advice of an orthopaedic surgeon I saw after being taken ashore in Salcombe, locked solid from neck to knee.

We hadn't even been anywhere. We had been invited aboard someone's boat moored to a pontoon and I was opening a bottle of Sauvignon Blanc when I felt as though I had been hit by Prince Nazeem on a good day. Doing what the lads described as an imitation of a bullock struck by lightning, I fell backwards, spraying the wine across a neighbouring teak deck. We were not invited again. Pausing only to recommend as many aspirins as I could take with half a bottle of whisky, the surgeon hurried off to catch the tide.

I had already noticed that in most sailing clubs bad backs were usually at their worst when people were required for manual work like hauling boats in and out or tidying the car park. Sometimes skiving became a minor art form prohibiting anything involving the slightest exertion. 'Then here's a job you can do,' said an exasperated secretary, handing over a book of raffle tickets. 'Write numbers on these.' 'Sorry, squire,' said the sufferer, 'I haven't got the right trousers on.'

My own back problem continued from time to time at the most inopportune moments. On one occasion we were taking the smack into Exmouth docks with a spring ebb tide running hard across the narrow entrance, using a well-tried technique of aiming the boat at full speed against the upstream wall. Just as bystanders were gleefully anticipating the worst, an eddy would swing us to starboard and the huge brass gear lever was slammed astern. As the smack slid into the calm water of the outer harbour, the lads would step jauntily ashore with mooring lines. It was impressive when it worked, and even more impressive when, as on this occasion, it didn't. As I leaned from the helm to engage reverse gear, my back jammed solid. I remained immobile, like some Soviet statue depicting the downtrodden proletariat, as sixteen tons of boat surged into the congested entrance at a good six knots. Someone pushed me aside and sent us full astern, but not before the 20-foot bowsprit had gone through an open saloon window of the *Devon Princess* passenger steamer, moored nearby, clearing the tables of plates of crab salads and several Victoria sponges. I still have the bills somewhere at home.

We were now being noticed by organisations dedicated to old-boat preservation, particularly the Old Gaffers Association – a national network of devotees of gaff-rigged sailing craft – which invited us to their south-western area race off Dartmouth followed by 'a knees-up at a convivial watering hole.' The OGA had been formed in 1963 by a few enthusiasts, mainly from the east coast, who were perturbed that the traditional four-sided sail with a spar known as a gaff supporting it diagonally at the top, used on working boats since the eighteenth century, was being forced into extinction by the more efficient modern triangular Bermudan rigs.

The golden age of gaff rig was from about 1880 to 1914. By the late 1950s most yachts had been converted to Bermudan rig and very few new gaff boats were being built. But by then, what were almost secret societies of gaff devotees were holding their own small races and demonstrating the charm of old boats and archaic rigs. Over the years the OGA attracted several thousand members in a dozen UK areas, with affiliated organisations in Ireland, France and Australia. We were soon to find that although they thought they were a rather rollicking lot, Old Gaffers took themselves pretty seriously.

Although they naturally had reservations about knees-ups and watering holes, the lads, to my surprise, decided we should go racing with the Gaffers. They now had an almost mystical belief in *Shamrock*'s invincibility, and the chance to beat toffs in posh boats was eagerly anticipated. When I pointed out we would be competing against retired racing yachts and nippy dayboats, in a boat built for dredging oysters, I was angrily accused of disloyalty. 'Call yourself Smartie Smacksman?' said Phil. 'You should be ashamed of yourself.' In vain I pointed out that it was them not me who had invented the name and that I was only being realistic. 'It's a working boat and we're working men,' Paddy said. That, as far as the lads were concerned, was a satisfactory end to the argument.

The race was on a Sunday and we prepared to leave Exmouth for Dartmouth one Saturday afternoon only to find that the engine had seized solid. The sun was out and spirits were high. It was only twenty-five miles and wind and tide were fair. Who needed an engine? Seven hours later there was dead calm, a foul tide and darkness. By midnight we had drifted into the harbour entrance and were fending off the rocks with brooms. A massive ethnic sculling oar was completely ineffective. So was towing with our stout traditional dinghy. Eventually the twentieth century fortuitously arrived in the form of a crabber, back from a night's pot-hauling, with diesels roaring and lights blazing, which towed us up the river and put us on a mooring off the town quay. Only one man saw us arrive – the owner of a small shabby ketch – and he didn't say anything. There was a south-easterly gale the next day and the race was cancelled but not the knees-up at the watering hole. We got a trophy for making the most seamanlike passage to the race. It was festooned with intricate knots and ropework and we were delighted with it. The man from the ketch came up afterwards and said, 'You ought to give that back. It wasn't seamanship. It was bloody madness.' He was right, of course, but I didn't give it back. I just lit my pipe and looked ethnic.

We did several Old Gaffers' races that year. The first was with an authentic Smartie Smacksman, David Green, who drove down from Essex in his red carpenter's van, once again bringing his own anchor. It was a hot and cloudless July Saturday and Start Bay was dotted with forty-five gaffers with white and tan sails of every shade. The wind was a fitful south-westerly and small light boats had an advantage, which David refused to acknowledge.

Skipper for the day, he revealed himself as what the lads approvingly defined as a 'shit-hot racer'. With the honour of the east coast at stake, he shook the boat out of the slovenly habits it had acquired under its new management. As he had advised, what now seemed so long ago, everything was sweated up and bowsed down until the sails stood stiff as boards in the sunlight.

Paddy was sent up the topmast to smooth out creases in the topsail invisible to the normal human eye. When the wind came on the beam, we were ordered to lie full-length beneath the bulwarks so as not to impede every breath reaching the sails. Under David's magic helmsmanship we crept slowly through groups of boats apparently motionless on a glassy sea, the lads shouting derisively at each crew we passed. Les and Sid had long since lost interest in the race and motored to nearby Slapton sands where they anchored, took off their clothes and joined the female occupants of a nudist beach for a light lunch. When the wind finally failed entirely, the race was terminated at the end of the third leg. We came seventh in our class and eleventh overall, but to the lads it was a famous victory, particularly as we had beaten Captain McWhirr, who had employed a professional sailing master for the day. That evening in the Royal Dart Yacht Club, someone celebrated the occasion by taking the bust of a Victorian yachtsman from the secretary's office and putting it on the roof of a public lavatory.

That season we raced in the Solent and in a series of races in the Channel Islands sponsored by a whisky company and managed not to disgrace ourselves. After one race, due to the eccentricities of the handicapping system, we found we had actually won three trophies: for first boat home in class one, first working boat home (we were sole entrants in both classes) and a cup for coming last. In the Channel Islands the lads pursued their vendetta against the rich and privileged by persuading David Green to skipper us again in three races, pledging themselves to beating

Captain McWhirr in all three, which we did. Captain McWhirr did not take kindly to defeat. After the first race he tried unsuccessfully to persuade Smartie Smacksman to jump ship and after the second asked if I would sell him the boat.

*******

Every trip was an adventure in those long hot summers of the late seventies and caution played little part in our plans. Against all advice, we sailed away one stormy night for France, only to return hollow-eyed the next day with the sails in shreds and the fuel tank torn from its mountings. But we didn't learn and didn't want to. For instance, against the most basic common sense, we never had guardrails on *Shamrock*. Working smacks never had them of course, and after she was yachtified we kept her looking as authentic as possible, with her foot-high bulwarks and exposed tiller, and trusted to luck. One evening, off Portland Bill, a huge following sea swept the helmsman up the deck and mercifully wedged him behind the mast, but we continued to pretend to be intrepid smacksmen and joked about nailing a pair of wellies for the helmsman to stand in on that long and lonely counter stern. It was the waders and faded smock syndrome and our only excuse was that in the world of old boats it was highly contagious.

We were constantly being re-infected. 'The two most useless things on a sailing boat are an engine and a depth-sounder,' we were told by a man who looked like Grace Darling's granddad but in fact was a teacher of media studies in Swindon. We last heard of him when he was hauled off the rocks by a boat which fortunately had both. Another man, Richard, owner of an ugly and painstakingly restored Cornish workboat, generously offered me a couple of peak-purchase blocks as a present to the boat. 'Unfortunately I can't let you have them today,' he said, 'I haven't got my wicker block basket with me.' Richard had a pale sad-eyed wife whom he called Red Leader. She skilfully cut Ritz biscuits in half and silently served them with tiny pieces of cheese on a grubby doily. 'Red Leader is an ace with refreshments,' Richard said. 'She was a stewardess on cruise-liners. She was proposed to by a gangster.'

Richard was a chiropodist renowned among his clientele of old ladies for his gentle touch, but at sea he was fearless and thoughtless. On one occasion he told Red Leader he was nipping down to the moorings to check the boat and would be home for supper in an hour. He returned three weeks later after taking in the Scillies, Brest and north Biscay, and Red Leader felt she was justified in making a mild complaint.

He had, she pointed out, missed their wedding anniversary, their daughter's birthday, forgotten to pay the gas bill which resulted in their being cut off, and reneged on his promise to take the dog for an ear operation. And why hadn't he phoned? 'How could I?' asked Richard. 'I had hardly any change for the phone and I wanted to keep it for emergencies.'

Many of the old gaffers we met around this time did their sailing safely away from the sea, pottering with dried-out wrecks in landlocked gardens and dreaming of the wide blue yonder, safe in the knowledge that nothing would come of it. There were, however, heroic exceptions. One was Charlie Force, an elderly Newquay inventor who spent a decade bringing back to life a boat which had spent thirty-five years embedded in ten feet of mud. When we came across him on the River Tamar, Charlie's nautical experience was limited to building an underwater JCB digger. He had just read about an 1895 51-foot sailing barge called the *Lynher* in a book called *Lost Ships of the West Country* he had picked up in a Truro bookshop, and was determined to save her from extinction.

Finding the *Lynher* sunk in the mud of a Cornish quarry, he spent a summer single-handedly digging her out and putting iron bars through the hull to hold it together. For the next eight years he rebuilt the boat from stem to stern using a book on carpentry from the library and sleeping in a van parked nearby. After the immaculate restoration had won a national award, Charlie sold it at a £40,000 loss and looked for something else to do. He went on to build a wind generator that supplied his house with so much hot water that he had to keep the bath taps running to get rid of it.

Other men, while no longer at sea, still managed to exert an impressive influence. Digger Rodgers, who ruled Exmouth docks from a shed near the swing bridge, was tall and fierce with a chapped red face. He supervised the movement of small freighters bringing in bulk cargoes from Holland and strode the quays in clouds of sickly-smelling poultry meal, usually followed by his assistant, known as Brian the Tooth, inspecting the mooring lines that held the creaking rusty ships and shouting a litany of criticism which usually included 'That rope wouldn't hold up my missus's knickers.' Digger was not supposed to allow yachts into the commercial dock but occasional bottles of Teacher's whisky would persuade him to make *Shamrock* an exception when we needed fuel and provisions. He admitted a grudging approval of the old boat, 'although if 'twas mine I'd cut all they ropes 'n sticks off un and put a big diesel in.'

Digger never explained how he became dockmaster. He came from a fishing family in nearby Budleigh Salterton, and told stories of epic hardship and hauling boats up the shingle in winter gales. He had fished for many years with his brother but eventually they were hounded out of business by bigger trawlers and had to sell their boats. He couldn't understand why people went to sea for pleasure. To him, small boats were synonymous with danger and misfortune. Once, to my surprise, Digger invited us for a drink at his house one Saturday afternoon near Christmas. The shed next to his cottage at Budleigh Salterton was stacked with bottles of Teacher's and lemonade. The lads were soon loudly drunk and inexplicably arguing about education when the sitting room door opened and Digger's wife ushered in an elderly woman who had apparently been invited to join the party. She sat in a corner as the noise steadily rose, smiling encouragingly. Then, when there was a momentarily break in the hubbub, she leaned forward and asked, 'Would anyone like to talk about speedway or the supernatural?' She continued to nod and smile and when Mrs Rodgers put her head round the door to ask 'Are you all right, Edith?' she replied, 'Oh yes. I think they're getting round to me now.'

I bought another of Digger's acquaintances, a small sandy-haired man known as Coastguard Len, a bottle of Teacher's that Christmas, feeling it was the least I could do after he had possibly saved my life, but I did it with a heavy heart knowing that I was now under deep obligation to Len and that he would undoubtedly mistake this obligation for friendship, which, as it turned out, he did. Len was an undertaker and one would have thought he would have been hardened to tragedy, but he took many of his customers' deaths personally and was seen crying at funerals and being comforted by mourners.

His stories of the funeral trade had a grisly fascination and attracted an audience in pubs. He had been apprenticed to a prosperous undertaker in the nearby seaside town of Sidmouth, then the richest retirement area in England, and had been appalled by the scandalous practices of his employer who, according to Len, cut the feet off corpses to fit them into standard-size coffins, tore the rings from their hands and sold them to the local jeweller and filled caskets with birdcage grit rather than bothering to sieve the ashes of the deceased.

Len had left Sidmouth as soon as his indentures expired and joined a funeral firm in Exmouth, eventually becoming a partner by marrying the proprietor's daughter. 'I came with my own grasses,' Len said, referring to the green lawn-like cloths spread over the earth around an open grave, 'so they knew from the start I had the right attitude.' It was puzzling to know why everyone tried to avoid Len, as he was warm-hearted, socially responsible and tried hard to please. When he joined the local Coastguard as a volunteer, a long-serving member resigned, saying 'I don't want to be anywhere near that bugger when he shits himself being winched down a cliff.' That was unfair – Len turned out to be a brave and resourceful coastguard. His only problem was that he had absolutely no empathy with boats or the sea and was forbidden from using the Coastguards' high-powered inflatable after he overturned it in shallow water and lay inert with fear under the boat as the propeller of the huge outboard engine flailed only inches away.

It seemed that Len couldn't climb aboard a boat without pulling off a fitting or damaging the paintwork. A cigarette he thoughtfully threw away before boarding a yacht landed in its furled cotton mainsail, which smouldered undetected before igniting at 3 am. He also took a hired liferaft in a canvas valise into a phone box and tripped over the ripcord that released the raft and filled it with compressed gas. Instantly the liferaft burst its bonds and filled the phone-box, trapping Len in a foetal position on the floor. A passer-by stabbed the monster with a knife and its flailing death-throes broke his glasses. He was not pleased. 'A pity it had to be him,' Len said. 'We're burying his mother tomorrow.'

When Len volunteered to abseil down a church tower for charity he fell twenty feet onto a gravestone, broke his leg and for weeks led funeral processions on crutches. Len asked people to autograph or decorate his plaster cast, but they were too busy or hadn't got a pen. The only person to oblige was a young nephew who drew a large explicit representation of two skeletons copulating, with the caption 'Love Never Dies.' Sensing it might cause problems at funerals, Len got his wife to give the cast a coat of magnolia emulsion paint.

Len was desperate to join what he called the 'comradeship of the sea', and for this he needed a boat. He bought a small wooden cabin-cruiser and, as he was a religious man (he referred to God as The Skipper), took it on a trailer to a local church to have it blessed by the vicar. After a month of refurbishment in his front garden, Len launched the boat for a gentle potter up-river with his wife and mother-in-law, but soon found himself out at sea due to the fact that the boat would unaccountably only steer to starboard. Its progress was mercifully halted by the bow sinking through a hole in the stem and the stern catching fire from an uncooled exhaust. The boat was finally beached and Len later swapped it for a static caravan at Dawlish. But he still kept up his membership of the yacht club and wore a knife and a shackle-key on a lanyard.

Len was always anxious for new experiences and a visit with his daughter to one of the early Glastonbury pop festivals provided him with several anecdotes for his pub monologues. The most unlikely concerned an apparent encounter with a drug dealer at an organic bagel stall. 'I was waiting in the queue when this bloke came up and said, "Can I interest you in any class A drugs?" I twigged this could be a set-up so I took out my Coastguard beret and put it on. Then I said, "Would you like to rephrase that?" and he said, "Well, what about some rolling tobacco at half price?" I took off my beret and bought ten packets.'

One damp autumn afternoon, with mist already on the hills, I pushed a wheelbarrow containing chain, two small concrete sinkers and a spade onto the mudflats at low tide, to lay a drying dinghy mooring for a friend. It was hardly an onerous job, just a question of finding enough vacant space for the boat to swing, digging holes for the weights, connecting them with chain and shackling on a buoy and a bit of rope. The only factors to bear in mind were that the mud was soft and the spring tide came in at four knots, but anyone with one of Andrew Archer's Yachtmaster's tickets would presumably know that.

The vast expense of mud was empty except for two men collecting cockles on a distant bank. I walked about a quarter-mile from the shore to where the mud was shiny and smooth. No boats were moored there and I soon discovered why. When I had dug a two-foot hole and lowered in a weight, I stepped back to check my handiwork and found I couldn't move. I was up to my knees in mud and sinking fast.

The pile of chain had already disappeared and the wheelbarrow was following. Leaning my weight on the spade and trying to lever myself out only accelerated the sinking process. When after ten minutes of struggle the mud had risen to thigh level and there was still nothing solid beneath my feet it dawned on me that I was probably in mortal danger – a situation which at first produced a strange feeling of lassitude followed by disbelief and then irritation that I would have to make a fool of myself by asking for help.

There was no need to panic. Then I caught a glimpse of the first of the flood tide sliding over the mud a few hundred yards to the south and decided that probably there was. I waved and shouted the word 'help', which was strangely difficult to enunciate at volume. At that moment I was very much alone in the world, my feet and legs were numb and I was convinced I was about to die. The two men with their baskets of cockles, now walking back to shore along a rocky ridge, paused, made a diversion, stopped at the edge of the shingle, some hundred feet away from where I lay in what now looked like a small lake of chocolate mousse, and stood watching the drama. One lit a cigarette but didn't put his basket down. They obviously had no intention of venturing onto the mud.

'Help!' I shouted defiantly.

'Are you alright?' one of the men said.

'No,' I said. 'I'm drowning. Can't you see that?'

'You shouldn't be there,' said the younger of the men. 'It's not safe.'

I watched incredulously as he began to walk away. The older man followed. Then he paused and shouted: 'We'll try to find someone. Don't go away. It's best if you keep your legs together.' They moved off towards the shore without a backward glance. I reckoned I now had fifteen or twenty minutes before the tide arrived. The early evening was cold and still and the mud made a faint bubbling sound like soup on a low light. The rate of subsidence seemed to have halted at just below waist level but only because I was no longer moving. Any activity and the slow descent immediately resumed and, far below, the mud gripped my calves like a snake. While I waited I tried to think of something jolly but it wasn't easy. Instead, my mind unaccountably slipped back some twenty years to a report of a minor fifteenth-century tragedy discussed in a school history lesson and which had obviously made a deep subconscious impression. For want of anything better to do, I found I could still recite it almost verbatim:

> In the doleful circumstance of a Jew, who on a Saturday fell into a midden in Maiden Lane and when suffered to be drawn out would not allow it, on the grounds that exertion was prohibited on his Sabbath. Thus he remained until the Sunday when he entreated Christians to draw him from the midden, which they would not, on the grounds that Sunday was their day of rest. On attending the midden on Monday, it was found that the Jew had meanwhile perished in the gonge.

I was getting some idea of how he must have felt, when

there was suddenly a movement on the shoreline, and when two Land Rovers with blue lights drove onto the mud, despair was quickly replaced by overwhelming relief, followed by what could be described as a vague annoyance. Was such a flamboyant show really necessary when someone could have just strolled out with a rope? There was worse to follow. When the vehicles stopped on the edge of the firm sand and men in yellow helmets got out I saw that one was Coastguard Len, who was apparently in charge. I needn't have worried: coastguards are obviously trained not to embarrass the customers and I got little more than a curt nod from Len as he supervised ladders and planks laid across the mud. Soon I was being eased up by a winch fixed onto a tripod above my head and gradually the mud let me go. It took a long time. 'We have to do it slow,' Len said. 'Otherwise the suction could pull you in half. We killed a horse that way last winter.'

As I was pulled out gently, like a large carrot, Len gave a short lecture about the irresponsibility of going out onto the mud alone without telling anyone, and of the expense and inconvenience I had caused. I imagined it was a speech all coastguards had to learn, and to his credit Len stopped in mid-sentence and said: 'I expect you've got the message. Let's clean you up and get you home.' Dripping with black slime, I was carried to a Land Rover and put on a tarpaulin in the back. As we drove away, I saw the tide entering the hole in which I had stood. Back at headquarters the incident was logged as 'Man recovered from foreshore'. I was blasted with a pressure hose after being advised for the second time that day to keep my legs together, lent a boiler suit and a pair of pumps, given hot tea and driven home. I was ashamed and deeply grateful. That night, despite extra blankets, I shook with cold and couldn't sleep.

Next day I expected the incident to be all over town, but no one said anything. I casually asked a friend who drank in the Pilot, Len's local, whether Len had been telling stories about rescuing anyone from the mud, but apparently he hadn't. It occurred to me that Len was sacrificing a potentially spiffing yarn out of pity, but it turned out he was slightly more devious than that. In return for not saying anything, he wondered if there might be a berth for him on *Shamrock* when we were going somewhere interesting. 'I'll have to ask the lads,' I said, knowing what their reaction would be, but luckily the decision was taken from our hands when one of Len's hearses ran over his foot at Exeter crematorium and he was in plaster for the rest of the sailing season. I gave him the whisky and hoped that would be the end of it. It was. Len's firm was taken over by an American funeral conglomerate and he moved to manage a funeral parlour in Plymouth.

We never saw him again but we heard the transfer was not a success. Len's wife left him for a member of the crew of the Torpoint ferry and the conglomerate closed Len's branch and demoted him to a hearse-driver in Torquay. One Sunday afternoon Len tried to commit suicide by drowning himself in the sea at Paignton but he had misread the tide-tables and the incoming tide repeatedly threw him back up the beach until, exhausted and thoroughly fed up, he went home. Next day his branch manager, a kindly man, hearing of the incident, took Len out to lunch and persuaded him he still had a lot to live for. There was a possibility of promotion and the manager, a yachtsman, offered to propose him for membership of his sailing club. Len left the office that evening with a spring in his step and sadly was later was knocked down by a tour bus full of pensioners from Scarborough. We had every intention of going to the funeral but somehow we didn't get round to it. We were all sorry to hear about Len and agreed that if The Skipper would do that to him, who was in the same trade so to speak, what hope was there for the rest of us?

CHAPTER 5

# Captain Jelly and Captain Custard

'Board the car, sailors, if you please,' Shahid Hamid said. He threw in our luggage, climbed in, slammed the door and the taxi plunged into the midst of the Karachi rush hour. Apart from the people, the noise, the heat, the bedsteads on the pavement, the camel carts and the professional letter-writers sitting at desks outside the post office, it could have been Manchester. Classic mid-nineteenth-century civic architecture and Gothic extravagances in maroon and yellow stone surrounded us on all sides. I learned later it was designed by a man called Strachan from Aberdeen.

The crawling cab, hemmed in by bicycles each carrying up to three people, stopped suddenly at a junction to avoid two camel-drawn carts being driven neck-and-neck at suicidal speed with total disregard for the traffic. In one of the tiny carts the driver held the legs of a wiry youth who hung out of the front grasping something between the camel's legs. 'If you squeeze their balls they run faster,' Shahid Hamid explained. 'For your information, people bet a lot of money on these races.'

The Squadron Leader, recently retired, small and severe, with grey hair which appeared to have been painted onto his scalp, his son Captain Bulpin and I were in Karachi in the winter of 1982 to take an 80-foot Dutch harbour tug through the Arabian Sea and the Gulf of Oman, and into the Persian Gulf to the port of Sharjah in the United Arab Emirates, a journey of some 800 miles and likely to take, without stops, four or five days. Bulpin, a tall dark man in his thirties whose long sideburns and saturnine expression made him look like a rake in a Gillray cartoon, was skipper of the expedition. The Squadron Leader was navigator and I was there to make up the numbers and also because I was Bulpin's new and special friend.

The tug was reasonably fast and comfortable and was being leased to Sharjah harbour authorities after a year working in Karachi on a construction project. Normally it was a trip that any Karachi harbour pilot would have regarded as a pleasant holiday, but these were not normal times. The Iran–Iraq war was at its height and neutral shipping was being apprehended indiscriminately, particularly in the 50-mile-wide Straits of Hormuz, which effectively controlled over half the world's tanker movements, and through which the tug would sail. Apart from the danger, the high insurance premiums and mediocre fees made the job unattractive to big delivery services and eventually the contract ended up, of all unlikely places, on the waterfront at Dartmouth and on the desk of Captain Jelly.

Captain Jelly was a youngish man with a liking for bright blue and white striped shirts and the pink damp look of someone who had just emerged from a very hot shower. He ran a small repair yard and boat delivery business, which seemed to exist in a state of suspended animation, with workmen sitting silently in the shadow of some dismantled hulk eating cake and Captain Jelly in his office talking to his girlfriend on the phone or chatting to someone with time to waste. Occasionally a customer would come in to ask why a job estimated to take two days was still uncompleted after a fortnight and Captain Jelly would send out for éclairs and settle down for a chat. The explanation was invariably the same 'We're still waiting for the bits. The moment they come we'll have it done in an hour. The guys out there are just aching to get on with the job' – indicating a lachrymose youth reading the *Daily Mirror*. The rest of the workforce had gone to lunch.

It was hard not to like Captain Jelly. He was friendly and obliging and knew everyone on the river. It was just unwise to do business with him if the job was remotely urgent. At the root of most of Captain Jelly's problems were what he referred to as merchants. These included rip-off merchants, cloud-nine merchants, Thatcherite merchants, woe-woe merchants (pessimists), suede-shoe merchants, blah-blah merchants, all of whom conspired to make life difficult. There were even ear-blowing merchants – sinister Lotharios who apparently had designs on his girlfriend.

Our private nickname for him came about after I had unwisely asked him to replace the 40-year-old Lister diesel engine in *Shamrock* with something more powerful, a job which he estimated would take three weeks at the most. The Lister was removed, an 80-horsepower converted lorry engine arrived in the Dartmouth yard from Brighton and there it stayed for the next five months while we waited for the bits. As *Shamrock* lay unused during one of the best sailing seasons for years the lads urged me into action. One Saturday, feeling distinctly liverish, I drove down to Dartmouth with Martin and Phil determined to sort things out once and for all. I would sue the yard, report it to the Board of Trade, refuse to pay, take the boat away.

But over coffee and several large teacakes in the yard office I began to wonder if I was being unreasonable. After all, the bits had finally come and the engine would be installed and ready by the end of the month. As we left we shook hands warmly. 'Bloody hell, what a pair,' said Phil to Martin as we walked back to the car. 'Talk about Captain Custard meets Captain Jelly.' The engine, needless to say, remained in the yard for another three months. When eventually installed, and christened Black Betty, it ran faultlessly for the rest of the time I had the boat.

Captain Jelly later became the right-hand man of a dynamic nautical celebrity who organised round-the-world yacht races. To the astonishment of all who knew them, the partnership was highly successful. All we could assume was that Captain Jelly must have had to buy an awful lot of cake.

It was in Captain Jelly's office that I had first met Captain Bulpin, who was both a friend and Captain Jelly's regular delivery skipper, taking a variety of pleasure craft and small commercial vessels from place to place for people who maybe hadn't the time, the experience or the bottle to do it themselves. The rest of the time Captain Bulpin was a deliberately peripheral figure on the traditional boat scene. He had an almost pre-Raphaelite dislike of modern marine developments, particularly glass-fibre and engines, and a stern disapproving gaze.

He was hard to categorise. He came from a military family but had been expelled from public school for leading a juvenile mutiny. He could be curt and tended to make enemies but was loyal and considerate to the people he liked. He played the guitar and spoke several languages. He had an ambiguous relationship with a woman of mature beauty to whom he appeared to act as some sort of house-husband before running off with, and marrying, the partner of his best friend. It was only at sea that Captain Bulpin seemed at peace. He was a superb sailor, and could read a weather situation more precisely than anyone I've known. His own small boat, an engineless gaffer, was always among the leaders in local races. Distance didn't daunt him: we once came upon him in the Channel Islands, sculling through a windless dawn. Later he built a larger boat and cruised Spain and Portugal for a season under sail and oar.

Despite his consummate seamanship, Captain Bulpin had no formal qualifications and had no time for bodies like the RYA which could bestow them. Once in Bayona in southern Spain, a regular call for delivery crews, he was asked by some yachtsmen in a café what his qualifications were. Pausing from excavating his paella, he replied, 'I was a radio announcer in Hong Kong.' On reflection, it seemed as good an answer as any.

I was surprised that Captain Bulpin approved of *Shamrock* and that the lads took to him. He helmed for us in several races and once we got an unprecedented third place. We sometimes saw him socially and when he was short of crew for an interesting delivery, as opposed to taking a rusty dredger to Goole, he would occasionally ask me along. It never ceased to astonish me that a man so jealous of his independence as Captain Bulpin had become what was in effect a waterborne chauffeur in the service of people who, for one reason or another, seemed intent on giving him a hard time. Commercial deliveries were usually no problem but many private owners of posh yachts and powerboats seemed intent on convincing themselves that delivery crews were a bunch of wasters who would put their feet on the mahogany chart table the moment their backs were turned.

What turned out to be pretty typical was one of my first deliveries – a ketch from Plymouth to Ireland. By definition most deliveries are done in difficult conditions and this was the coldest January for five years. We went to bed in our oilskins and the halyards froze on the cleats. It was rough enough to disable a freighter twenty miles to the south, but the yacht arrived safely, looking smarter than she had in the marina. We'd hardly expected any medals but we could have done without a letter from the owner complaining that we had stolen a 90p shackle-key and a tin of tomato soup.

I soon found that most boat-deliverers had such stories to tell, particularly when the owner, and even worse, his wife, decided to come along for the ride. This was a situation which seemed to bring out the worst in everyone. I was told about the case of a Contessa 32, plus owner and wife, being taken from Southampton to Majorca. At least that was the plan, but the trip ended abruptly only four days out. From the moment of departure the boat had two captains, the owner and the delivery skipper. Both maintained they were legally in command and neither would give way. What began as comic became farcical and then positively dangerous when the delivery skipper set a course to ride the tide south down the Chanel du Four and the owner ordered a diversion to the west of Ushant. While they argued, a five-knot tide was pushing the boat fast towards the rocks of Les Trois Pierres.

Apparently this seemed to temporarily bring some sanity to the proceedings and they motor-sailed to Brest for a peace conference. But before they arrived there had been a fight after the owner accused the skipper of fancying his wife, and the delivery crew hitchhiked home.

Another man I was helping deliver a motor-cruiser up the Thames said he had recently declined to take a boat to France on the grounds that it was sinking. 'Just keep the pump going,' said the owner. 'She's got a good battery. You'll be all right!' He also remembered that a big motor-sailer delivered to Portugal had a gearbox leak so serious that it needed topping up every forty minutes. The owner, who kept the paint and brightwork immaculate, admitted it had been like that for years. 'Oil's cheap enough, after all,' he said.

Indeed, an owner's priorities were sometimes hard to fathom. A man whose Roberts 34 cruiser was being delivered from Spain to Brixham by Phil and me, some years later, spent £300 on a farewell dinner at Santander Yacht Club but refused to lob out £12 for a corrected chart of north Brittany. 'I'm not made of money, you know,' he explained. It was hard to believe that some boats scheduled for delivery had ever actually been to sea. A large power-cruiser bound for the Mediterranean had a three-piece suite. Only after we left port did we realise it wasn't fastened down. By then the sofa was chasing us around the saloon.

*******

We weren't expecting any such problems when we flew out of Heathrow one cold wet Wednesday in February. Captain Bulpin had worked for the tug company before and assured us that their vessels, though old and somewhat rusty, were usually reliable. We were met at Karachi airport by Shahid Hamid, a thin young man in a blazer who said he was the assistant port manager – in fact he made tea and sandwiches in a shed behind a crane – and took us by taxi through the city to a house in a northern suburb rented for its workers by a British construction company, and where we were to stay for two days while the tug was fuelled and victualled.

The house was large and considerable effort had been made to erase any traces of Pakistan from its interior. One room had been expensively converted into a replica of the saloon bar of a gloomy northern pub, complete with dart board, pool table and John Smith bitter. The six north-country construction workers who lived there spent their spare time reading old copies of the *Sun* and the *Daily*

*Mirror* and trying to convince themselves they were really in Gateshead. Sean, a small sallow man in his forties, was the foreman of a team extending a jetty at a Russian-built power station. He said he had been in Pakistan for nearly two years but had never been into the centre of Karachi or had any social contact with the indigenous population, eaten the local food or tried to learn a word of the language.

'I'm just here for the money,' he said. 'I've earned more this year than I'd get in ten years at home but it's like being in a prison. There's nothing to do here or to spend money on. It drives you mad. I count the days when I can get out of this bloody shit-hole, but I keep signing on for a bit longer. Last time it was because the wife wanted a conservatory. Before that it was a sauna in the garage.' Sean's wealth – he claimed he was earning over £50,000 a year plus bonuses – had made him a tax exile.

'I can't go back to Gateshead when I get leave. They fly me to the Isle of Man and the wife meets me there. We have a few days in a hotel and she goes back on the ferry with a couple of grand stuffed up her jumper.' He didn't see the slightest irony in his situation but he seemed to be slowly becoming aware that his chances of going home to any sort of normal life were decreasing the more he earned and the longer he stayed away.

Life in the construction hostel was uncannily like a space station with the alien environment firmly excluded. Self-sufficiency extended to junk food and ingredients for fry-ups being flown in from Manchester. No native vegetables were allowed apart from potatoes, which were only served when there were no frozen chips. All meals, cooked by a petrified youth called Ranji, were carefully inspected for any foreign content. Our first evening meal, eaten in oppressive silence behind a line of sauce bottles, was enlivened by a terrible scene involving a plumber named Ken who had asked for creamed potato – a dish obviously unknown to Ranji, who had used his imagination to provide a baked potato covered with artificial cream topped by a glacé cherry. The Squadron Leader had gone to bed with a headache but both Captain Bulpin and I were tempted to defend Ranji's initiative. We thought better of it and watched in silence from behind the sauce bottles as the creation was thrown out of the window.

We were relieved to move from the hostel to the tug, now alongside a largely derelict wharf on the edge of the main docks where we were to wait for what Shahid Hamid called 'documentation', which meant giving backhanders to a succession of officials in return for largely meaningless documents certifying the height of the mast or the capacity of the oven, but without which we could not leave Pakistan. A doctor even got in on the act, charging us £25 each for a 'medically verified' smallpox vaccination certificate. 'What about a vaccination?' asked the Squadron Leader. 'That's £25 extra,' the doctor replied.

The wharf was run by a large man in the traditional gho, a male garment like a knee-length overcoat, but also wearing jeans and trainers. Despite his long black hair, beard and deep tan, his name was Kevin and he was a former sidewinder-trawler skipper from Hull, who had been driven out of business by a cut in cod-fishing quotas ten years earlier, joined a Greek tanker, jumped ship at Karachi and stayed. 'The money's good and I do bugger-all,' Kevin said, which seemed a pretty fair assessment: he drove a Mercedes and sat all day in a hut drinking tea and smoking Marlboro Lights. The tug and a rusty dredger were the only vessels in his dock.

Kevin, like his compatriots in the hostel, was contemptuous of all aspects of Pakistani life except one. 'I'll say this for the buggers,' he said, looking up at his cigarette smoke swirling in a slowly turning fan, 'they're bloody good thieves.' He had had the shoes stolen from his feet while asleep in the office, and his belt with its ornate

Hell's Angels buckle stolen out of his trousers. 'They'd take the steam off your piss if they thought they could sell it,' Kevin said, lighting another Marlboro. He explained that bunkering the tug had been delayed because a fuel bowser containing 500 gallons of diesel had been siphoned dry overnight despite being in a floodlit barbed-wire compound watched over by CCTV. The thieves had completed a good night's work by unbolting the floodlights and the TV system and stealing them too.

That afternoon, while Captain Bulpin checked the engines and the Squadron Leader was busy with his charts, I was sent by taxi to buy a long list of provisions including a large quantity of cabbages, ice cream and Marmite, check the accuracy of the ship's chronometer with an officer on a distant freighter and change some traveller's cheques. The expedition was not a success. The cabbages already reeked of rot, Captain Bulpin didn't believe I had properly checked the clock, the Squadron Leader said the ice cream tasted like frozen face-powder and the Marmite was found to be a cheap substitute made in Calcutta. I had also been swindled of half the value of my traveller's cheques but I kept that to myself. Later the Squadron Leader was heard to wonder if they had chosen the right man for what could prove to be a difficult voyage.

In search of friendlier company, I visited Kevin in his hut, finding him with his feet on the desk, smoking and drinking tea with a small dark man introduced as Jamal, captain of the stevedores. I later found that the stevedores in Kevin's dock consisted of Jamal, his brother and his uncle and that they hadn't unloaded a ship for two months. They were talking about the ship-breakers of Gaddani Beach a few miles west of Karachi, a major employer in the area. Jamal's nephew had been one of nine men killed a week earlier when a cable snapped and their cradle fell 100 feet from the bow of a beached tanker. More than a hundred men had died in that one shipyard in the past year and none of the families had received any compensation.

From Kevin's window we could see at least thirty ships at anchor in the bay waiting their turn to be broken up. Some were comparatively modern tankers, others archaic freighters, and there were even a couple of redundant cruise-liners. 'They call it death bay,' Kevin said, 'both for the ships and for the people who break them up. It's like something from another century.' He said that before 1970, ship-breaking was done in highly mechanised European shipyards, but it was now being carried out at a fraction of the price in India, Bangladesh, Turkey, China and Pakistan. There were now over 130 shipyards on the twenty miles of Gaddani sand where ships could be beached and torn apart, largely by hand, by a workforce which in the early 1970s was as high as 35,000.

'You've never seen anything like it,' Kevin said. 'On a really big tide they'll fire up a 50,000-tonner and drive it at full speed up the beach. Everyone gets off except the pilot and he ties himself to something in the wheelhouse. The further up the beach they can get it the better. The noise and the smoke and all that crashing and banging. It breaks your heart to see some lovely old ships end up like that.' Jamal said that the work was hard and dangerous but you could earn £5 a day on skilled jobs like operating a cutting torch, and about half that as a labourer literally pulling ships apart with your bare hands. 'I've seen fifty men twisting a metal plate backwards and forwards until it breaks. By then it's so hot that if burns their skin,' Jamal said. 'They give you no safety equipment. If you want gloves or goggles you have to buy them. Some of the men are in clothes that have been burned into rags by the sparks. But it's work. If they don't do that, they do nothing.'

He said that spillage of oil and chemicals from the ships being dismantled was now a major environmental problem, but one which the authorities chose to ignore. 'The beach and the sea are black with oil and there are dead birds and fish everywhere. It was a very beautiful place when I was a boy,' Jamal said. He wasn't angry but deeply disheartened. He said that in the village where he lived the fishing industry had been ruined because of the pollution and people were suffering from stomach, eye and respiratory problems. 'But who will listen to us? The government will never upset the people who bring business to this country.'

That evening we took a taxi into the city to sample, at the Squadron Leader's insistence, some classic Pakistan cuisine; but after an hour spent peering into restaurant windows and bickering over menus and prices, we ended up in a Chinese takeaway. Returning in a taxi, we saw everywhere the sight, fundamentally disturbing to home-loving Westerners, of ordinary respectable families setting up beds on the pavements, often bolting together bedsteads and arranging bedside tables. Others apparently preferred to sleep on the move: we stopped at traffic lights behind a lorry loaded with a dozen huge concrete drainage pipes. In each one was a man woman or child peacefully asleep. Back at the tug the Squadron Leader went to bed and Captain Bulpin and I were sitting on deck in still-stifling heat under a blazing full moon when we were invited to go crab-fishing by the crew of a passing small lateen-rigged dhow.

'How much?' asked Captain Bulpin, deeply suspicious. 'Nothing', he was told. 'You come as our guests.' The boat was sailed by the owner, Ali, and his small son. They fished most nights for crabs a mile out in the bay, and sold them to cafés and small hotels. In the day Ali drove a taxi to the from the airport. The bay was calm and pure silver in the moonlight and the dhow sailed silently and surprisingly fast on a barely discernible breeze. To tack, the son had to climb the mast, lower the sail and reset it to leeward, a manoeuvre done without fuss in a few seconds. When the dhow was anchored, father and son fished with lines, hauling aboard crabs the size of large ashtrays. While Ali continued to fish, the son lifted a couple of floorboards and lit a fire in a small metal tray, dismembered several crabs and boiled them in a saucepan of water. We ate them with small pieces of dry brown bread and drank bottles of German lager, produced from the bilge. 'Illegal,' Ali said, raising his bottle in a toast. They returned us to the tug after an hour and sailed away, accepting neither thanks nor payment. A minor incident, but one I have remembered.

We left early the following morning, threading our way through condemned ships at anchor in the bay. It was a doleful experience, despite the bright sunlight and sparkling sea, and we were glad when we had cleared Gaddani Beach and were steaming eastward at twelve knots towards the Iran border just beyond Gwadar, some 300 miles distant. The Squadron Leader was at the helm, high in the wheelhouse which resembled a small Victorian signal box, and Captain Bulpin was arranging a hoist of assorted neutral flags which we hoped would spare us from military attention. I sat in the shade of the funnel reading Evelyn Waugh's *Officers and Gentlemen* and hoping this level of inactivity would last the whole voyage.

Extracts from secret unofficial log:

THURSDAY    Crisis: cabbages, put whole and uncooked in deep-freeze, dissolve from iron-hard cannonballs into yellow slime in hot water. Silent lunch of cheese sandwiches and ice cream. All the vegetables we froze raw are proving to be uneatable.

FRIDAY    Sea surprisingly smooth considering there's no land south of us until the Antarctic, but wind picks up at lunchtime and we roll about sickeningly for two hours until it suddenly drops. Deck too hot to walk on. CB rigs a pump and we sit under a canopy with our feet in tepid water. Off Chah Bahar only a few miles offshore and hopefully out of the tanker channels. At least six tankers in view at any time. SL shouts down that we should be keeping watch not reading.

SATURDAY   Now in Gulf of Oman leading to Straits of Hormuz. Tankers converge from all sides. SL says that if they can see you it's too late for them to take avoiding action, so it's up to us to up to keep clear. Two Iranian gunboats come to look at us. CB puts up more Dutch flags and adds what we think is a Swiss flag for good measure. We have been warned to expect illegal searches of neutral vessels, but they lose interest after a few minutes and steam away.

SUNDAY   The heat, tiredness, boredom and soporific thump of the diesels takes its toll. I fall asleep at the wheel at 4 am and wake to find that somehow the tug has turned 180 degrees and is heading back to Karachi. Unsuccessfully try to edge back on course without waking anyone. Scolded for irresponsibility.

MONDAY   Off watch when at midnight we round the northern tip of Oman for the last 100-mile leg south-west to Sharjah. Wake momentarily to see enormous moonlit rocks through the porthole less than a mile away. In the morning, to make sure that what I'd seen at night was no dream, check the chart and find we had squeezed through a narrow unbuoyed channel in a ragged archipelago called the Musandam Peninsula, past Perforated Rock and Elphinstone Inlet, on a course recommended only to those with local knowledge. Useful information for any further discussion on irresponsibility.

TUESDAY   Arrive Sharjah before breakfast, but no one takes any notice of us until after lunch. In the outer harbour are about fifty 60-foot open wooden dhows shaped like slices of melon. Sharjah is high-rise, rich and bustling but the dhow harbour must be much like the Emirates were before they struck oil. Cargo is loaded by hand from rusty pickup trucks. Cargoes vary from washing machines for Somalia to radios and bicycles for Ethiopia. CB and I inspect a dhow loading milk powder for Bombay, approving its massive lateen sail and rigging. The captain smiles from the wheelhouse. 'All for show,' he says, gesturing aloft. He walks forward and opens a hatch to reveal two huge red Volvo diesels and says, 'These are the business.'

WEDNESDAY  No one seems to know why we have brought the tug to Sharjah. There are plenty here already. But eventually someone signs for it and we are free to go. At Dubai Airport, ring home to find that a trawler has dragged its mooring in a gale, snapping off *Shamrock*'s bowsprit and badly damaging the bulwarks. Spend most of the flight worrying about what the damage will cost. Already Perforated Rock seems a very long way away.

## CHAPTER 6

# The last voyage of Major Ferchbind

*Shamrock* looked a sorry sight with her bowsprit broken off at the gammon-iron and her bulwarks beaten in along the starboard side. We took her up the Exeter ship canal to the city basin and alongside the Exeter Maritime Museum, whose director, David Goddard, kindly allowed us to use some of its workshop facilities. The work was done in their spare time by the lads, who once again had the tender of their fictitious boat-building company accepted by my insurers. As usual the repairs were immaculate but the damage was extensive and time-consuming and there was little chance of the smack being in commission before the summer. So when delivery trips came along I usually took them.

One was a three-week idyll in a new 35-foot yacht

Skegness 1946. On his first seaside holiday, Tony returns from an inspection of the beach.

Phyllis, Jamiez and daughter Geraldine enjoying a joke around the fire.

Tony's mother was unimpressed by the circumnavigation of the pond.

Tony, right, in his mother's jumper, with his mentor 'Cap'n' Lumbers.

Moored securely in the broad-bean bed, Tony's first boat never moved again.

*Shamrock* dredging oysters on the Blackwater circa 1950, before she sank and was re-registered. Navvy Mussett is in the white jumper.

*Shamrock* close-hauled in an Old Gaffers' race, Dartmouth 1978. She came last.

Captain Custard takes full command.

David Green asleep in his deckchair. George Robbins and Liz Brown in the foreground.

*Shamrock* on passage from Scillies to Plymouth during the long hot summer of 1977.

The crew going ashore for refreshment. Freeboard was even less on the way back.

The Ancient Mariner, alive and well and helming *Shamrock*, summer 1977.

▲ *Shamrock*, right, momentarily ahead while racing from Guernsey to Jersey 1978.

▼ Tony's new macho image was not regarded as a great success.

Tim and Sophie's land-based yachtmaster's course would stand them in good stead.

Tim on his first Cornish cruise in 1978. Now he takes his dad sailing.

Sophie strikes a pose in St Malo 1978. She is now a successful actress.

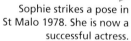

through the French rivers and canals from the Hamble to Marseille with a skipper and his new wife who were regarding the trip as their honeymoon. The mast had been lowered at Le Havre and the hull protected with tyres and planks to prevent damage in the 180 locks we would encounter on a voyage down the Seine, through the canal system and the River Saone to Lyons and thence by the ferociously tidal River Rhone and under the bridge of Avignon to Marseille, where the owner, a Swiss banker, would join us and be taught how to sail.

At sunset, when all canal traffic stopped, we moored on grassy banks and ate in the cafés of tiny villages. In the early mornings we bought hot bread which steamed in the mist. One day near Dijon we sailed over a small mountain using nearly thirty locks. Many were automatic, controlled by electronic eyes accustomed to giant barges rather than small yachts and reluctant to let us through until we were taught how to fool them by clapping a hand over the eye for the time it would take for a barge to pass. At Lyons we descended a sea-lock so deep the sky was a pale rectangle far above, and shared it with two barges which surged above us and hammered at our boards and tyres. One had come from Belgium and had flowerbeds and a small car on board. We needed a pilot for the last hundred miles down the Rhone but he rode in the first of a string of barges and we tagged on behind as best we could. There were tidal rips and eddies, rocks, sandbanks and floating trees. The skipper was grim and preoccupied and his new wife read a magazine.

Years afterwards I remembered details of the trip, like sailing under the bridges of Paris on a warm evening, passing so close to vineyards that they could, had they wished, have thrown a bottle on deck. I remembered sitting at the railway station at Arles, near the house of Vincent Van Gogh, waiting for a train back to Paris at the end of the delivery and seeing a poster advertising what I translated as a performance by the Terrible Ass Concordia. I also missed the ferry at Le Havre and had to sleep in a park.

Sadly, not all deliveries were so pleasant – including most of those organised by a man named Topsy Turner, a former Royal Navy petty officer who ran what he called a general maritime agency from the front room of his house under a motorway flyover on the outskirts of Bristol. In the Navy anyone named Turner seems to be called Topsy, but in this case his real name, Cyril, seemed more appropriate for a small overweight white-faced man with pimples and a permanent three-day beard.

Why Topsy went into the delivery business was a mystery. Most of his service had been done deep in the bowels of aircraft carriers where he had been a purser's assistant, and he had little knowledge of the sea and virtually none of small boats. He had for a brief period been a crewman on a dredger in Avonmouth docks, where his tattoos and stories of Tahitian brothels had given him a certain amount of respect, and when asked if he knew anyone who could take the dredger up the Severn to Sharpness, he invented a delivery company and did the job himself with his brother-in-law, a retired Avonmouth docker. From then on, he managed to get occasional delivery work which he supplemented by driving a minicab and helping in a fish and chip shop.

I heard of Topsy through Captain Jack Flowerdew, the broker, and after I helped him take a motorboat on an uneventful passage in flat calm from Swansea to Plymouth during a July heat wave, Topsy got the mistaken impression that I knew what I was doing when it came to taking boats from place to place. It was also the first time I heard the incantation with which Topsy ritually ended all deliveries: 'Well, that's another one the Queen knows nothing about.'

Topsy spent most of his spare time sitting in his vest at the kitchen table, smoking and drinking tea and putting the world to rights. He once spent an afternoon telling me that healthy eating was a load of bollocks after I had unwisely mentioned that perhaps he needed to lose a little weight. 'I'm not fat – not for my size. I'm quite happy with my stable diet thank you very much. OK, I like arbocarbodrates [carbohydrates] and teutonic [tannic] acid but they're natural foods aren't they? All right I'm full of toxeroxins [toxins], but you rarely see me doing moodies. I can't see that eating carrots improves your temper if I might say so. Went down the chippie lunchtime. Wouldn't suit you of course. Big piece of cod, double chips, gherkins and white bread and a nice cup of teutonic. That's proper food. You can stuff your nutmeat cutlets and goat's cheese.' When I protested I didn't actually eat such foods, Topsy said he didn't believe me.

Once when I tentatively asked if we could open a window in the smoke-filled kitchen, Topsy immediately gave me the benefit of his medical experience. 'Most normal people smoke,' he said. 'It would be a good thing if a neuratic like you had a smoke. It would calm your nerves. Princess Margaret smokes. I suppose you think you're better than her. And the old king wasn't averse to a fag neither. We took him on the old Vanguard battleship to South Africa and he was sick in the piano. The Vanguard went seventeen feet on a gallon of fuel. Bet you didn't know that.'

Topsy was secretive about his shortcomings as a sailor and it was left to others to reveal some of his more spectacular aberrations, which included placing a lager tin next to the compass on a night passage from Poole to Cherbourg, causing a ninety-degree deviation. His young nephew, on his first delivery, stuck obediently to his course when Topsy went to bed, and the boat ended up in Yarmouth Isle of Wight. Topsy, so the story went, was as puzzled as everyone else on board that no one in the shops spoke French.

On another occasion, bringing a boat into harbour at St Mary's in the Scillies in thick fog, he went aground and fired off a red flare, which luckily wasn't seen in the murk. When the fog lifted, it was revealed that Topsy had gone aground on the lifeboat slip. During another delivery, arriving in Alderney at high tide in a converted lifeboat, he moored it tightly to the quay and went to take ale at the Albert public house up the main street. As the hours passed he was vainly reminded that the tide was ebbing and that the lifeboat would need attention but was too busy propositioning a retired woman traffic warden.

Returning to the quay at half-tide, he found the lifeboat hanging from its moorings a foot from the water and cut the warps with a borrowed hacksaw, watched by a crowd of interested onlookers. The boat fell heavily into the water, causing a minor tidal wave which rolled across the harbour, upsetting a pan of boiling pasta in the galley of a nearby yacht, which scalded the leg of a small dog asleep under the chart table. The owner unsuccessfully tried to get Topsy to pay the vet's bill. 'I told them I had lost an eye when the *Sir Galahad* was blown up in the Falklands and they agreed to drop the claim,' Topsy said. 'All right I was in a shore station in South Shields at the time, but I did have a stye. Bloody painful it was.'

My last delivery with Topsy involved taking a motorboat from Jersey to Guernsey, a distance of about thirty miles, on a calm sunny day in July. It was, as Topsy said, a doddle – at least it was until just west of Sark with about five miles to go we ran into thick fog. With visibility less than fifty yards, no radar and a VHF which wasn't working, a cautious crawl until conditions improved seemed the sensible option, but Topsy had no intention of slowing down. 'We're only doing twelve knots and I'm not hanging about out here,' he said. 'And besides, I know St Peter Port like the back of me 'and.' Twenty minutes later, the doleful tolling of what I took to be the Sardriere bell-buoy put us unpleasantly near the rocks off Jethou and less than a mile from the busy harbour of St Peter Port.

Now the fog was if anything thicker and Topsy was still doing twelve knots. 'Slow down, you bloody fool,' I cried. 'You'll have us up the beach in a minute.' Moments later the fog on the port bow changed from white to blue and we were scraping down the side of something huge and metallic which ripped off our guardrails and rubbing strake and disappeared as suddenly as it had come, leaving us rolling violently in its oily wake. We had, it turned out, hit a thousand-ton Guernsey–Portsmouth Sealink ferry which had just left its berth and was moving slowly out through the harbour entrance, obviously as unaware of our presence as we were of its.

Things could have been worse. We could have been hit head-on, sunk and drowned without anyone being any the wiser. As it was, the damage though expensive was largely cosmetic, and a few minutes later the fog thinned and we limped to a nearby mooring. But by then, Topsy had apparently decided to be very angry indeed. 'Why the hell didn't you see it?' he shouted. 'I told you to keep a proper look-out. That's the last time I sail with bloody amateurs.' 'Well,' I said, 'That's another one the Queen knows nothing about.' But since then, I've occasionally wondered whether I should at least have dropped her a line. It's too late now. Not long afterwards Topsy dropped dead while serving two portions of cod in the fish and chip shop.

*******

Shortly afterwards I was asked by an elderly retired army officer named Stephen Wilkinson to help him bring back a 40-year-old wooden Nicholson 35-footer to the Solent from Cherbourg. I would be doing it as a favour. The owner, a friend with whom he had served in the war, had died on board two days earlier and was now in a coffin in the main cabin waiting to be brought home. 'The family have arranged everything with the authorities and the undertaker will meet us at Portsmouth,' Stephen said. 'I hope you don't mind travelling with a corpse. Some people think it's unlucky.'

Stephen Wilkinson, generally known as Wilks, was a mild and courteous man, full of contradictions. A widower, he lived alone in a terraced house overlooking the sea on the Isle of Wight and sailed a small gaff-rigged cutter, but occasionally he would put on shiny black leathers, a lilac-coloured scarf, and take off on a huge Japanese motorcycle he kept behind the coal shed. Although not poor, he had never been known to buy a drink in a pub, but in his own home would gladly cook tasty meals for anyone who visited.

I had sailed with him in several Solent races and we had invariably come last because Wilks was more interested in philosophical argument than sail trimming and navigation. We were once disqualified for going the wrong side of a course mark after Wilks had dropped his lighted pipe next to the fuel tank under the cockpit grating.

On the ferry to Cherbourg to pick up the yacht, Wilks told me about his time in the army and about a dichotomy which after all this time obviously still disturbed him. As a Captain in the Royal Artillery during the Italian campaign, gunnery fascinated him, particularly the trigonometry involved in range and trajectory, and yet he hated the carnage accurate shelling caused. 'All those innocent people and lovely buildings, but when my guns hit the target I was thrilled. A lot of the gunners were decent chaps with families and they felt the same.' He said that to take their minds off killing people and destroying the Roman heritage they got drunk and behaved badly.

'We held a big party in a theatre we had captured in Arezzo and asked the local people, including the mayor. We took out the seats in the stalls to make a dance floor. Some of the chaps jumped down from the dress circle onto the backs of couples dancing below to see how many they could knock down. I came second with five, I'm ashamed to say.' Another regular off-duty diversion was something Wilks called the dance of the blazing arseholes. 'You rolled up newspaper, stuck it in your bottom and lit it. The winner was the one who let it burn the longest. It's sad that war brings out the worst in people,' he said.

The yacht, moored on the Quai des Meilles, was being guarded by a gendarme when we arrived. Silently he led us aboard and unlocked the main hatch. An oak-veneer coffin had been skilfully manoeuvred into the boat and now took up the entire floor-space of the saloon. 'We don't want to trample over poor Leonard,' Wilks said, 'but he would appreciate that we've got to get to the bog and the galley.' We solved the problem by covering the coffin with a sheet of plywood and an old carpet found on the dockside and for the next two days tiptoed across it in what Wilks called 'a respectful manner'.

Before we left on the afternoon tide, I found myself buying Wilks a meal at a restaurant behind the church of Sainte Trinité. While I paid the bill, he went off to buy a few bottles of duty-free wine – I think the current allowance was about three bottles each – which he said he would have delivered to the boat. It was a warm September day with high pressure and a steady breeze from the southeast and I loitered for a while watching a ferry dock on the Quai de Normandie. When I got back, Wilks was signing the last of the documents delivering Leonard's coffin into our custody and handing them to a man in a brown suit who put them in a briefcase. Six bottles of 1971 Chablis and a 1975 Bordeaux were prominently wedged between the coffin and the starboard pilot berth, for all to see, held secure by the previous day's rolled-up *Daily Telegraph*. 'Leonard loved a nice glass of red and the *Telegraph* crossword,' Wilks said. 'Appropriate, really. I don't like to ask, but can you settle up for the wine?'

The eighty-mile overnight passage was largely uneventful

except for an interesting moment in the eastbound shipping lane when Wilks fell asleep at the helm in the path of a large Japanese car transporter which we somehow missed with the help of a burst of the engine and an all-standing gybe. Apart from that, we sailed comfortably with a soldier's wind on a broad reach, letting the tide take us east for a dead run towards Portsmouth, leaving the Isle of Wight comfortably to port the following morning. Then, with our destination less than ten miles away, Wilks unaccountably decided to anchor for lunch, choosing the narrow busy strait between Bembridge and Nab Rock. 'Ah, Bembridge,' he said as he unwrapped some paté and broke up the last of the French bread, 'I had an aunt there who had been in the original Tiller Girls. She once gave me a shilling.'

'It says we shouldn't anchor here,' I said, consulting the late Leonard's Pilot's Guide to the English Channel. 'It's a main fairway. The *Queen Elizabeth* comes through here. 'Bollocks, dear boy,' Wilks said, 'I once anchored here before the war in a westerly gale snug as anything, playing baccarat and winning a packet from a chap who couldn't pay up so I took his car, a Sunbeam Talbot. Ran it for years and then sold it to a vicar. Never saw another ship the whole time.' 'Well there's one here now,' I said as a large grey Customs and Excise cutter loomed alongside and informed us through a powerful megaphone that two officers intended to come aboard.

Most customs officers I had previously dealt with had been affable men in seeming semi-retirement in out-of-the-way harbours, who demanded little more from yachtsmen than an occasional Form C1328 stuffed through their office letterboxes on a Sunday evening saying that you had nothing to declare from your weekend in Alderney, had no firearms, uncooked poultry, plants, bulbs and trees or indecent literature aboard and no one was suffering from yellow fever, beriberi, or a high temperature.

But this was something else. The legendary Customs and Excise roving rummage crews in their fast armed cutters were the hard-eyed scourge of drug-runners and immigrant traffickers, who could stop and search any vessel on a whim. It was therefore with some surprise that we watched two figures climb down the cutter's side onto our deck. One was a small middle-aged man with a paunch whose flushed unhealthy complexion reminded Wilks of a pork butcher he had known in Cowes. The other looked about seventeen and seemed thoroughly ill at ease on a small boat. Neither was remotely hard-eyed.

The pork butcher explained that as we had come from the direction of France and were now in United Kingdom territorial waters we should be conspicuously flying a yellow flag (the Q flag in the international code of signals) requesting customs clearance. Failure to do so could in certain circumstances lead to prosecution and a fine up to £100 on summary conviction. 'The truth is, old chap, we just haven't got round to it,' Wilks said. 'As you can see, we were just having a spot of lunch.'

Asked if he was the owner of the vessel, Wilks immediately explained the situation. 'I am technically in charge, yes. You will find the owner, Major Leonard Ferchbind, below in the cabin, but unfortunately he is dead. I have all the documentation to hand. My name is Wilkinson and I am a former officer in the Royal Artillery.' When we went below and removed the carpet and plywood to reveal the coffin, the senior officer quickly decided that corpses were none of his business. The fate of the late Major Ferchbind should be reported to the port health authority at our destination within four hours of arrival and a Maritime Declaration of Health completed. No one should leave the vessel until the arrival of the health authorities and in the meantime a red light over a white light should displayed at night and the signal flags ZW in daylight. But everything else in the yacht appeared to be very much the customs officer's business and he announced that he intended to search us for unauthorised goods and if we had anything to confess now was the time to do it.

'We have these seven paltry bottles of wine, as you can see, and I have a small amount of tobacco in my pouch,' Wilks said. 'Anything else you can find, you're very welcome to.' Taking him at his word, the younger customs officer soon had his head and shoulders inside the cooker and the senior officer was throwing things out of the saloon lockers. After thirty minutes of unsuccessful rummaging, during which they tipped out the contents of all the galley cupboards, dismantled the oilskin locker and poked under the engine with a wire coat-hanger, the senior officer returned to the cockpit to notify Wilks that he was considering a 'deferential examination of the casket' under the Customs and Excise Management Act 1979 and did Wilks have any observations?

I had never met Leonard Ferchbind, who according to Wilks had been a somewhat mediocre conveyancing solicitor in a family firm on leaving the army, but violating an honourable man's coffin in search of booze struck me as so outrageous that before Wilks could make any observations I found myself saying very loudly and angrily that the customs service should be thoroughly ashamed of itself. Not only would Captain Wilkinson and I feel we had a duty to Major Ferchbind's family to resist any desecration of the coffin, but as a journalist on *The Times* (which I wasn't) I would make sure that their scandalous behaviour got national publicity. 'Quite so,' said Wilks, who was now sitting on the coffin eating a bag of crisps. 'And if you have my word as a commissioned officer that we have absolutely no contraband aboard, surely that can be the end of the matter?'

Much to our surprise, it was. After a muttered conversation and a half-hearted examination of the stern lockers, the senior officer, obviously furious, announced that no further action would be taken. 'You'll have a good tale to tell them at the yacht club,' he said as he climbed back aboard the cutter. 'Luckily, you caught me on a good day.' They steamed away towards Chichester Harbour, leaving the yacht in chaos. 'They're not obliged to put anything away,' said Wilks, opening the bottle of Bordeaux. 'Thank you for your timely intervention. Here's to what has been quite an interesting cruise.'

We reached Portsmouth without further incident and after the formalities had been completed and the coffin removed, I returned home by train. Wilks, now wearing Leonard's expensive Royal Thames Yacht Club blazer, remained on board until the following day to 'tidy up and get things shipshape.' He was sorry if I was out of pocket on the trip but obviously he could hardly ask the grieving family for expenses. He also hoped I didn't mind that he had given the remaining wine to Leonard's solicitor.

Over the next few years I occasionally saw Wilks to wave to on a quayside or in a crowded bar but we never sailed together again. As he grew increasingly frail from the illness which eventually killed him, he gave up his motorbike and finally his boat and his dog. He died in a military nursing home and a friend took his ashes in a cardboard box and threw them in the sea off the Needles. Occasionally, people remembered Wilks and told stories to illustrate that he was a bit of a rascal. There was one about a time he brought a friend's coffin back from France which he'd filled with bottles of wine and packets of tobacco. Customs nearly caught him but he talked his way out of it. He also got £500 for the trip and the bloke who sailed with him never got a penny. It was a good story, but personally I prefer to believe that Wilks, for all his faults, wouldn't have done anything like that.

*******

The majority of boat-deliverers I came across in the early 1980s seemed solitary men, usually single or refugees from some marital disaster, who preferred when possible to work alone. But sometimes they needed crew and once again on the recommendation of Captain Flowerdew I was invited to do several short deliveries with a tall shy ex-public schoolboy in his late thirties, who had been a coding officer in the Navy and was generally known as Codes.

Codes came from a wealthy family who owned several provincial department stores but he had no wish to go into business and had been virtually disowned by his parents. He had a small cottage on the Suffolk coast and made a modest living delivering small vessels, usually motorboats, on short coastal trips to dismal east-coast harbours. Codes would stay overnight in bed-and-breakfast establishments and return in cold empty trains across the dreary East Anglian landscape doing the *Telegraph* crossword and eating Maltesers. It was not my idea of a full and happy life but Codes seemed to enjoy it.

He had once been married to a successful artist who apparently discarded him because of his lack of ambition, and since then Codes had lived with only an old dog named Mark, who sometimes came on trips and lay comatose at his master's feet, oblivious of wind or weather. One wintry evening we had secured a small dredger to the quay at Orfordness and were making a cup of tea before going to the chip shop when Codes looked down at the sleeping dog, so thin it could have been made of coat-hangers, and said with unusual feeling, 'My God, Mark, I wish you'd die, but I fear you're in rude health.'

Over the years, Codes had collected a variety of idiosyncratic tales, which he was always pleased to share. He said that a few weeks earlier after a vicious take-away curry, he had booked into a particularly bleak bed-and-breakfast in Lowestoft, put his bag in the room, and hurried to the nearest lavatory. Seconds later the landlady knocked on the door. 'We don't do solids in that one, lovey,' she said.

On another occasion, while waiting for the tide off Felixstowe, Codes shared an incident which occurred when he was coding officer on a minesweeper on a south-coast patrol. 'One day, a leading seaman, a young chap with glasses called Graham, came up and said would I mind if he asked me a question. He said he knew I had gone to a good school and could I tell him what was real music? 'The wife and I listen to a lot of Semprini and Mantovani and Eddie Calvert and we think that's real music. Do you think it's real music, Codes?' Flattered to be asked, Codes felt that in all honesty he could not identify Semprini and Mantovani or even Eddie Calvert as real music. To him, composers like Bach, Beethoven and Mozart produced real music. As it happened, there was a concert by the Bournemouth Symphony Orchestra the night the minesweeper put into Portsmouth, and if he wished to hear real music, Graham was welcome to come along.

The first-half programme included Beethoven's Second Piano Concerto, the overture from *The Marriage of Figaro*, and Vaughan Williams's *Fantasia on a Theme by Thomas Tallis*. In the interval Codes asked Graham what he thought. After a long silence he replied, 'Codes … I think I've got a gumboil.' When they emerged after a second half of Benjamin Britten, Gluck, and Elgar's concert overture *Cockaigne*, Graham delivered a considered verdict: 'Codes … I *have* got a gumboil.'

'We served together on the ship for another year,' Codes said, 'but real music was never mentioned again.' I enjoyed trips with Codes and was sorry to hear that lack of work had finally forced him ashore. The last I heard he was teaching English as a foreign language in Ipswich.

\*\*\*\*\*\*\*

I had soon found that yacht delivery, like most forms of boating, involved a lot of hanging about, usually on rain-swept quays as the boat surged against its warps in a greasy swell, or in grim out-of-season towns waiting for the tide or for the weather to improve. Much time was spent reading in half-empty cafés or walking alone at dusk looking into flyblown shop windows and wishing you were at home with someone nice. In Bideford, the highlight of two days spent waiting for the weather one stormy February was finding a shop which had in the window a teapot depicting the Last Supper. Inevitably it was closed.

When you weren't hanging about, you were in a mad hurry, as typified by one short but interesting assignment to take a large luxury motor-cruiser down the Thames from Maidenhead to Ramsgate on a cold wet winter's afternoon. Picking up the cruiser from a deserted boatyard, we swept past shuttered riverside bungalows and jetties empty of launches and punts, with Fleetwood Mac on the boat's stereo. Leaves blew across uncut lawns. As we approached west London, there was little moving on the river apart from the occasional police patrol launch and a tug pulling a solitary lighter. As the light faded, mist looped across the flat grey water. It was a bleak scene but inside the cruiser, with its central heating, black leather nightclub decor, and consoles of winking lights, it was as timeless and insulated as an airliner. I was cooking scrambled egg in the microwave for an early supper but the skipper, steering with a wheel which looked like something from a Ford Probe, had a preoccupied look. The evening tide, just starting to ebb, was one of the biggest of the year and if we continued at our present speed there was a real possibility that the gleaming plastic superstructure would be too high to pass under several central London bridges.

Above Kew bridge, we tied up to a deserted water-police pontoon and lowered the radio aerials and the burgee masts before continuing cautiously towards central

London. The tide was now falling fast and with the engines idling in reverse we drifted under the central arch of Kew bridge with about three feet to spare. The next, Hammersmith, was the worrying one – at the top of a spring tide there was little more than nine feet of clearance, and although we should now have more than that, the skipper wasn't taking any chances. Reasoning that he would have more power and control when going forward, he turned the boat round and stemming the tide at full throttle allowed us to go slowly astern, foot by foot, under the bridge. I stood on deck and watched. At one point we had less than a foot between us and the dripping black girders before we burst out into the twilight amid a cloud of diesel smoke.

Under Putney bridge we had about two feet clearance and under Battersea and Chelsea slightly more, but all three were traversed backwards to be on the safe side. So was Westminster Bridge. As we passed the Houses of Parliament, a woman watched us sternly from a window. I could have sworn it was Mrs Thatcher. The skipper said we were probably breaking some ancient by-law but they would never catch us now. The rest of the trip to Tower Bridge was done pointing the right way. Beyond the bridge we rafted up for the night on a pier alongside a Thames sailing barge. In the morning I left the boat as I had an appointment in London and the skipper took her on alone to Ramsgate.

If we'd allowed ourselves more time we could have saved a lot of anxiety, but the delivery was, as usual, being done for a fixed fee and the skipper couldn't afford to hang around. It still puzzles me why boat owners invariably quibble over the cost of transporting something which, apart from their houses, is probably the most expensive thing they own. But they do, and consequently skippers are usually intent on keeping expenses to a minimum, which usually involves, among other things, hitchhiking rather than taking a bus or train. I once travelled 200 miles across Normandy in a lorry containing thirty near-hysterical pigs destined for slaughter. I hitched a ride in Holland in a hearse. In Marseille, I stayed in a bed-and-breakfast establishment next to the station which turned out to be a brothel and was invited to an out-of-hours birthday party. Six girls wearing slippers and faded dressing-gowns, and their two protectors, in belted camel-hair coats, ate cake with green icing and drank sparkling wine in a damp basement at 10 in the morning. One of the pimps explained that as the girls started work at noon this was the only convenient time for a celebration.

It was also in France around this time that a bizarre incident occurred which could have had many different consequences depending on the reaction of the person experiencing it. Few would surely have come out of it with less credit than I did. On a sweltering hot autumn afternoon I found myself with time to spare in the ancient Brittany port of Douarnenez with its retained-water harbour containing a treasure trove of vintage sail and unlikely maritime relics, among them the retired Scarweather lightship which for years guarded the sandbanks of Swansea Bay. To photograph the lightship I had to walk down a narrow tree-hung track and climb down a bank thick with brambles and nettles towards the water's edge.

There was no one about and the few houses nearby were behind high hedges. As I began to climb down the steep bank, holding tightly on to my photographic equipment, I paused and then momentarily froze. In a nettle-filled dip in the bank about 100 feet away was the body of a boy. He was lying under a tree, face down, arms out. He wore jeans and a white T-shirt and was probably about twelve. His arms were thin and brown and the fingers were spread out. I took in the entire scene in about two seconds and it is with me still. No one would lie face down in nettles unless they were dead. That being so, there was nothing I could usefully do. I had seen nothing which would help the police with their inquiries. If I reported the incident they would quite rightly want to know what a middle-aged man was doing scrambling through nettles with a camera. And how could I convincingly explain, in my inadequate French, that I wanted to photograph a Swansea lightship? The British consul would be summoned from Brest or perhaps even from Paris. In any event, I would be detained until things had been sorted out in the usual long-winded French way. My companion would be stranded. We would miss the tide.

It was inconceivable that a body lying so near a well-trodden path would not be seen, probably by the next person to pass, the body identified, the distraught parents informed. Any interference on my part would only be a hindrance, and in another two seconds after seeing the body I had decided what was best for all concerned. I turned and walked away.

That evening we ate dinner at an expensive restaurant but I wasn't hungry. We would leave Douarnenez in the morning and the fate of the boy in the ditch would be an unanswered question for the rest of my life. Halfway through the oak-smoked breast of duck and apricots, I pushed the plate away. 'Something happened this afternoon,' I said. 'I saw a dead boy in a ditch.' As I told the story my companion ordered another bottle of Blanquette de Limoux to go with the warm marinated goats' cheese and said that there was only one thing to do: in the morning we must return to the scene of the crime and find out what actually happened.

I didn't sleep much that night. As we walked along the path early next day, I fully expected to find the area cordoned off with red and white tape, a tent over the fatal spot and weary detectives pouring coffee from a thermos. There was nothing. The ditch was empty and not even the brambles had been trampled down. As we stood, my friend, whose eyes were sharper than mine, pointed out that there were in fact no nettles in the ditch but only tall harmless weeds. The previous day had been one of the hottest of the year. The boy, perhaps on his way home, could have flopped down momentarily under the trees for a rest. It was easy for a mind conditioned by countless episodes of Maigret, Poirot and Inspector Morse to have come to the wrong conclusion. We left Douarnenez that morning and I never got a photograph of the lightship.

It was soon after this that I encountered my only female delivery skipper, a legendary figure known as Auntie Joan. Not only had this redoubtable woman rebuilt almost single-handed the wreck of a small yacht found lying in ten feet of water, but she could drink anyone under the table and once threw overboard a man who had the temerity to suggest that she was wearing his wellies.

Joan was a sturdy well-educated woman in her fifties with a complexion which suggested she had spent too much time near pans of boiling water. She had once been married to a man who had a job in East Africa and Joan joined a colonial yacht club mainly for company while he was away. She began to crew dinghies, and found to her surprise that she was both good at it and enjoyed it. When they returned to Britain with their young son in the 1960s they bought a second-hand Nicholson yacht which they kept at Lymington and soon got a reputation for being what Joan called 'good sports'. In the 1970s they changed the boat for a larger Moody fin-keeler and started to do some serious sailing, including an Atlantic crossing and six months spent cruising the coast of Guyana and Brazil.

In 1976, back in the Hamble, Joan prepared the boat and checked its equipment for a Mediterranean cruise while her husband returned to Africa for three months to finance the trip. They left on passage for the Mediterranean via Gibraltar and a month later Joan flew back alone. There were reports in the papers that her husband and son had been lost overboard in a gale off Ria de Pontevedra in north-west Spain, just north of the Portugese border, and inquests returned verdicts of accidental death. The effect on Joan was catastrophic: she hired a cottage outside Lymington, refused to see anyone, and proceeded to try to drink herself to death. She very nearly succeeded. Just before Christmas 1976, a postman trying to deliver a parcel saw Joan lying unconscious in the kitchen and called an ambulance. After a week in intensive care she discharged herself, returned to her cottage, stopping off to buy a case of Scotch at Sainsbury's and carried on where she had left off.

Only a month later, sober and in apparent good health, Joan flew out to Vigo with two friends to bring the Moody home. This minor miracle of recovery came about not by expensive rehabilitation but by a dog named Norman who had been dumped on Joan's doorstep with a carrier bag of tinned food and a note asking whether she could look after him for three weeks while they were on holiday. The dog was owned by neighbours who later claimed that they knew nothing about Joan's state or the tragedy which had caused it, but if it was a shrewd bit of animal therapy, it certainly worked. 'I couldn't look after the poor old bugger if I was pissed, so I chucked the booze and just got on with things,' was Joan's explanation of her remarkable recovery.

Enjoying sailing and needing an income, Joan took up yacht delivery, first crewing with friends and then as a one-woman business specialising in the feminine touch. 'I always gave the surfaces a rub over with lavender furniture polish and put a few flowers in a vase and crap like that,' Joan said. 'The customers liked it.'

The terrible events off Ria de Pontevedra remained largely her secret, although the newspapers had reported the basics: the yacht was on passage from La Coruña to Oporto when a westerly gale caused it to heave-to behind d'Ons island. Clipping their safety-harnesses to a central lifeline, Joan's son and husband were pulling down more reefs when a huge wave swept the deck and the lifeline's anchor-points parted. Joan sailed the boat into Vigo. The husband's body was washed up on the beach at Moaña a week later but the boy was never found. Just why Joan blamed herself for the tragedy only became clear to me years later when we were in Poole readying a small family yacht for a trip to Torquay on a bright summer's morning and I found Joan on hands and knees giving the lifeline fittings a microscopic inspection. 'I do this on every boat and on every trip,' she said, obviously feeling an explanation was necessary. 'I always have since the time when – well, you know …'

Joan was as experienced and qualified as anyone I've sailed with and yet her appearance at the helm of a boat rarely failed to trigger the most extraordinary reactions. On one occasion when she brought a Sadler 32 into a Hamble marina and tied up perfectly properly on a vacant visitor's pontoon, yachtsmen paled, put down their coffee cups and hurried to lay out more fenders. One man in a blazer stood on his side-deck clutching two boat-hooks and obviously intent on defending his varnish-work with his life.

Joan wasn't worried. Such behaviour, she said, just confirmed that although your average yachtie may have a boat stuffed with twentieth-century technology, his attitude, when it comes to women sharing his hobby, usually dates back to about 1885, or maybe 1901 on a good day. 'The majority of blokes still seriously believe that women have no place on boats and if they do manage to catch the right rope or tie the right knot, it's just a fortunate fluke,' Joan said. 'Sod them all, I say. Present company excepted.' When Joan died three years ago, I was really sorry.

My last delivery involved taking a racing yacht up the Bristol Channel to a muddy creek near Weston-super-Mare after a delivery crew had propped the fin-keeler against the wall of a small drying harbour and disappeared. The new owners, a farming couple in their seventies, came bemusedly on board. They had bought the boat on impulse in Torquay after seeing a video of the TV yachting soap *Howard's Way* but had never actually seen a yacht at close quarters before. They could hardly have bought a less suitable craft for beginners.

Two friends and I agreed to finish the delivery fifteen miles up the channel. A north-westerly force four gave us a brisk broad reach. It was sunny and warm and almost perfect sailing, but the owners, huddled below in lifejackets and safety harnesses, were appalled. Would the boat sink? Had we ever been in such seas before? If this was yachting, they wanted none of it. Reaching the creek, the farmer gave us his instructions: 'You drive the bastard up on the mud as far as he'll go and take they big ropes and tie him down like a roaring lion. We don't want him moving again. We'll come down weekends and use him as a summer house.' Only when we got home did we remember we had forgotten to ask for any money, and we never did. As a lesson in common sense it was priceless.

## CHAPTER 7

# Mr Gregory and the dog bowls

*Shamrock* was never an easy boat to sail, and while the previous owner had literally taught himself the ropes by taking her out alone one Saturday afternoon and charging up and down the Blackwater River until he felt he was some way towards getting the hang of things, I never felt happy about putting to sea with less than four able-bodied hands. Most smacks had built-in weather helm – the tendency to come up into the wind – as oyster-dredging was usually carried out with the smack hove-to. But *Shamrock*'s weather helm was prodigious, mainly caused by the mast being moved a foot forward in the distant past, and often the helm would need to be kept at least twenty degrees to weather by brute force if she was to sail in anything like a straight line. Twice the tiller, a massive nine-foot piece of oak, had cracked under the strain.

Efforts had previously been made to reduce weather helm by lengthening the bowsprit and putting more canvas forward of the mast, but to little effect. Helming on the exposed counter was tiring and often worrying, particularly at night. There were no sheet or halyard winches, the mainsheet, despite a three-part purchase, often needed the attention of two strong men, and the sheets of the jib topsail, the smallest sail on the boat, could lift a heavy man off the deck.

Obviously such power needed cautious handling, and over the years I had compiled a small grubby notebook of tips and gratuitous information from smacksmen we had sailed with when visiting east-coast races and rallies. Much of it the lads dismissed as bullshit from boring old farts, but there was also priceless information distilled from decades of smack-handling on the Essex marshes. Guidance under the heading 'In a blow' included 'If pressed, ease the smack by letting the peak run, but never ease her by starting the throat. Don't scandalise the main but sweat up the topping lift to keep the boom up. When driving hard to windward, over-peak the main to get the best out of her.' In the margin someone had neatly written 'Bollocks' in red biro.

Later that season, *Shamrock*, now repaired and back in commission, was booked to take part in an old-boat rally at Plymouth, which meant a twenty-hour overnight sail of nearly 100 miles. Only Martin could get the time off. The other lads would drive down with the cook the following day and sail back after the rally. It would be breaking all our rules about adequate crewing but with the noon forecast predicting a pleasant force two to three easterly and good visibility, surely two of us could manage a leisurely sail down the coast with eleven hours of favourable tide without too many problems?

Unfortunately we had failed to hear the 5.55 pm shipping

forecast, which painted a very different picture: a complex low had drifted south into central Europe while a high had suddenly moved into Shannon. This, we learned much later, would result in gale-force northerlies kicking up a nasty sea against the tide. But rowing out to *Shamrock* on that golden evening, we had no notion of the treats that lay in store.

The estuary was still and silent except for curlews on the distant shore and the smack was beginning to turn with the tide as we rowed out to the mooring and climbed aboard. The glass above the chart table was high and steady but it could be a deceptive instrument and I should have remembered the story of Sir Anthony Eden's father, a noted eccentric, who was apparently once seen to open the front door of his house in Belgrave Square and throw a barometer into the pouring rain, shouting, 'Get out, you fool, and look for yourself.' There can be a lot of truth in these cautionary tales.

We left at 9 pm and motored with jib and staysail through the mile-long channel to the sea. Away from the shelter of the cliffs, the wind was northerly and already stronger than expected. We set the mainsail but in the darkness something had jammed and we were unable to peak it up properly. By midnight, the wind had increased to a force five northerly, giving us almost a dead run, and a following sea made steering difficult even with two on the helm. Already I was regretting the lack of manpower: With more hands we could have further reefed the main but it was now too dark and rough for any major adjustments. At 2 am, after Martin had gone below for a nap, the wind backed and further strengthened. To hold our course meant sailing by the lee so I decided to curtail the night's entertainment and put into Dartmouth, continuing in the morning when we could at least see what we were doing. I dropped the staysail, scandalised the mainsail and edged into Start Bay, hoping to find some shelter in the lee of Froward Point – only to find that the wind funnelling down the cliffs made matters worse. As the weather helm increased, *Shamrock* suddenly screwed round to starboard and, with a thunder of canvas and a shrill yelp of breaking wood, gybed all standing.

A helpless spectator, I watched as the port gaff jaw snapped, jamming the gaff and sail high in the starboard shrouds. Now on a broad reach, *Shamrock* revealed one of her less likeable traits: when heavily over-pressed she refused to steer, and was now plunging at full speed towards the breaking water of Castle Ledge. 'Martin,' I called, 'could you spare a moment? I think we have a problem.' At least I have always maintained that's what I said. He always maintained that he replied, 'Be with you in a minute, squire. I can't find my trousers.'

For once, the awful old engine started first swing and *Shamrock* turned with agonising slowness into the wind, but not until the rocks were less than fifty yards distant. Now it was a case of dropping everything and getting the hell out of there. We handed the jib without too much problem but the mainsail was a different matter, and only after Martin had gone aloft to cut the mast lacing and disconnect the halyard blocks, as the smack rolled in a breaking beam sea, could we eventually wrench it down and Martin could resume his search for his trousers.

It took an hour, against both the wind and a foul spring tide, to reach the sanctuary of the Dart, little more than a mile away. The sky was lightening as we picked up a mooring off the town and there was hardly a ripple on the river. On shore we could hear the whine of an electric milk float and the dawn chorus was starting in the trees below the naval college. It was going to be a beautiful day. Looking at the shambles of torn canvas, hacked ropes and splintered wood, Martin said, 'Anyone would think we've been round Cape Horn or some bloody place.' 'I'm beginning to wonder if we imagined the whole thing,' I said. 'I'll put the kettle on.'

Surveying the wreckage, it was obvious there would be no sailing that day, and later we motored home disconsolately over a glassy sea, taking the shattered gaff ashore for the lads to prepare a favourable quote to accompany yet another insurance claim. But this time there was a problem: the gaff jaws needed to be made of wood with a grain which followed a natural curve to give the jaws their necessary strength. What we needed was a forked ash branch shaped like an enormous catapult, but Ron Lavis had nothing suitable. 'Unless we cut down someone's bleeding tree, I don't know where we can get something,' Phil said. 'Don't worry,' I said. 'I know a man who will.'

\*\*\*\*\*\*\*

'Why, Mr Gregory,' my father said, 'we're looking for a nice bit of grown ash for my lad here.' We were standing in the office of a timber yard in north Derbyshire with the owner, Mr Gregory, an elderly man in tweeds, who was pouring out three small sherries from a bottle he had taken from the safe. 'Will you have a sherry, Mr James?' he asked. 'Why, that's very kind of you, Mr Gregory, just a small one if you would be so kind. Your very good health, Mr Gregory.' 'Thank you very much, Mr James.' 'Not at all, Mr Gregory.'

Although they spoke as though they had been introduced for the first time five minutes earlier, my father and Mr Gregory had done business together for over forty years. Gregorys specialised in making veneers and my father was always looking out for mature walnut trees he could chop down and sell to Mr Gregory, who put them through a machine resembling an enormous pencil-sharpener. Negotiating the price of a walnut tree involved a pointless ritual they both enjoyed during which Mr Gregory said he could get an identical tree cheaper somewhere else and my father maintained that he couldn't. 'He's a hard man, your father,' Mr Gregory said. 'Fair's fair, Mr Gregory,' said my father, opening a packet of Craven A cigarettes. 'I bet you got half a mile of veneers out of that tree we got you from Chatsworth. Can I offer you a cigarette?' 'I won't have a Craven at the moment if you don't mind, Mr James,' said Mr Gregory hastily. 'I find Players are better for my throat.'

As we drove away in my father's new Rover with the newly sawn six-foot-long ash catapult from Mr Gregory hanging out of the back, there were the long silences I remembered well from childhood but which I now regarded as comforting rather than irritating. 'He's a rum chap, Mr Gregory,' my father said after we had been driving for about ten minutes, 'but he knows his onions regarding veneers. I'm just going to pull in for a few minutes and take a look at a parcel of oak.'

We pulled off the main road, down a series of lanes and stopped at a large wood. I had long noticed that only in woods did my father seem fully at home. He could calculate the cubic content of a tree by sight without ever using a tape-measure and although he rarely spoke of it, his knowledge of local fauna and flora was profound. He loved woodland and yet he had destroyed thousands of acres during a lifetime in the timber trade, replanting with spindly saplings and vulgar conifers without a twinge of conscience. 'Why, trees are a crop, like everything else,' was all he would ever say on the subject.

As a child, going out with my father for a day in the woods during the school holidays was something I automatically tried to avoid and then found to my surprise that I usually enjoyed. We often drove into adjoining counties to woods in which my father's timber-fellers were working – small freckled men who cooked rabbits on open fires and drank cold tea from lemonade bottles. Huge trees crashed down into glades and were set upon with axes and there was the sharp smell of newly cut wood. We would stop for lunch in the silent back rooms of small hotels in country towns, invariably lamb or pork with cabbage and roast potatoes followed by plums and custard, and Camp coffee, served by middle-aged women in black dresses. The carpets of the hotels smelt faintly of gravy. My father would have a small glass of beer and I would have a lemonade. The other diners were usually two or three salesmen sitting separately at small tables. Their Hillmans, Vauxhalls and Standard Tens were parked deferentially beside my father's Wolseley.

Usually we would sit in silence on the drive home, but occasionally he would tell me about times when he was young. Once he told me about when he rode a motorcycle to Cornwall with his friend Harry Dale, who was apparently my godfather. 'We were told there were no garages down there so we took all our petrol in cans tied on the back, and we had spare tyres round our waists and pockets full of sparking plugs. Of course there were garages, the same as everywhere else.'

Back home in the early evening after a day in the woods, we might have tea together and companionably share cold meat and tomatoes, but soon my father had imperceptibly retreated back into his own world and I had returned to the one I shared with my mother and sister. Now, thirty years on, we were back together in the woods and my father was scribing his mark on the bark of some trees he had bought with the folding hooked implement I had known all my life. He was bulkier and slower and his hands were very red. He was past retirement age but no one had ever dared to suggest he stop work and spend his days at home with my mother. We reached the edge of the wood and looked down into a shallow valley and onto an extraordinary and completely unexpected sight. In the depth of the countryside was a huge factory straight out of Chaplin's industrial nightmare, *Modern Times*.

Steam spurted from pipes connecting a row of drab buildings reminiscent of Rochdale at its worst. Lowry-like figures scuttled to and fro with heavy trolleys while overhead a monolithic chimney decanted the sort of fumes you'd expect from a fire in a launderette washing rugby-players' socks. I stood transfixed in the shade of a silver birch. 'What do they make in there, for God's sake?' My father, obviously slightly irritated by my ignorance, paused and replied, 'Why, they make dog bowls.'

I had arrived at my parents' home the previous evening with my son and daughter. They were always delighted to visit their grandparents. To them, the middle-class comfort and tidiness, the fluffy carpets, shining furniture and pristine soft furnishings had the sumptuous security of a hotel. They were spoiled by my mother, who treated them as pitiable waifs, and washed and ironed their clothes while they were asleep – my ex-wife regarded ironing as bourgeois. They had secret talks in her bedroom in the early morning and were allowed to eat ice cream at all times.

They were blissfully unaware of the convention of silent dinners and chatted and laughed throughout the meal, asking my mother questions about her own childhood. When she had overcome her surprise that anyone should be interested, she told them about going to school on a steam train and shutting the windows in tunnels to prevent sparks getting in her eyes. When she travelled alone, she would be locked into her carriage by the guard, a friend of her father's, to avoid the attentions of commercial travellers. My father took no part in these conversations, flinching slightly when there was a rise in decibels, and keeping a watchful eye on food dropped on the carpet, which he removed with the Hoover the moment the meal was over.

One lunchtime he seemed particularly uneasy, directing meaningful glances at my daughter throughout the meal. I noticed that whenever she moved, her chair, one of a set of ornate Tudor replicas my father had made when he was twenty, gave a soft mouse-like squeak. At the end of the meal my father rose and folded his napkin. 'I'm taking that chair down to the workshop,' he said. 'That squeaking is driving me mad.' 'How long has it been like that?' I asked, seeing the chance of some semblance of conversation. 'Why,' my father replied, 'just over forty-two years.'

The following day, my parents stood side by side in the large half-timbered porch my father had recently added to the house in defiance of the planning regulations, and waved in unison, as though practising semaphore, as we drove away. The departure had been delayed when Tim disappeared without trace and was found to have locked himself in the boot of my father's car. He was already in disgrace for making a pair of stilts out of some pieces of antique oak, from which my father had intended to make a Jacobean-style gate-leg table for a Masonic friend, and for treading chewing gum into the carpet.

My parents were still waving as the car turned up a hill and out of sight of the house. 'I don't think Grandpa likes us much,' Tim said. 'I think he's just a bit shy,' Sophie said. The following day my father phoned to ask if the wood had arrived safely and I told him the lads were impressed with it and were already fitting it to the gaff spar. From then on, whenever we spoke on the phone he usually asked about the health of the gaff jaws. I said they were doing their job well and he said he would pass on the information to Mr Gregory, who had generously made no charge for the wood. The following year my father died suddenly in hospital during routine treatment for blood thinning. In fact, the ash had unaccountably split down the middle only days after being fitted to the boat and the lads had replaced it with a pair of gaff jaws beautifully made out of laminated plywood. I never told my father about the inadequacies of the Derbyshire ash, feeling that he would have taken it personally. It was only one of many secrets I never felt able to share with him.

*******

That summer was the last we sailed in *Shamrock*. One by one, the lads had got engaged to be married and started spending their weekends putting together MFI wardrobes. Getting crew became more time-consuming and tedious and repair bills were becoming increasingly large. An expensive rebuild was not far distant and it would be hard to justify the expense. It would be sad but sensible to sell the boat and get something smaller and newer that just the cook and I could handle. We put *Shamrock* on the books of Captain Flowerdew, who warned that we would be besieged by dreamers and time-wasters who wanted to sail round the world, and when *Shamrock* was advertised in the yachting magazines this proved to be the case.

Moored in the Exeter canal basin next to the maritime museum, *Shamrock* became the target of a succession of visitors who saw the boat as a passport to a new and exciting life. Some had no sailing experience and others had never actually been on a small boat in their lives, but knew someone who had. Sometimes these friends were brought along, taciturn men in jumpers, who stuck their penknives into the planking and stared intently at the mast.

Many of the would-be buyers seemed more interested in their own lives and aspirations than seriously looking at the boat. A typical example was a middle-aged man named George, who drove down from Coventry with his wife and three small children. His family stayed in the car, staring glumly at the boat, while George told us his life story. He had been made redundant after operating a drilling machine in the Rover car factory for nearly twenty years. A robot could now do his week's work in twenty minutes and there seemed no reason for George to stay in Coventry. He could sell his house, buy a boat and take his family adventuring. He was, he said, a practical chap who could get casual work and the children would learn a lot from being in foreign countries. He had to admit that his wife was not too keen on the idea, but he was confident that he could talk her round. 'We'll never get the chance again,' George said. 'The sunshine and the freedom. Up to now the most exciting thing we've done is a week at Butlins.'

He had never been sailing but he had, as a youth, done canoeing in the scouts and thought that handling a boat would be largely a matter of common sense. He could learn navigation from books. He thought he could probably handle *Shamrock* by himself with a little help from his wife. He was impressed by the engine but thought it could do with an oil change. He was interested to see that some of the electrical equipment had been made in Coventry, but spent most of his time on the boat telling us of his plans to cruise America's Pacific coast and visit relations in San Diego. For my own peace of mind I felt I should tell him that *Shamrock* was an 80-year-old inshore fishing smack built for the Essex creeks, not a round-the-world cruiser or a blue-water racer. George's response was to frown at the scrubbed pine of the saloon and say, 'What you need down here is a nice bit of carpet.'

To bring some reality to the situation I suggested that at least he should look at a recent survey report, inspect the sails and rigging, perhaps check some of the hull fastenings and planking, and invite his wife aboard what could conceivably be her home for the foreseeable future. The first three suggestions got no response from George, now posing at the tiller like a figure from a Player's Navy Cut tobacco advert, but he did shout across to where his wife was still sitting in the car and ask whether she wanted to come and have a look. Eventually a large woman in mock leopardskin climbed from the car and stood scowling at the boat from the quayside. 'How can I get in that?' she asked. 'It hasn't got a door.'

'I'd better go,' George said. 'Is there anywhere I can get the kids some chips?' He seemed relieved to have an excuse to leave. He said he would be in touch, but Captain Flowerdew never heard anything more from George. In any event I had planned to say the boat was sold. I didn't like the thought of having George and his family on my conscience.

A very different prospect, or so I thought, was Commander X, who drove up from Plymouth in his Alvis and said *Shamrock* was exactly what he was looking for on his forthcoming retirement from the Navy and he would have her, subject to a survey. There was no haggling over the price but he did have a vintage Dragon racing day-boat to sell and was also moving house, so could he give me a deposit and pay the rest very shortly? Meanwhile, could I take the boat off the market? Captain Flowerdew and I heard nothing for over a month. Then I had a midnight phone call from someone who sounded as though he was speaking down a length of plastic hosepipe. 'Sorry not to have been in touch, old chum,' Commander X said. 'There have been a few changes lately and I'm temporarily abroad.' He said he would be returning shortly and still wanted the boat. Then he used a phrase I thought was only found in P.G. Wodehouse novels: 'There will be a cheque in the post, along with a very nice cigar.'

There was silence for three weeks, followed by two phone calls made in the small hours. Commander X was reluctant to give his exact location. We talked about cricket and scuba-diving and he said he had been waiting for the exchange rate to improve before sending further money. When the original deposit cheque bounced, that was the last we heard of Commander X. Captain Flowerdew put the boat back on the market when he found that there was no sign of Commander X's name on the Navy List. 'I told you boats bring out the worst in people,' he said.

One chilly Sunday afternoon, after showing round an asthmatic cyclist who used my ownership of the boat to attack me as a member of the capitalist classes, I was locking up *Shamrock* before going home and was certain I was starting a cold, when David Goddard, curator of the nearby Exeter Maritime Museum, appeared on the quayside and asked if it were true I was having trouble selling the boat. Hearing that it was, he said, 'I think we'd better have her for the museum. Come and have a cup of tea tomorrow and we'll sort out the money.'

David Goddard had been a major in the army and his connection with maritime history was not clear. He had founded what was then the West Country's biggest maritime museum in the dock and warehouses at the head of the Exeter ship canal, which he filled with an eclectic array of craft ranging from steam tugs and Tahitian dugouts to a rowing boat in the shape of a white swan. This eccentric approach had made him enemies among the city councillors who provided much of his finance and constantly urged him to organise the sort of themed collection which was currently fashionable. *Shamrock* had wintered in the canal basin for several seasons and Major Goddard had always been friendly and helpful but never seemed particularly interested in the boat. Now this had apparently changed and the following morning, when we met in the museum café, Major Goddard was waiting for me with coffee, cakes and a signed cheque for the full amount of my asking price. 'There'll be a hell of a row about this,' he said cheerfully. 'I know she's got bugger-all to do with the West Country, but she's a pretty boat.'

As with George the drilling operative, I self-righteously urged him to at least have the boat surveyed and to conduct a full inventory, conveniently forgetting that all those years ago I had offered to buy *Shamrock* within twenty-five minutes of ever seeing an Essex smack 'I know you've looked after her,' Major Goddard said, pushing the cheque under my saucer.' And I've always liked the colour.' A week later, Captain Flowerdew had transferred the boat to the museum and Major Goddard had organised a Friends of *Shamrock* group to take on the responsibility of looking after her.

Arriving at the dock one evening to collect a sleeping bag my son had inadvertently left in a locker, I found that a reception was being held in the museum to announce a scheme to use *Shamrock* for teaching delinquents to sail. Sneaking on board hoping not to be noticed, I was accosted by a man wearing a guernsey sweater newly embroidered with the boat's name who said that he was *Shamrock*'s bosun and that if I had any questions I would like to ask about the boat, he would do his best to answer them. I said I couldn't think of any. 'Of course we're going to put her back to her original working trim,' the bosun said. 'It's criminal what they do to these old boats. We'll have our work cut out, I can tell you.'

I went and sat in the car. When everyone had gone back to the reception to toast the success of the venture, I returned alone to the darkness of the quay and thanked the boat in a formal and slightly embarrassed manner for the ten years we had spent together and wished her well. I was surprised to find I felt no particular regret about the parting. I had a cheque in my pocket for nearly three times the original purchase price and there were a lot of nice boats on the market which would need less expensive maintenance. I looked up at the mast and at the high shadow of the burgee moving in the night breeze and walked away with the sleeping bag under my arm. I never saw *Shamrock* again.

CHAPTER 8

# In at the deep end

'Put on these goggles, hold your breath and walk down the ladder to the bottom,' Keith said. 'Keep your eyes open and pretend you are a crab or something.' We were standing on the edge of an open-air swimming pool of a rather select country hotel near the small Devon town of Ottery St Mary, where Keith taught people to swim who had previously maintained they were the human equivalent of blocks of concrete. His successes had included a one-legged man and a woman who had never entered the water until she was eighty-two and subsequently swam every day summer and winter until she was drowned at ninety-one. Keith said that's how she would have wanted it. He was a small fishlike man with smooth skin and short greased hair. He had an evangelical belief that swimming was a natural blessing bestowed on the human race and the world would be a better place if everyone did it. 'Have you ever seen anyone swimming with a cross face?' Keith asked. 'No you haven't, because swimming promotes a psychological and physiological state of wellbeing which is impossible to resist. And that's a fact.'

Certainly there was no sign of an angry face in the Ottery St Mary swimming pool that Sunday afternoon. Indeed, the only occupant was a large mottled woman who was floating face down at the shallow end. Keith caught my glance and hurried away calling, 'Give us a mo. I'll just check on Mrs Marsden. Are you alright, ducky?' Mrs Marsden's scarlet face rose from the water like a miniature sunrise. She had been holding her breath as requested, peering down at the bottom through small round goggles, her inflated body floating gently just below the surface. As she opened her mouth to reply, she was no longer airtight and gravity promptly reasserted itself, returning her to the vertical in a flurry of foam. 'Bugger me, Keith,' Mrs Marsden said. 'I was going along like the *Queen Mary*. What did you have to stop me for?' She was out of breath and apparently near-apoplectic, but she didn't appear to be cross.

Back at the ladder, Keith explained his theory. 'If you hold your breath when you're in the water you're like a football, see, and you can't sink even if you wanted to, and that's a fact. Once you accept that, you'll get confidence and then you'll be floating and then you'll be swimming. Then you'll find that you're not holding your breath any more and that's it. Job done. Bob's your uncle.'

I admired his confidence, but I was Ironbones, the incredible sinking man, and in me he had met his match. At school, Dozy Woodward, the sports master, with certificates and medals for swimming instruction, had in desperation on the last day of summer term had me thrown into the slime-ringed deep end of the school pool, shouting, 'It's sink or swim time, James, you bastard,' and stared in disbelief as I cartwheeled into the water and lay inert on the bottom. Dozy had plunged in, still in his flannels and sports jacket, and dragged me out. He wrote 'As far as swimming is concerned, I suggest he lives in the Sahara' on my term's report.

Now, some thirty years later, Penelope had insisted that I should try once more to learn to swim. As she pointed out, there had been at least three occasions in the past year when, but for the intervention of the lads or other well-wishers, I would have gone over the side, two of them at night when the chances of rescue would have been minimal. 'It's no good always saying that you read on a cigarette card that Nelson couldn't swim,' she said. 'One of these days your luck is going to run out, my lad.' I could see the sense of all this, hence my appearance in my late dad's trunks, among the congenital non-swimmers at Ottery St Mary shortly after *Shamrock* had been sold. As Penelope pointed out, when we bought a smaller boat the lads would no longer be there to save me and she could only swim well enough to save herself.

I put on the goggles and began to walk down the ladder at the deep end. 'Keep you eyes open and hold your breath,' Keith shouted. When the water closed over my head it felt as though I was encased in cellophane. The shrill scratchy sounds of the world above reminded me of the noise of the small Bakelite radio set my Auntie Madge kept switched on day and night throughout the war, tuned to German frequencies in the belief that it was draining the Nazi electricity.

I reached the bottom of the ladder and, holding on to the rungs, stood on the tiled floor of the pool. In the distance, through a blue haze, I could see Mrs Marsden's legs gyrating in a silent ritual dance in time with the deep banging of my heart. Estimating that the pressure inside my body must now at least equal that found in a small lorry tyre, I decided it was time to return to the surface before something actually burst. Not that I had much choice: the instant I loosened my grip on the ladder, I was whirled upwards to the surface, ears fizzing and eyes dilating, into the afternoon sunlight. Keith was bending over the edge of the pool peering into the water. He looked relieved. 'You see,' he cried, 'if you're full of air, you can't help but come up, and that's a fact. Now go down the shallow end and float with Mrs Marsden. We'll have you swimming by teatime.' Twenty minutes later, emerging from the pool after I had propelled myself half a width without putting my feet down, I almost wished that Dozy Woodward was still alive to see my triumph. Then again, he would have found some reason to disparage it.

After three more lessons from Keith, I felt justified in buying a pair of Lycra swimming trunks and a season ticket for the local open-air pool. I had a pair of round goggles which Penelope said made me look like a perverted welder, and took to wearing a damp towel, worn like a scarf, in cafés and saying 'Just been doing a few lengths.' When I expressed disappointment that no one seemed impressed or even interested, Penelope pointed out that to most people knowing how to swim was normal, and if I'd wanted to attract attention I shouldn't have learned, or, better still, I should have drowned in public on a bank holiday. The lads, too, seemed disappointed that they would no longer be able to tell their mates how they regularly saved me from drowning.

By the end of the season my eyes were red and weepy with chlorine but I could swim several lengths with the jerky strokes of a Victorian clockwork toy and tentatively floated in the shallow end among the toddlers and inflatable plastic fish, holding my breath to be on the safe side, but finally convinced of my innate buoyancy. It was a small achievement, maybe, but one I treasured, and one which, as it turned out, probably saved my life only a few months later.

*******

It was a rainy March morning when I took *Swift* down-river from Dartmouth for the first time, heading for Exmouth, some twenty-five miles north. A spring ebb was hurrying towards the sea and the wind was almost dead astern. There were two of us, young Jimmy, the son of a friend, at the helm and myself, up forward, tidying up after setting the mainsail and working jib. There was little traffic on the river this early in the season and most of the boats which had wintered on their moorings still had a frowsty neglected look. In yellow oilskins and wellies I stood on the port side-deck, admiring the fast-receding view of Dartmouth through the rain and feeling the loping movement of the lean long-keeled yacht. I had completed the purchase of *Swift*, a 30-foot gaff cutter built by Philips of Dartmouth in 1932, and now we were taking her home.

The previous owner, with small children, had prudently corralled them behind stout stanchions and high guard-rails. We had spent the last weekend taking them off. They spoiled the line of the sheer, and anyway, sailing a boat like *Swift* from behind a wire fence didn't seem right. This was thoroughbred boating: brass and mahogany, teak toe-rails, gimballed oil-lamps over the chart table, a kettle singing on the saloon stove, a blazer in the hanging locker, the *Telegraph* crossword, a nice bottle of Chablis on the mooring. The days of Captain Custard and Smartie Smacksman already seemed long gone. As I stood with my back to the mainsail, Jimmy, in the cockpit, held up a lifejacket. 'Maybe you ought to have this,' he said, but fate had already decreed otherwise. As though at some prearranged signal, the wind veered sharply and *Swift* gybed all standing. With a majestic hay-making stroke, the boom caught me at waist level and sent me in a graceful arc over the side.

Coastguard information on man-overboard procedures:

> *Remain calm. Keep your legs close together and restrict your movements to stop flushing cold water under your clothing.*

It was very peaceful under the water and, as I sank, I passed a large mooring chain leaning away from the tide which made me wonder in a desultory way about how far I would be taken by the current and what were the chances of eventually emerging under the hull of *Swift*, which by then would presumably have her propeller turning. I was interested to find that none of this caused panic or even alarm, but noted that the lung-full of air I had managed to gulp before sinking wasn't going to last much longer. I was continuing to sink and if I was going to survive I would have to get my boots off. I kicked out experimentally, not expecting any result and was astonished when both boots promptly fell off and I immediately began to rise. Keith's theory of natural buoyancy, demonstrated so convincingly in the Ottery St Mary swimming pool, had been triumphantly vindicated in real life.

> *Panic at this stage can be counter-productive. Remember in cold water your ability to assist in your rescue will be greatly diminished after ten minutes.*

It was only after I broke the surface that I began to behave more like a traditional man overboard. I shouted and flailed my arms. I shook with cold. I coughed and sneezed so violently that I was sick. I was shocked by the potential peril I had been in rather than what had actually happened and more than anything I longed for a cup of a tea and a chocolate biscuit. But first I had to be rescued. A fish's-eye view at water level gives a surprisingly distorted impression of distance and location, but as I trod water and gathered my wits I realised I had been carried several hundred yards towards the Kingswear shore and was within hailing distance of the Royal Dart Yacht Club, of which I happened to be a lapsed member.

I remember wondering if they would pull me out if I promised to settle up, but fortunately the matter became academic when the bulk of *Swift* loomed into view and

Jimmy leaned over the side with a lifebelt on a line and an expression which was a mixture of relief and irritation. He had dropped the sails, fired up the engine and was idling out of gear to see where I would surface. Now there was a question of actually getting me back on the boat.

Reaching up, I grasped the bobstay with both hands and hung like a waterlogged figurehead, submerged by the waves which still surged around the bow.

> *In rough conditions, turn your back on the waves and keep your mouth and nose clear of spray.*

As the water sluiced into my mouth and nose, and my hands and arms supported my dead weight, I knew I couldn't hold on for much longer. I would be the man who drowned outside the window of the Royal Dart Yacht Club, the location pointed out with a shake of the head to visitors on the club balcony. But fortunately this time it didn't happen. Jimmy was leaning over the bow lowering a rope containing a bowline loop into which I managed to put my stockinged foot. As he hauled the rope tight, the weight on my hands magically lessened. At least I was now attached to the boat.

> *Getting a person on board can be difficult. If they are unconscious or exhausted a form of lifting gear will need to be improvised.*

Seeing that I was in no state to pull myself onto the boat, Jimmy went busily about the job of trying to get me on board without any further consultation. He obviously knew what was required, quickly unhooking the throat halyard, with its double purchase, from the gaff, lowering it down the side of the boat and hooking it into a rope he had managed to tie around my waist. Then, tailing this back to a winch on the mast, he slowly and painfully wound me up the topside like an enormous yellow banana. Only when I reached the level of the toe-rail was I able to contribute anything to the proceedings by rolling face downwards onto the safety of the side-deck and lying inert as water streamed out of my clothes and hair. My chequebook had disintegrated, my watch had stopped and my glasses had disappeared. It was hard to believe that the whole sorry incident had lasted less than five minutes.

Jimmy, a thoughtful youth of nineteen waiting to go to university, was deeply ill at ease. His father was a competent experienced yachtsman, and being called upon to rescue a middle-aged skipper who had fallen helplessly out of his own boat was not only completely outside Jimmy's experience but disturbed the status quo so severely that he was at a loss how to react. Embarrassed by my thanks and obviously feeling that to make light of the incident would be disrespectful, he handed me the tiller and went below to put on the kettle, remaining out of sight. I rearranged my sodden clothing, there being no dry garments on board, smiled what I hoped was a faintly laconic smile, and resumed command of the yacht.

The wind died as we passed the twin castles at the entrance to the Dart, the rain increased, and the sea was flat and sullen during most of the five-hour trip under engine. It was a miserable, largely silent voyage and my only consolation was that I couldn't get any wetter. Off Teignmouth, Jimmy made some toast and we passed an anchored tanker in ballast, so still and silent it could have been bolted to the bottom. Off Exmouth, a brisk offshore breeze from the north-east allowed us to finally cut the engine and scud up the estuary under foresails on the spring flood. We found four biscuits and Jimmy offered me an apple his mother had given him. The rain had stopped. We passed wide deserted beaches and shuttered hotels. Near the lifeboat slip a man waved and shouted but at that distance he was neither heard nor recognised. In the dock, as we passed, a small blue freighter was unloading hen food in a halo of dust and high above, gulls rode the wind. I was now almost dry under my oilskins and Jimmy, sensing that the journey was almost over, became more relaxed and spoke of his plans to take a business degree. It began to rain again and we could hear the clang of hatch covers as the freighter shut her hold to keep the hen food dry.

Jimmy was busy with the sail covers as, once more under motor, we traversed the broad sweep of the estuary towards our mooring on the western shore a half-mile away. An hour later, when the boat was snug and secure and we had rowed ashore, Jimmy said goodbye. 'It's not often you get to do a real man-overboard,' he said. 'Could have been a lot worse. There are a lot of people on boats who can't swim, you know.' 'That's unbelievable,' I said. 'Can I buy you a drink?'

So far as I know, Jimmy never told anyone about the man-overboard debacle, but I certainly did. I wrote about it at length in an article which appeared in *Yachting Monthly*, illustrated by the fashionable cartoonist Mike Peyton and purporting to draw some philosophical conclusions from the incident, particularly the removal of the guardrails and stanchions and their subsequent replacement. There was no mention of the recent swimming lessons. If I remember, part of it read:

> Hopefully, though, an important lesson has been learned: when you are busy recreating a fantasy of yesterday's sailing there's always a chance that you won't be around for tomorrow's.

It struck what I felt was the right note of portentous disapproval used by yachting writers at any sign of irresponsibility at sea, and indeed several readers wrote in to congratulate me on 'saying things that needed to be said' and 'having the courage to admit mistakes and put them right.' I honestly did mean to put the guardrails back but somehow never got round to it and eventually sold them for £10 at a boat jumble.

\*\*\*\*\*\*

Writing about boats had started to become part of my journalistic output the previous year when a south London publisher asked me to write a small paperback to fit the title *Boating on a Budget*, for which they had already commissioned a cover. I was recommended for the job by a photographer friend with whom I briefly shared a London flat. He had already written a handbook on marketing photography for the publishers, and certainly no one was better qualified than him to sell dodgy pictures. We had worked together on a number of what were then called 'photo-features' which my pal had somehow managed to sell to tabloid picture-editors.

They included a mermaid apparently sitting by the Serpentine (the home-made plastic tail was made by my sister), a man being fired into space in a rocket made from a telephone box, and half-naked girls serving ice cream to commuters in a packed tube-train. All were obviously fake. There was also a sequence featuring a dog pulling a bone which was tied on to a roller-skate, for which I supplied the caption 'Drawing his own conclusions.' My ex-flatmate has long since given up photography. He took a doctorate in psychology, changed his name, and is now a regular pundit on radio talk-shows and the *Today* programme.

*Boating on a Budget* was part of a series the publishers had optimistically called 'The Secrets of Success', and which included such companion volumes as *The Bike Buyer's Guide, Questions and Answers About Caravanning,* and *Electronic Projects for the Not-so-Brave*. Looking at it some thirty years later, I was surprised by how much work I had been persuaded to do for what was a derisory one-off payment, but the cost of sailing had preoccupied me for so long that information had obviously been absorbed by a process of osmosis and it was not difficult to formalise it into a book. As the title implied, the book was entirely concerned with the money involved in all aspects of boating, with chapters ranging from detailed breakdowns of basic costs, down to maintenance, insurance, repairs and depreciation. Information was gathered from manufacturers, brokers and chandlers, but whenever possible I persuaded friends and acquaintances to share the secrets of their boating budgets, and one man who worked out for the first time exactly what his hobby was costing was so appalled that he put his boat up for sale.

Some of the best financial horror stories came from a man I called Roger who had come to boating in early middle age as a way of spending some of the money he was earning as a partner in a successful advertising agency. For the first few months, unable to afford an office or a phone, the two partners actually ran their business from a remote AA box on the edge of Dartmoor. The stoutly built box, on a little-used carriageway superseded by a nearby link road, had been all but forgotten by its owners, which suited our heroes just fine. Using an AA key borrowed from a relative, they spent the mornings making free calls and the afternoons planning business strategy and cooking simple meals on a primus stove. It all came to an abrupt end when an AA man, accompanied by a broken-down motorist, opened the door in a hailstorm to find the creative director dictating an advertisement to a newspaper and the financial director cooking a mushroom omelette.

Recovering from this setback, the enterprise became successful, mainly due to winning a national slimming club account, but Roger seemed unable to transfer his business expertise to his boating activities and spent a small fortune on a pretty 18-foot wooden centreboard sloop in which he intended to take his wife and two children on short coastal passages. In fact they never went anywhere. The centreboard case was so large that the family couldn't get into the cabin, and the drying mooring bought with the boat meant that for more than twenty hours out of the twenty-four the craft was unusable. After Roger's wife refused to even go on board, the boat was sold at a thumping loss.

The nearest I got to actually writing about sailing was in a chapter called 'All aboard the *Skylark*', which featured a fictitious eight-day West Country cruise in a 27-foot sloop crewed by Tom, Dick and Harry and Tom's wife Thomasina, who seemed to spend most of her time counting her small change and haggling over cut-price bacon. Tom was distraught at having to buy a new water-pump for the engine in Dartmouth (£18.50 plus double time because it was Sunday) and there was some unpleasantness with a harbourmaster in Salcombe over a 97p mooring charge, but by and large the cruise was considered a success at £47.50 a head and Thomasina had £7.89 worth of unused groceries, including a considerable amount of bacon which the crew took home.

You could hardly blame her for that. 'Breakfast,' the book had stressed, 'is perhaps the most important meal of the day. A really huge breakfast seems to fill people up for longer than the largest lunch or supper. Bacon, though expensive, is a vital food on many boats.' Where I got that from, I can't imagine.

There was inevitably a chapter on old boats. 'Buying an old 'un' gave a bleak warning that 'a vintage boat will eat up your attention, your time and your money with a gluttony which deserves a severe bout of indigestion', before promptly undoing the good work and going misty-eyed about 'the charm and fascination that glass-fibre will never possess and a deep satisfaction from relearning the sailing crafts that most yachtsmen forgot more than half a century ago.' All I can say is that I must have meant it at the time.

Several owners of old boats contributed accounts of their expenditure, vying to produce stories of horrendous expense and near-disaster, as in the case of the man who asked a boatyard to put three new bolts in the rudder pintles of his 1910 Medway Bawley. When the boat was hauled out and the worn bolts removed, the entire transom fell out onto the startled shipwrights, resulting in a £5,000 rebuild. The owner reflected that he had sailed over 2,000 miles with the boat in that condition. A similar saga started with a soft spot on the deck of a Falmouth quay punt and ended with replacing the entire side of the boat. The owner had to sell his car to pay for it.

Les the artist claimed to have spent £2,000 on navigational and safety equipment for his boat, including self-steering gear, log, echo-sounder and liferaft, in the hope that the Inland Revenue would read the book and take it as proof of a tax-deductible expense. Sadly Les had little opportunity to use any of it: shortly afterwards he discovered massive rot in the deck and cabin and decided to return *Certa* to her original open-boat state by running riot with a chain-saw one Sunday afternoon. Appalled by the resulting devastation, he moored the wreckage under the trees near his farm on the Tamar where I assume it remained. But *Certa* as she once was still sails into the sunset in a picture Les painted from a photograph I took when we were sailing in company off Start Point one autumn evening. Les called it 'Going Home'.

Much of 'Buying an old 'un' was taken up with the dangers of impulse-buying and the perils of ending up with a 'a jaunty ketch which may well be a rotting worm-eaten hulk beneath her new paint and sparkling brightwork. So it goes without saying that a detailed professional survey is absolutely vital.' The theme was repeated even more forcibly in a chapter 'How to buy', which detailed the precise negotiations necessary to complete a sale to everyone's satisfaction and advised: 'It is absolute folly to buy a second-hand craft without a thorough professional assessment of its condition. This way you will not only know exactly what you are buying but you will have the peace of mind which comes with owning a boat which is thoroughly sound and seaworthy. And that, to me at least, is beyond price.'

The chapter ended with another cautionary tale, this

time supplied by Captain Flowerdew, of a surveyor who examined a boat so thoroughly that his report contained the observation 'Engine – none' when the craft actually contained a monolithic single-cylinder diesel with a five-hundredweight flywheel. A few weeks later, when the boat had been bought on the strength of the survey, the bow planking parted company from the stem and the boat sank in six feet of water. The parable ended, 'Such incidents are happily very rare but they are worth remembering if you are tempted to get a cut-price survey.'

The flyleaf of the book contained a picture of the author, bearded and scowling, against a seaweed-encrusted wall with the caption, 'Tony James has sailed a wide variety of craft in venues as varied as the Caribbean, the North Sea and the River Trent!' I objected to the exclamation mark but by then it was too late to change it. The book was briefly reviewed in the yachting magazines and commended by *Practical Boatowner* for its meticulous price-lists. It sold quite well at £1.25 and I was asked to sign a copy by a man who had been given it by his daughter as a birthday present. He didn't have a boat. The magazine *Small Boat* asked me to convert 'Buying an old 'un' into a two-page article and I spoke to the local Rotary Club in exchange for a ham-salad lunch.

One mildly interesting upshot of all this was that as a published author I had apparently transmogrified virtually overnight into someone who knew about boats. And as it was also known that I was looking for a *Shamrock* replacement, anyone with a dodgy boat would surely think twice about offering it to the author of *Boating on a Budget*, a book now boldly displayed on the bargain counter of the Exeter branch of W.H. Smith. But, as the events of the next few weeks would show, this would not be the case at all.

*******

My friend Black Pete (so called because of his long black beard) rang up one Saturday morning in February while we were still having breakfast. '*Swift* is for sale,' he said. 'I thought you'd like to know.' Pete was a tall bearded man who ran a yacht-rigging business in Dartmouth and was a friend of Captain Jelly's. Together they kept a careful watch on what was happening on the river and invariably were the first to know when boats were being bought or sold.

Pete sailed a beautifully restored engineless Edwardian day-boat in local gaffers' races in fierce rivalry with Captain Bulpin, matching him in skill and local knowledge. Invariably, they were both in the first three across the line but Pete was more gracious in defeat and had a more relaxed attitude to life in general. Years later, when Captain Bulpin and I irrevocably fell out, Pete tried several times to effect a reconciliation but was unsuccessful.

When I was in the ex-working-boat fraternity, we made a point of pretending that yachts were generally of little interest, but I had noticed *Swift*, moored on the Dart near the upper ferry, mainly on account of her unpleasant hull colour, a strident grapefruit yellow, and because she was so rarely used. She was a typical deep-keeled West Country coasting yacht of the early 1930s with a fine entrance, an easy turn of bilge and a transom buoyant enough to keep her stern up in a seaway. She also had a coal stove on which to dry your socks, a period washbasin with brass taps, a wardrobe with a tie-rack and some very nice art-nouveau berth covers. According to Pete, she was 30 feet, plus bowsprit, nine-foot beam, five-foot six-inch draft and 7.63 gross tons. She slept five but could be easily sailed by two and the 20-horsepower diesel was almost new. She was for sale for £11,000.

Pete said that the owner, a recently retired Royal Navy officer with young children, wanted to spend the money on house improvements. His family hadn't taken to sailing and he disliked seeing the boat lying unused. As far as Pete knew,

*Swift* had been well maintained and a boatyard up the river had done some work on her. 'Of course you'll get a survey if you're interested.' Look mate,' I said, 'you're talking to a man who's just written a book about buying boats.'

A week later, at the end of February, Penelope and I drove to Dartmouth and took the owner's dinghy across the river to take a look at *Swift*, lying to a swinging mooring near Philips' boatyard. There was ice on the decks and the cockpit cover was stiff with frost. When we opened the teak cockpit doors and slid back the hatch the cabin was damp rather than cold, something I only remembered later. We went below deep into the boat, dark with wood and tarnished brass. There was nothing fancy or particularly stylish about her fitting-out: just high-quality austere joinery in teak and mahogany, dovetailed drawers, high fiddles, sturdy handholds, a spacious chart table and a galley easily worked at sea.

Already the old boat's class and character were having their effect. We turned on the gas to make tea and sat with our mugs either side of the cold stove like figures in a period advertisement for marine insurance. All the subconscious sales aids were cunningly, if unintentionally, in place: a pot of soft pencils on the chart table, gimballed brass lamps, a builder's blueprint framed on a bulkhead, a bucket of kindling wood by the stove, a chart of the Western Approaches, an oilskin on a hook behind the door. Last year's tide-tables, curling at the edges. There were memories there and also anticipation. Penelope saw warm evening dinner parties on a sheltered mooring with plenty of wine after a lazy day's sail. I saw broad reaches, safe but flashy, pulling down a reef in a warm strong wind, opening a beer on the mooring after a cold wet beat to windward. Neither of us could have guessed what was actually in store when *Swift* eventually became ours.

For the next hour we did all the right things: we ran the engine, found an acceptable amount of bilge-water for a laid-up wooden boat, looked at the standing and running rigging and checked the sails in their numbered bags in the forepeak. Everything seemed fine. The boat, despite being rarely used, had been kept in good order and all equipment was expensive and well maintained. Back ashore, I told the owner that assuming an examination of the hull proved satisfactory, we might have a deal. The author of *Boating on a Budget* could hardly have complained about the way things had been handled so far.

The following weekend's weather was sunny and unseasonably warm, and when, with the owner's permission, we took Swift from her mooring and leaned her against the town quay to dry out for a preliminary look at the hull, we quickly became a focal point of the Dartmouth Saturday morning social scene. Soon the quay railings were thick with nautical know-alls discussing the efficacy of our lazyjacks and double topping-lift and whether cockpit drains would have been part of the original specification. Captain Jelly and Black Pete, who had taken our lines and moored us up, came aboard for a brew, Captain Bulpin and his wife appeared with a bag of cakes, Ken Harris, skipper of the restored Brixham sailing trawler *Vigilance*, moored on the town buoys, asked if he could have 'a quick squint at the old girl'. By the time *Swift* took the ground and gently settled against her fenders there was a full-scale nautical tea party and Penelope had gone ashore for yet another dozen cakes and several small pork-pies.

Boats look curiously vulnerable when out of the water and I felt it was only proper that I should be alone when I first saw Swift in a state of undress. As she stood on the shingle, propped against the dripping green wall, her waterline was at head height and the turn of the bilge curved elegantly down to the long iron keel, and swept backwards to a wineglass-shaped transom. The hull was surprisingly clean and the blue antifouling had obviously only recently been applied. I tried to remember the warnings

I had catalogued so graphically in the book: nail-sickness, rust, rot, dodgy caulking, leaking butt-joints, suspect hood-ends, corrosion, sagging, hogging, electrolysis, cracked frames, gribble damage ... the list was endless and deeply depressing. But by now men were descending the steps and wall ladders and gathering round the boat. Captain Jelly and Black Pete were on their knees examining the garboards – the planks nearest the keel – which had apparently been replaced by an up-river boatyard the previous autumn. 'Bit of a woe-woe merchant,' (a pessimist) said Captain Jelly of the yard owner, 'but he seems to have done a fair job here.' Captain Bulpin pressed a long narrow knife into the planking and found nothing worthy of comment.

Two men stood at the stern discussing the merits of inboard and outboard rudders. Swift's was outboard, hung on the transom, but they were talking of other rudders and other days. 'Very tidy little craft,' said one man, who lived on a small boat on a creek up the Dart which had never been known to move, 'but I'd want self-steering gear for blue-water work.'

In the course of the afternoon, at least a dozen owners of old wooden boats visited in relays to poke about in the seaweed-scented gloom beneath the boat as part of an unspoken competition to find something wrong, but they were unable to come up with anything significant and were reduced to saying that the antifouling clashed with the colour of the topsides or that if I bought the boat I wouldn't be allowed to fly the owner's defaced blue ensign. Captain Jelly, who had stayed on for more cake, voiced the general approval of *Swift* as a well-preserved 50-year-old gaff cutter and a useful coastal cruiser. 'But of course,' he added, his bright blue eyes clouding with what I now assume was instinctive caution, 'I'm not a qualified surveyor.' There would be several occasions in subsequent months, when I was casting around for someone to blame, that Captain Jelly had to tactfully remind me of that.

By early evening, waiting for enough water to motor *Swift* back to her mooring, the non-stop advice and reminiscence from a constant stream of largely uninvited visitors had become almost more than flesh and blood could bear. For the previous half-hour, as *Swift* began to stir with the tide, Penelope and I had sat in numbed silence in the saloon, as a man who claimed his father-in-law had probably helped build the boat in Philips' yard told us that boating was no longer what it was.

'I nearly fell over the other day when a marina quoted £300 for slipping and antifouling a 26-footer. I told them my first boat cost less than that so they told me to go and find someone who would do it cheaper. I couldn't of course. When I started sailing I used to go to a man in a little boatyard up a creek who sat in a shed and always had the kettle boiling. You could get a scrub-off and antifoul and a cup of tea and still have change from a fiver.' 'I think I better start the engine,' I said. 'If I can remember how to do it.' 'I'll tell you this,' the man said, eyeing the last Eccles cake, 'if my father-in-law, God rest his soul, built this boat, you'll have no problems with it, no problems whatsoever.' When I turned back from starting the engine, the man had gone and so had the cake.

There was mist on the river and the sky was nearly dark by the time we had moored the boat, turned everything off and locked up. Before we rowed back to the shore, Penelope and I sat in the cockpit for a while enjoying the silence broken only by the swirl of the tide round the mooring and the murmur of traffic in the lamp-lit town across the river. It was getting cold. 'I think we should buy the bloody thing,' I said. 'I can't go through all this again.'

Back home, it was hard to imagine that a surveyor would find on *Swift* anything that the old-boat fraternity of the Dart estuary had missed. They had taken up floorboards and picked at the keel-bolts with their knives. And all the while they had told terrible stories of what you

154

can find in old boats and to a man had gone away empty-handed. The following day I phoned *Swift*'s owner and agreed to buy his boat. I put my copy of *Boating on a Budget* back on the sitting-room shelf next to the *Ashley Book of Knots* and remarked to Penelope that there was only a certain amount you could learn from books. The rest you had to find out for yourself.

CHAPTER 9

# A sinking feeling

On a warm spring Sunday some three weeks after Jimmy and I had brought her from Dartmouth, *Swift* lay at anchor on a flat windless sea half a mile or so off the resort of Budleigh Salterton and Penelope prepared afternoon tea. It was our first trip with guests – a mere five-mile dawdle largely under engine – but we wanted to impress two of the lads, Martin and Phil, and their girlfriends, with the elegance of our new acquisition, and soon the teak cockpit lockers were spread with an array of cooked meats, salad, hard-boiled eggs and French bread warm from the oven. A bottle of sparkling white wine, towed astern in a net, was brought aboard and a toast proposed to a successful season. Already the lads had volunteered to crew in a couple of Old Gaffers' races and obviously bore no grudges about the departure of *Shamrock*.

We ate and drank and chatted about old times, and as we had mixed company Phil went below to use the heads. When he returned he had the all-purpose non-committal look that I knew from past experience heralded a crisis. 'I hate to spoil the party,' Phil said, 'but I think we're sinking.' Water was beginning to seep through the saloon carpet and could be heard surging in the bilges as the boat settled into a soggy sluggish roll. As in the past, the lads took over, taking up the floorboards and bailing vigorously with a bucket and the hand-operated bilge-pump. The electric automatic pump was ominously silent for reasons that were soon apparent: its valiant efforts to stem the leak had flattened the battery, which in turn meant the engine wouldn't start and the VHF radio was dead. Visitors strolling on the nearby beach and throwing stones for dogs would no doubt have been interested to know that the people picnicking on the smart little yacht anchored on the calm sunlit sea were at that moment seriously thinking about sending up a distress flare which would call out the coastguard and probably the lifeboat.

In fact, it didn't come to that. Instead, twenty minutes' bailing managed to reduce the water level, and from then on someone on the hand-pump could keep it generally under control. Some violent hand-cranking eventually started the engine and we set off cautiously towards home. No one had an appetite for any more food. Curiously, once the boat was moving, the inrush of water actually decreased and by the time we reached Exmouth dock entrance an hour later we had pumped the level down to a few inches in the bilge and could actually see the problem: water was leaking through the top edge of the garboard strake on the starboard side in a steady but not particularly violent stream.

Digger Rodgers, the dockmaster, was on the pier head holding a heaving-line. He had his official cap on.

'You can't come in here,' he shouted, 'I've got a ship coming in.'

'We're sinking and in distress,' I replied, 'you've got to let us in – that's the law.'

'You don't look in much distress to me,' Digger said.

'Come on, Digger,' Phil said, 'the girls are very upset. They've had a nasty shock. They're not used to being sunk. We can go up into the corner out of the way until we've sorted things out.'

A small grey freighter laden with yet more hen food from Scandinavia was making its way slowly up the channel towards the dock and Digger had to make a decision. 'All right,' he said. 'Just this time. But don't make a habit of it.'

We tied up in what was known as Calamity Corner among half-sunk dinghies and dead fish, in a part of the dock which dried out briefly at low water, and reviewed the situation. We agreed there was nothing we could do while *Swift* was in the water and that she should be taken out as quickly as possible and put in the hands of professional repairers. Lavis's, for whom Tom and Phil worked, hadn't the heavy equipment to lift the boat but their rivals, Dixon and Sons, had, and their yard adjoined the dock. I spent the night alone on the boat pumping out every hour or so, apart from the two hours from midnight when she was aground, and eating the remnants of the previous afternoon's tea, which had now become more of a funeral feast.

In the morning I went to see John Dixon in his yard across the quay. Some of the letters had fallen off the name-board which now read DIXO SONS, but the workshop was large and busy. Dixons were one of the last south-west yards to still build wooden trawlers, largely paid for by subsidies. There was a beautiful carvel-built 50-foot hull on stocks in the shed. Two men were painting it with crimson red lead. John Dixon was in a small office at the back of the shed. He was a quiet man in a sports jacket. He walked back with me to *Swift*, which had taken in some nine inches of water in my absence, and arranged to have her craned out later that morning. They were busy trying to finish off the trawler, but he could spare a good man to do the job.

When *Swift* was propped up on the quay, the weight of the boat closed up the seams, thus hiding the source of the trouble, so on John Dixon's suggestion I rang the previous owner to ask whether there had been any history of leaks so that we would at least know what problems we were facing. The previous owner said the boat had been regularly maintained and he had no knowledge of leaks. With no alternative, Dixons removed what appeared to be sound wood and caulking hoping to find some obvious fault, but planking, frames and fastenings showed no deterioration or movement. John Dixon was mystified, particularly as the leak was greatest when the boat was stationary and there was minimum strain on the hull. The garboards as we knew had only recently been replaced so over the next two days 12 feet of pitch-pine was scarfed into the hull above the garboard on the starboard side and the whole area caulked with looped cotton and sealing compound. John explained that it was important that caulking should be under even tension. Excessive caulking in one place can sometimes cause opening and leaking elsewhere and it was wise to replace caulking for a greater distance than might appear necessary. Eventually nearly half the starboard side of *Swift* was recaulked and repainted and the antifouling replaced. There seemed, at least to the untutored eye, no way she could leak now, and this was confirmed on the fourth day when the boat was craned in and the bilges remained mercifully dry.

A few days later, with my son Tim, now a teenager, as crew, we left on a Saturday morning for a weekend cruise to Salcombe, where we had arranged to meet friends. The predicted force four to five north-easterly should have meant we bowled down on an easy reach, but off

Dartmouth at mid-morning it perversely veered south-west and increased, putting us hard on the wind and making it necessary to change the foresails for something smaller. I was on the foredeck dropping the staysail when a violent gust tore it from my grasp and lashed a shackle into my face. At the tiller, Tim watched mesmerised as I staggered and fell on the deck like an extra in the Charles Lawton version of *Mutiny on the Bounty*.

'You're not dead, are you, Dad?' he asked. 'No,' I said, 'just blind.' As my eyes were now full of blood this seemed a reasonable assumption as I groped my way back to the cockpit. Assessing the damage with a wet face-flannel, Tim found that the left eyelid was badly cut. The eye was obviously damaged although how seriously he couldn't tell, as the eyelid was swollen and closing fast. It was obviously time to curtail the cruise and put into Dartmouth for medical attention, which I received at a small empty hospital up a hill from the harbour. A nurse at the reception desk was reading a Mills and Boon novel and had obviously got to an exciting bit. She looked at my face wrapped in a blood-soaked towel, reluctantly put down the book, and asked if I had been in a fight.

A young Indian doctor washed out the eye, found no permanent damage and supplied medication and a black eye-patch. Back on the boat, with the wind nearing gale force, we took the soft option and motored up-river to a remote stretch beyond the village of Dittisham, where we picked up a mooring in a pool fringed with reeds and thick spring foliage. We lit the coal stove and could hear the gale high in the trees, but at water level it was calm and peaceful and well away from the sea. There was hardly any traffic on the river. After supper, as we sat in the cockpit in the last of the evening sun a small cabin-cruiser motored slowly past and an elderly man cried, 'Good evening, Nelson,' and raised his hand in salute.

Having the use of only one eye gave the world a curious

two-dimensional quality and distance was hard to judge. The injury was painful and Tim suggested that it would be wise to go home. The next day the wind had subsided to a stiff breeze and after returning briefly to the hospital to have the eye dressed, it seemed prudent to head back before the next southerly gale, which had been forecast for late evening. As we emerged in the grey mid-afternoon from the Dart into Start Bay, well reefed and with everything lashed down ready for some heavy-weather sailing, the wind instantly died and *Swift* rolled and pitched on a long greasy swell. For the next four hours we motored towards home with that mixture of boredom and morbid apprehension which constitutes a good seventy per cent of sailing but is never mentioned in the books. It began to rain as we reached the bell-buoy at Straight Point, marking the beginning of the Exe fairway, a narrow channel in places less than a cable wide separated from the sea by Pole Sands, and running parallel to the beach for two miles. It was two hours after low tide and in the middle section of the channel there would be less than six feet of water. *Swift* drew five feet six inches and the depth-sounder wasn't working.

> *Entrance at night or in bad weather should not be attempted by strangers. The channel changes frequently and buoy positions can be misleading. The estuary should not be depended upon as a refuge, particularly in southerly winds. For yachts a reliable engine is essential* – Pilot's Guide to the English Channel.

As we rounded the fairway buoy and made for the first channel mark, a conical black buoy moored on Orcombe Ledge, the engine stopped and the wind piped up from the south. Immediately the sea began to break across Pole Sands and the boat, taken by the flood tide, headed for the shore.

> *The fairway has strong tides, with numerous rocky dangers and unmarked ledges.*

Tim set the small jib and the reefed mainsail. I tried to restart the engine only to find it apparently dead, and abandoned it to concentrate on sailing. We had steerage way, but already the wind was veering towards the west and increasing. The further it veered, and the narrower the channel became, the less we would be able to sail without numerous and largely pointless tacks, and the slower we went through the water, the more we would be at the mercy of the spring tide, soon to be running at around four knots.

As Tim put on the kettle and made himself a jam sandwich I pondered the logistics. The channel ran north-west as far as the dock entrance and so long as the wind remained where it was we could just about sail close-hauled and keep in the deepest water. After that, the channel took a curve to the west, turning north in a gradual semicircle to the remote village of Cockwood on the western bank of the estuary and to our moorings on the edge of the mud from where, as evening fell, the calls of mallard and oystercatcher could already be heard.

It was this western curve, following the line of a deserted and almost tropical beach called Warren Point, a popular venue for antifouling boats and illicit sex, which would cause us problems. Turning west into the wind, we would lose steerage and the tide, then at full flood, would push us north and directly onto a submerged hillock known as Bull Bank. The tides were dropping each day. Depending on how hard we went aground and how far up the hill we slid, we could be stuck there for a fortnight.

> *The tide is at its strongest just north of the dock entrance, increasing even further towards Bull Bank. It should be noted that the current running past Warren Point is like a rapid.*

There was worse to follow. Whatever happened, Tim would not be returned to his mother's Exeter home until some ungodly hour, his weekend homework still to do and his school shirt covered in his father's blood. The terms of the children's access order would have been violated yet again and Mr Horsey's now-familiar threat of further court appearances would almost certainly be on my doorstep by the end of the week. But there was little time for further surmise about what might happen in Exeter: on the water the scenario was quickly being overtaken by reality. *Swift* was now off the town, sailing parallel to the beach about a cable's length from the red beacon on the pier head of the dock and travelling with the tide at about seven knots over the ground. The problem was now how to stop her.

With the wind heading us from the west and sandbanks all around, there was little chance of tacking onto the mooring, but a possible destination was the Town Buoys, three large rusty cans in deep water off Warren Point used by coasters waiting to dock but now unoccupied. Any chance of reaching the buoys before the tide took us onto Bull Bank involved going as hard to port as possible, cutting the corner into the curve of Warren Point, and in the process sailing the wrong side of the Checkstone Ledge buoy, a red port marker specifically put there to discourage such behaviour.

> *Checkstone Ledge presents the greatest danger in the channel and the tide runs over the ledge with great strength. Do not attempt to pass south of the buoy as it is moored very close to the ledge.*

Without a depth-sounder there was no way of telling how close we came to hitting the ledge, but Brian Rowsell, a Trinity House pilot who was watching the proceedings from his office on the dockside, said afterwards it was probably less than a foot and that he had seldom seen such irresponsibility. He didn't know it was me. He thought I still had *Shamrock*.

As the buoys approached we rounded up, dropped the

sails and anchored some twenty yards upstream of the cans. Tim rowed out in the dinghy with a line which he attached to the nearest buoy. We won our anchor, laboriously warped the boat up to the can and made fast. Exmouth was still half a mile away but we could row ashore in the dinghy when the tide slackened. No harm could come to us now and the engine could be sorted in the morning. It was another one the Queen knew nothing about, and with a little editing could have all the makings of yet another homily for *Yachting Monthly*.

We sat in the cockpit and listened to the tide drumming on the buoys. 'Go and put the kettle on,' I said, adjusting my patch. 'Then I'll take you home. Never a dull moment, eh?' Tim went below, but he was soon back. 'Dad,' he said, 'there's water coming through the carpet.'

\*\*\*\*\*\*\*

I pumped out the bilge, rowed Tim ashore and Penelope drove him back to Exeter. Returning to the boat, I spent the night aboard, pumping out every hour, and in the morning rowed over to DIXO SONS to tell them the news. Later that morning John Dixon towed *Swift* into the dock with his launch. As she was once more craned out the problem was immediately apparent. Water poured from the boat in a steady stream – but this time from the port-side garboards which had previously showed no sign of leakage. John Dixon was aghast. He took the new leak personally and although once again he could see no obvious signs of damage or decay there was nothing for it but to replace the garboard and recaulk a large area of the port side.

A week later, after the engine had been checked and found to have a fuel blockage, John Dixon and I sat side by side in the cabin silently staring into the bilge as the boat was lowered back into Calamity Corner. Whatever the problem was, it seemed to have been solved, and after half an hour the bilge was still completely dry. John Dixon allowed himself a bleak smile and went back to his yard. I said that I hoped the worry and inconvenience I had been caused would be reflected in the bill, and motored *Swift* back to the mooring.

If I thought that was the end of our troubles I was mistaken. A week later, during a succession of unseasonable north-east gales, there was yet further disaster. In the night a heavy steel trawler broke adrift from further up-river and collided violently with *Swift*, smashing off the bowsprit and damaging the topsides and varnish-work. Hopefully it would be an insurance job for which the lads could once more submit a tender, but when Martin and I went out to assess the damage we found to our utter disbelief that the saloon carpet was once more under water. Like some malign curse, the leak had once again returned.

The rest of the sorry story can be condensed into a brief précis. The boat was craned out yet again and virtually rebuilt. Extra knees and frames were fitted in the hope of strengthening the hull and preventing the mysterious movement that apparently opened the seams. John Dixon came to the conclusion that the boat must have been built with an inherent weakness, but if so why hadn't it shown itself in the previous fifty years?

Despite John Dixon's assurance that he would take into account my worry and inconvenience, the repair bill, when it arrived, was so enormous that it took all the profit previously made on the sale of *Shamrock* and forced me to sell a small insurance policy. The good news was that during the remaining three years we had the boat, *Swift* no longer leaked – but I was never completely confident that we had solved the problem and for ever afterwards the automatic pump remained unconnected and the first job after climbing aboard was always to check the bilges for water.

When we moved home and boat to Cornwall, to

accommodate Penelope's career ambitions, we found an idyllic mooring on the River Tamar in a sheltered backwater at the village of Cargreen overlooking the Spaniards pub and surely well out of harm's way. In fact the catalogue of misfortune had merely been transferred from Devon to Cornwall. Soon after we arrived *Swift* broke her mooring in a gale and went ashore into a small plantation of silver birch with surprisingly little damage. We were less lucky one night shortly afterwards when some unknown vessel snapped off the bowsprit and damaged the stem, requiring the attentions of two elderly shipwrights in a willow-hung creek, recommended to me as masters of the imaginative insurance claim and who eked out a living when trade was quiet by making exquisite clinker dinghies and selling chandlery from the back of a three-wheeled Trojan van. Years later they came to a sticky end – teaching carpentry at the local technical college.

There seemed no end to the boat's misfortunes, which Captain Bulpin seriously believed were caused by painting her green, considered an unlucky colour. Returning up-river on a falling tide on August Bank Holiday, we went aground actually under the massive new road bridge at Saltash and the boat lay on its side like a dog in a heat wave. Acid ran from the batteries into the breadbin and tins of fruit fell out of lockers and broke my glasses. As the tide rose, water poured through the top seams of the hull and soaked a fruit cake we had bought for tea.

On another occasion we arrived at the riverside for an afternoon sail only to find *Swift* with her bow deep under the water and the stern high and dry like a miniature version of the last moments of the *Titanic*. The mooring had snagged on some underwater obstruction on a rising tide and the chains were dragging the boat under, carving deep furrows in the topsides in the process. It was back to the willow-hung creek for more expensive repairs.

I was beginning to have increased sympathy with the

attitude of a man called Bob Brooks, whose carefully preserved wooden ketch was moored a few hundred yards up-river and who was derided for not having sailed beyond the protection of the Plymouth Sound breakwater, some eight miles away, for at least ten years. We soon observed that Bob's weekend sailing ritual seldom varied. A crew, usually students from the college at which Bob taught technical drawing, was assembled and briefed for an overnight cruise, maybe a run to Falmouth if wind and tide served. Courses were plotted, tide-tables were consulted, stores stowed. Those who hadn't been on the boat before really believed they were going somewhere. Those who had, apparently mouthed two words: 'Cawsand Bay'. The mooring was slipped and as they drifted down the Hamoaze on the first of the ebb tide, a subtle change would be observed in Bob. He would scan the cloudless sky and say something like, 'Don't like it. Too bright too early. There'll be a real blow from the east. Spoke to the weather boys this morning. They're none too happy.'

By now Claud Worth's morbid anxiety (described in the dictionary as 'unwholesome uneasiness') would be running riot from stem to stern and when Bob suggested a stop for lunch there was eager agreement. They would drop anchor in Cawsand Bay, a cosy inlet on the landward side of the breakwater, and after visiting the village's excellent fish and chip shop, catch the flood tide back to the mooring.

By the summer of 1983, I was beginning to suspect that Bob might have the right idea. Continuing mishaps, domestic problems and other diversions meant that the boat lay largely unused until August when we sailed to Falmouth in company with Captain Bulpin and his wife in their boat for a week's cruise dogged by accidents and bad weather. To escape what had every appearance of a winter gale, we motored far up the River Fal past the mothballed freighters and rusting obsolete tankers moored among the trees at King Harry Ferry. We anchored in a wood off

Magotty Bank so silent you could hear the tide sucking at the stones. We dinghied up a dark creek to a ruined church far from the sea and saw no one all that day. At night we lit the stove and Captain Bulpin sang softly to his guitar. In the morning as we motored down-river on the ebb it was grey and raining again. We anchored briefly at Mylor to buy milk. We bought a passion-flower from a stall in Mylor churchyard and examined an epitaph which read:

> Here lies Joseph Crapp, shipwright
> Who died on board ship, June 1770
> aged 40
> His foot did slip and he did fall
> 'Help, help,' he cried, and that was all

The following day we sailed in company back to Plymouth on an unpleasant lumpy sea in a south-westerly gusting six to end what was our last cruise in *Swift*. In October she was put on the market and sold to a bookshop owner from Looe for £2,000 less than I originally paid, but I felt it was time we parted company and once again felt relief rather than regret. So *Swift* was dried out on a wall near the pub and subjected to merciless scrutiny by a the buyer's surveyor. I had expected his findings to be somewhat frank and so they proved. He had never come across a yacht of *Swift*'s age in such excellent condition at such a reasonable price. She was, he was sure, a boat which in the right hands would give many years of safe and happy sailing.

## CHAPTER 10

# Davy Jones never sleeps

A few weeks after *Swift* was sold, I discovered that Penelope was having an affair with our next-door neighbour and so one rainy November afternoon I drove my turquoise-blue Datsun away from our cottage for the last time. The car was full of clothes, books and kitchen utensils and I was towing a 13-foot wooden Enterprise sailing dinghy on a trailer. Under its green cover the dinghy contained a red-bound set of the Encyclopaedia Britannica, a selection of charts of the English Channel, a saddle and bridle – I had recently taken up riding – a small outboard motor, a trombone in its case, a steam-iron and several pot plants.

I was once more going through the ritual of leaving home, and while my objective that afternoon was the spare room of my sister's house in west Somerset some hundred miles to the east, any permanent destination was still unknown. I had bought the boat, as yet untried, from a friend for £350, seeing it as a possible passport to some future nautical scene, or at least as a useful topic of conversation. In convoy with me down the narrow lanes leading from the moor onto the Exeter-bound A30 carriageway was a Volkswagen Golf saloon stacked with more of my possessions including files, books and an electric typewriter, and driven by a blond bearded man who looked like a peripheral character in an Ingmar Bergman film. His name was Tony Hazzard, yachtsman, goat-keeper, writer of several major pop-hits in the 1960s and a loyal and long-suffering friend.

Penelope and I had bought his house, a granite cottage in a tiny windswept village on Bodmin Moor, three years earlier when Penelope became deputy head of a comprehensive school in the area and Tony needed the money to settle a large tax bill dating back to the heady days of his show-business success. Instead of shifting well away from Farm Cottage, the house they admitted they loved, and had hated to sell, Tony, his ex-wife Carol, Carol's lover (a young builder), a dozen horses, goats and Tony's very old dog merely moved a few yards to a piece of land they owned on the other side of the Farm Cottage garden hedge and set up a smallholding and livery stable in a barn, which they ran from two caravans parked together under a tree.

The authorities had been persuaded to allow the caravans on the understanding that the builder would construct a large agricultural bungalow which would accommodate himself and Carol, with a separate flat for Tony, who since their divorce some years earlier had a enjoyed a close but platonic relationship with his ex-wife. But the entire time we were there the bungalow never progressed much beyond the foundations.

None of this appeared to affect Tony Hazzard, known as H, who lived on the modest royalties from writing several of the Manfred Mann pop group's 1960s successes including 'Fox on the Run' and 'Ha Ha Said the Clown', and which still accrued from reissues of 1960s hits in distant emergent nations. Alone in the wind-rocked caravan, green with lichen and decorated tastefully with William Morris wallpaper and brass lamps, he lived a life, disturbing to someone like me, brought up under a rigid Midlands work ethic. True, he had a well-structured routine which included milking the goat for his morning porridge, baking loaves of wholemeal bread, preparing ethnic pulses for his vegetarian meals, writing letters to the *Guardian*, listening to the afternoon play on Radio 4, strolling on the hills when the weather was fine and going to bed early with a good book, but none of this could be strictly regarded as work as I knew it, particularly as he was still barely forty.

There had been talk of an album to revive his career and although he did produce some songs of haunting beauty nothing came of it. Very occasionally he and a guitarist he had worked with in the 1960s would do an evening gig at local folk clubs. H sang his own songs in a voice not unlike James Taylor's and the evenings were always crowded and very successful, particularly to attractive young women. H was invariably asked why he had given up show business when he still had so much talent and he usually replied that he didn't like going to bed late. A more likely reason was that he hated using lavatories other than his own, or in this case the lavatories at Farm Cottage which for some reason we had agreed to let him continue to use after the property had changed hands. After he had convinced Penelope that a daily bath was the only cure for conditions he described as hot knees and restless legs, it seemed logical to invite him for supper and soon he was spending almost as much time in Farm Cottage as he had when he owned it.

Originally from Liverpool, H had become involved in

music immediately after university, discarding it abruptly at the height of his success. He was easy to like, good company, yet curiously unobtrusive, and maybe it was this unthreatening quality which made him so popular with a wide circle of women, mostly married or in relationships, who regularly phoned and visited him for confidential talks and advice. Others were openly besotted with him, including a beautiful BBC television presenter who besieged his caravan for weeks until he asked Carol to tell her that she was seriously upsetting his routine.

H rarely left the village except to visit the nearby town of Liskeard to patronise a health-food shop, and he needed a lie-down on his return and, if possible, a bath. It was a minimal lifestyle, more suited to someone twice his age, and was accentuated by his clothing – usually pale grey pyjama-like tracksuits. His other regular visits were to his boat, a small wooden sailing cruiser called *Magpie*, moored on the River Fowey in a leafy creek below the town of Lostwithiel. It was reached by a lane which bore a sign reading 'If You Cannot See This Sign The Road Is Flooded'. H's cruising was also characteristically minimal. On warm windless afternoons, in company with what he called 'a lady', he would motor a mile down-river and out through Fowey harbour to nearby Lantic Bay, where they would anchor and swim. Afterwards they would make tea. He would always need a particularly long bath after one of these excursions, which were the extent of his cruising schedule. His dog, myopic and deaf and nearing twenty years of age, usually went, too. 'What a dog!' H would cry as the comatose creature was lifted aboard. 'What a corker!'

During the dismal terminal weeks of the relationship with Penelope, when I was once again blockaded inside my office in the cottage and communicating by solicitor's letter and notes pushed under the door, H and Carol were kindness itself, providing food, company and solace as things went steadily from bad to worse. H volunteered to help move what was required for my immediate needs and later another sailing friend lent me a small removal van. On a day when it was known Penelope would be working late at school we returned to the cottage and meticulously removed half of the entire contents. The operation took longer than we had expected and H nervously kept watch on the road as I wrote out a detailed inventory of what had been taken, including half the contents of the pepper and salt pots. Apparently, minutes after the van had rumbled away, Penelope's green Renault arrived from the opposite direction, but by then H and the corker were safely in his caravan.

West Somerset wasn't entirely a random destination. Apart from my sister, there was another connection. For reasons which were never entirely clear, a small newspaper features syndicate in which I was a partner had recently moved from London to a remote address in the Brendon Hills, and it was here that H and I deposited my possessions while I looked for somewhere permanent to live. In the meantime, there was my sister's spare room in a cottage in a deep combe on the edge of Exmoor where cows stood at forty-five degrees in fields above our heads. My sister, six years younger than me, had long been reconciled to the fact that when things went badly wrong I would usually come bleating to her to help me out when no one else would. Over the years she always has, with loyalty and forbearance, although apparently she did once confide in a friend that a few good thrashings as a child would probably have done me the world of good. After a career as a scenic painter with the Royal Shakespeare Company, Geraldine married the painter and sculptor Alexander Hollweg, and now makes exquisite jewellery in a converted pigsty. She is also a very good cook.

Near Alex and Geraldine's cottage was a field study centre converted from a mansion recently abandoned by a family of eccentric aristocrats. Now bespectacled girls in dungarees set up newt traps at dawn, lay in ditches watching spiders and walked in procession along narrow lanes carrying jars of frogspawn.

One day I came upon the bearded warden of the centre, reputed to be the world authority on the life cycle of the dog-whelk, painting a wooden yacht in a shady yard. We had previously met briefly and I admired the boat, a classic long-keeled south-coast design of about 25 feet, and asked where it was normally kept. 'Watch it!' he replied. 'Sorry?' Had I strayed onto his wet paint? What could have become one of those ponderous misunderstandings from a Will Hay film mercifully ended when I realised what he was actually saying. 'Oh, you mean Watchet.' 'Yes,' he said, 'it's cheap and it's only three miles over the hill. But it's a bloody awful place to keep a boat.'

> *WATCHET – a small drying Bristol Channel walled commercial harbour six miles ESE of Minehead. Used by coasters up to 200 ft, has a mud bottom and offers good shelter in most weathers. Approach with caution in offshore winds. Tides strong in harbour entrance. Town is friendly and rather salty –* Bristol Channel and Severn Pilot.

I had been to Watchet several times in the past and didn't like it much. When my father visited my sister and her family he had liked to make a short visit to Watchet, usually on Sunday afternoons when the docks were deserted, to view the imported timber piled high on the quays. We would stand in silence while he communed with the planks and speculated how many cubic feet of timber was contained in the piles. On one occasion, for something to say, I asked what sort of wood it was. 'Why, it's deal,' my father said. 'And that?' I pointed to something which looked quite different. 'That's deal as well, of course,' my father said. 'It's a good job you're not in the timber trade.' When I next went back to Derbyshire I had mentioned my confusion over deal to my father's long-time assistant,

Arthur Sharpe, who explained that to timber merchants of my father's generation deal was a measurement rather than a species of wood and was used to categorise planks nine inches wide and three inches thick. It was knowledge that I never had cause to use because my father never mentioned deal in my presence again.

\*\*\*\*\*\*\*

It was nearly a month after arriving in west Somerset that I found myself once more in Watchet. The intervening time had been spent setting up a temporary office and looking at a succession of damp and depressing rented cottages. In Watchet there was a flat in a gaunt Victorian house overlooking the sea but it had been lived in by a Hell's Angel who had painted all the walls with black enamel. The estate agent was trying to convince me that the place had character and potential but his words were largely drowned by a fight taking place in an adjoining flat. As we left, a nearby fish and chip shop caught fire.

Amid the rural sweep of Exmoor and the gentrified villages set deep in the soft plump hills, Watchet seemed a starkly urban community, rough, tough and defiantly working-class. The town of around 3,000 population housed many of the area's problem families. Young mothers queued at the post office for their benefits on Thursdays. There were five pubs, two cafés, a milk bar, two social clubs, two fish and chip shops, a cinema turned into a seldom-open amusement arcade and a bookie's.

There was industry in Watchet – haulage businesses, a massive paper mill, a bakery, three banks, a shirt factory – and the streets had a gritty northern feel. It was on the sea and it was reputed to be the setting for Coleridge's *Rime of the Ancient Mariner*, but it was not a holiday town. For a thousand years Watchet life had centred around the nine-acre drying harbour: most families had someone who worked on the docks. Some had lost relatives who had fallen into holds, been crushed by cargoes or trapped between ships and quays and whose names were now on commemorative plaques on several dockside seats.

In the early 1980s the docks were run by Watchet Marine, a subsidiary of a Welsh shipping line, and were busier than for decades. Three or four small freighters a week could usually be seen on the two commercial quays unloading timber and fertiliser or taking on scrap metal and bales of newsprint. Sometimes the bales burst and newspapers flew into the sky and lodged in trees and bushes around the town, contributing to the general seediness of the landscape. It was claimed that newsprint cargoes for Muslim countries first had to have all salacious page-threes removed from the *Sun* and the *Daily Star*, but this, like so many other things, was probably Watchet folklore.

The current prosperity of Watchet docks was mainly due to the fact that as one of the smallest commercial ports in the UK it came outside the Dock Labour Scheme regulations and so could work almost unlimited hours to turn vessels round in record time, a fact appreciated by both ship operators and customers. Later the regulations would change and that was the beginning of the port's decline and eventual demise in 1993. In any event, it was an odd place to have a port: coasters could only enter around two hours either side of high water and spent the rest of their time aground on mud the consistency and colour of chocolate mousse, which in places was ten feet deep. Watchet was without doubt the muddiest of all Bristol Channel ports, yet at one time it was apparently so clean that cricket could be played on the harbour bed and carts were driven alongside ships. The problems started after the western pier was rebuilt of solid stone after a calamitous storm in 1900 had sent brown frothing water into the town, and from then on the harbour became a sump for Severn mud.

Leaving the estate agent that cold winter afternoon, I passed a café with a poster reading 'Take Home A Tart For The Weekend' and reached the public walkway called the Esplanade, which ran along the southern edge of the docks. This was a narrow cobbled rectangle containing a terrace of low white buildings housing the coastguard station, the Esplanade Social Club, a chiropodist, the Watchet Men's Conservative Snooker Club, a small library in what had been the lifeboat station, the Red Cross and a closed amusement arcade called The Ritz. Someone had climbed up the high facade to carefully remove the leg of the R so that it now read The Pitz. The place later became the office of a fancy-dress hire firm called Auntie's Bloomers, owned by a man who had a small private aeroplane and business interests in the Balkans.

The tide, second only to that in the Bay of Fundy as the highest in the world, was inevitably out that afternoon, and some three-dozen small yachts and fishing boats, moored on posts and chains around the edges of the harbour, lay high and dry on the mud. Their hulls were thick with scum and weed. Sticking from the mud was a depressing detritus of old bicycles, shopping trolleys, car tyres, road signs, plastic bags and disintegrating armchairs. If there was anywhere more inconvenient and dismal to keep a boat I certainly hadn't found it.

At the end of the Esplanade, near the dock entrance, a group of schoolboys, presumably on an educational trip, gathered round a stocky white-haired man in a blazer whom I later knew to be Tommy Ley, retired Watchet harbourmaster and former Trinity House pilot. I heard him say, 'Remember this, my lads: Davy Jones never sleeps.' Pointing dramatically out to sea, like the fisherman in Millais' *The Boyhood of Raleigh*, he added, 'If you die out there, you're not drowned, you're murdered.' It only served to reinforce my already steely resolve to avoid sailing in the Bristol Channel if at all possible, and certainly never to keep a boat in Watchet.

Meanwhile, hearing that I had an Enterprise dinghy lying under a tree in my sister's garden, an acquaintance suggested I joined a dinghy sailing club based on a remote reservoir in the Brendon Hills. 'It can be a bit boring sailing round a field, but they do sell very good cake,' he said, 'and at least you'll be on the water.' When I eventually arrived at the lake, which had been made by submerging a village and several farms, I found the reservoir sailors quite unlike anyone I had met in my previous sailing adventures. With no tides, currents, navigation or other uncertainties to worry about, they were free to concentrate on other priorities.

Most of the men were called Mike and the women Jan or Jo and virtually everyone had responsibilities like safety strategy, social development and site security, which they took very seriously. Reservoir racing was the sole interest – few members had sailed on the sea, or had any wish to – and I was derided for providing my boat with a coil of line, a couple of fenders and a small anchor. 'You'll be bringing flares and a chart next,' said Mike, the flag officer of the day. 'We're not sailing the Atlantic, you know.'

When I arrived at the sailing area, with its imposing clubhouse and neat rows of parked dinghies, the site security officer of the day pointed out that my membership card wasn't signed and lent me a pen. Ignorant of dinghy club etiquette, I was wearing wellies and an old jumper and was immediately conspicuous among the sleek Lycra wetsuits and expensive gas-powered lifejackets.

Casual sailing was not allowed until the end of the racing programme and it was early evening when I eventually got afloat. The wind was strong and erratic, deflected from the hillsides and trees and constantly changing direction, but, fooled by the rural surroundings, I hadn't reefed, and the Enterprise was soon sailing at full speed on a broad reach, the lee rail under and the end of the boom skimming the water. OK, I didn't have the right clothes and hadn't signed my membership card, but no one could say I didn't know how to sail. In answer, the wind waited until the boat was level with the clubhouse terrace before it suddenly backed 180 degrees and the boat gybed and instantly capsized.

The water was flat and relatively warm and once again I lost my wellies and all vestiges of credibility. The terrace, previously almost empty, magically filled with men and women chanting 'Capsize. Man overboard. Safety boat please,' and men, buckling on their lifejackets, ran to a large and powerful rescue boat moored nearby. Any chances of climbing back aboard and sailing away out of their reach to some remote corner of the pond were dashed when I found the Enterprise's mast was stuck into the mud of the reservoir floor and the capsized boat was as immovable and waterlogged as a dead turtle. As the rescue boat came alongside I grasped its gunwale ready for some light-hearted banter and a tow back to the shore. Instead I got a dressing-down from Mike, safety officer of the day, which began 'I'm afraid I'm going to have to read you the riot act for this.' There was as yet no attempt to recover me from the water, nor much sign of any banter. The riot act, delivered in Mike's curiously ecclesiastical voice, was done alphabetically.

A. As a new and inexperienced member I should not have been out alone after 5 pm or 4 pm in winter.

B. I should have logged the time and the estimated duration of sailing in the duty officer's daybook.

C. My launching trolley had not been properly docketed and had been left where it could have caused problems in the case of emergency.

D. I was sailing irresponsibly in the prevailing conditions.

The water was no longer relatively warm. As I hung from the rescue boat looking up into Mike's pale eyes, my teeth began to chatter and the jumper tightened around my chest and when the lecture showed no sign of ending I eventually asked, 'Do you think we could continue this on shore? My hands have gone numb.' Curiously, the whole incident, made more ridiculous by taking place a few yards from a group of watching cows, was more disturbing than falling into the Dart.

By the time the dinghy had been righted and baled out, and I had been taken aboard the rescue boat, the spectators had lost interest and returned to the clubhouse. At the slipway, Mike and his crew hauled the dinghy out, helped me return it to its parking place, and I was left wet and shivering in the dusk. Not expecting to be submerged on my first outing, I hadn't brought a change of clothes. I found an old dressing-gown and a pair of slippers in the boot of the car, stripped off my wet things and put them on. Looking like something from a Spike Milligan sketch I returned to the clubhouse hoping for a cup of tea and a slice of cake, but the cafeteria had just closed and Jan and Jo were carrying the cakes away. They were chocolate, lemon-sponge and something decorated with almonds. I suddenly felt very lonely. As I turned to leave, Mike the safety officer came up. 'I'm glad I caught you,' he said. He asked me to sign a document absolving the club from responsibility in case the boat had been damaged. 'Just routine,' he said and, glancing at my clothes, added, 'I hope I haven't kept you up.'

I went out into the almost-empty car park and there was mist on the water. The cows were walking in single file up a steep hill and into the last of the sunset. It was quiet. I hitched the dinghy onto the Datsun and drove away from the reservoir, down the hills towards the sea, and never went back.

Soon afterwards I sold the Enterprise dinghy for £200.

*Shamrock* entering Plymouth Sound 1979. Martin at the helm as Tony tends the mainsheet.

In company with another gaffer, 1980.

*Shamrock* beached on the Exe estuary for anti-fouling.

The lads, (L to R) Martin, Paddy and Phil in their suits before wreaking havoc in St Malo.

A study in concentration – Phil helming *Shamrock*.

Tom, navigator on *Shamrock*'s trip to London.

David Green helming in an Old Gaffers' race. Phil and Martin stripped for action.

▲ *Swift* in Dartmouth on her first trip under new ownership.

▲ *Swift* (R) rafted up in the Dart before a Cornish cruise.

▲ Phil skippering the trip to Brixham from Spain.

◀ Geraldine and Alex, with their children Lucas and Rebecca, at Nettlecombe on their Silver Wedding Day 1987.

*Sophie*,
approaching
Watchet on a
broad reach.

*Sophie* setting
a topsail as she
approaches
Barry on the
Welsh coast.

Tony Hazzard,
yachtsman,
pop composer
and good
friend, fresh
from the bath.

Pilot Nigel
Stokes,
relaxing after
a successful
docking.

Tony with *Yankee Jack*'s stem-post, the most expensive piece of wood on the boat. *Photo: Bruce Scott*

Derek Vivian. He masterminded the flatner project and did the difficult bits. *Photo: Bruce Scott*

*Yankee Jack*, immaculate before the launch in 1997. *Photo: John Nash*

In Watchet Boat Museum (L to R) Ben Norman, Tom Head and Fred Routledge entertain with shanties prior to the launch. *Photo: Brian South*

◀

*Yankee Jack* heads for the harbour, pushed by the Watchet Sea Scouts and led by the Town Crier. *Photo: Brian South*

On the slip, watched by well-wishers and bemused holiday-makers.

▼

Somewhat over-pressed, *Yankee Jack* passes Watchet lighthouse. The picture made a half-page in *The Times. Photo: Tim Cuff / Apex*

▼

Tony with Sophie, Tim and Juliet at his niece Rebecca's wedding, May 2003.

Myrtle on holiday with ever-present bags.

Grandsons Ben, Harvey and Oscar at Falmouth 2005.
*Photo: Tim James*

Gentle sailing. Myrtle helms as Tony tends the sheets.

Tony demonstrating the Chiropractors' Association approved tiller. *Photo: Dave Hall*

◀ Bob Eaglesfield (left), Tony and Rick Pook return swamped but unbowed from the Brixham Trawler Race.

A sensible boat at last. Tony aboard *Kittiwake*, Watchet 2005.
▼

Without a boat for the first time for more than twenty years, I filled the vacuum by spending more time in pubs. One of the most popular was a former cider house in a small valley next to the sea, run by a large perspiring man who had previously been a postman in Kent. It was hard to define just why Ken was such a successful landlord but the pub was crowded most nights and closing times were loosely observed in this remote place. I preferred to visit early in the evening when it was more like a private club with a line of locals at the bar and Ken unashamedly eavesdropping on conversations and pontificating on topics which interested him.

One evening two customers were discussing an exhibition they'd seen of the nineteenth-century painter and engraver Samuel Palmer when Ken joined the conversation. ''Ere, I couldn't help hearing you was talking about that Samuel Palmer. I used to deliver his post at Sevenoaks. And do you know what he gave me at Christmas? F-ing nothing. Next day I chucked his post in the ditch.'

'What do you do about contraception?' he once asked as he handed over a bag of cheese and onion crisps. I said that unfortunately it wasn't a problem at the moment. 'Well take it from me that the best two contraceptives in the world are a F-ing great Alsatian on the bed and a bag of golf clubs,' Ken said.

A regular early-evening customer was Nobby, an elderly farm worker who stopped for a half-pint on his way home. Nobby's visits rarely lasted more than ten minutes and he had never had cause to use the pub's facilities but one evening he asked to use the lavatory and was directed to the gents in the yard. He was away for nearly twenty minutes. Eventually Ken, knowing that Nobby had heart problems, went to investigate and found the cubicle door closed.

'Are you all right, Nobby? You've been in there a long time.'

'Yes. It's just that there wasn't any toilet paper.'

'Sorry about that. Can I get you some?'

'No it's all right now. I've fastened all my cigarette papers together.'

Ken eventually moved to a pub in the Midlands and immediately trade declined. A succession of publicans seemed unable to revive it and eventually there was little to be seen in the car park in the early evenings but Nobby's green Raleigh bike.

*******

On either side, the Bristol Channel stretched as far as I could see. It was dusk on an early spring evening in 1984 and dead ahead, a dozen miles away, the coast of Wales stretched like a blurred line of type. Some thirty-five miles to the north-west the glow of Swansea faded into the shadow of the Gower Peninsula, running north to the Black Mountains and the Brecon Beacons. Twenty miles nearer, on the south-east corner of Swansea Bay the Nash Point light was already flashing, marking the narrow navigational passage through Nash Sands. East from the Nash, from where the Bristol Channel becomes the Severn Estuary, the lights of Barry docks and the loom of Penarth and Newport marked a low and almost featureless coast.

To the north-east, above Penarth, where the estuary narrowed and fierce tidal streams rattled through sandbanks and rocky shoals, two islands lay some four miles off the Welsh coast. Steepholm, some forty acres, part of Somerset, dark and straight-sided as a fruit-cake, was a bird sanctuary with a broken-down fort and the only wild peony in Britain. Two miles north lay Flatholm, slightly larger, part of Wales, flat as a sponge-cake, with a lighthouse and an old farm. Marconi sent his first radio signals to Wales from Flatholm. Now volunteers counted black-backed gulls. Spring tides of over six knots swirled between the islands and there were overfalls and eddies. At least twenty craft had been lost in the five miles of violent shoaling water between Steepholm and Weston-super-Mare since the war.

Two freighters were anchored in Barry Roads, waiting for the tide. Tides rule your life in the Bristol Channel: no yacht can sail against them. You have to plan your passages in legs rather than in absolute mileage. When you are running out of favourable stream it's time to look for some sheltered nook and to lay out a couple of heavy anchors and a good scope of chain. If you are sailing above Avonmouth with its 48-foot tides, there's no shame in taking a professional pilot. It's just good sense.

I knew all this, and more, because I had read pilot books and studied the charts, but I had never sailed the Bristol Channel and had no plans to do so. It was draughty now as an offshore breeze rose with the setting sun. As I shut the skylight in the loft and climbed down from the chair on which I had been standing, I wondered in a desultory way whether I would ever really understand exactly what had happened to put me into a house in Watchet, a town in which I had vowed I would never live, and why I had agreed to marry a woman who hated the sea. Once again, as so often in this tale, I had unaccountably floated free of the rocks only to drift inexorably back onto them.

*******

Five weeks after moving to west Somerset I had finally been persuaded by my sister to rent a flat she had found in a converted laundry attached to a Georgian mansion in the Quantock Hills. It was owned by a gentleman farmer and magistrate who had dismissed my offer to supply a reference with 'All good references are rubbish. Where did you go to school?' I wasn't particularly looking forward to living in the laundry, which was dark and damp and looked out onto impenetrable laurel hedges, but there seemed no alternative. I arranged to move in the following Monday but I never did. Two days earlier, while listening to jazz in a village pub, I was introduced to a very tall good-looking woman in her forties, wearing an orange miniskirt and carrying a book of poems by a well-known poet.

'We were lovers,' she said. 'He wrote some of his best poems in my house but he spent most of his time on the lavatory. He had problems in that department.' When I asked if I could buy her a drink, she turned to a woman she was with and asked, 'Does he look all right? I haven't got my contact lenses in.' When she replied uneasily in the affirmative, the tall women said, 'I'll have a very large glass of wine.' She said she was an actress but at present was teaching drama at a girls' public school along the coast. She had been married twice and had a ten-year-old daughter. She said her father had once been described as the most handsome man in London and had had a dashing career as a diplomat before being sacked for sleeping with ambassadors' wives. He spoke twenty-six languages and had written a sonnet every day of his adult life. He died after falling from a German train while translating secret Russian documents for the Americans.

She said that she and her second husband had owned a holiday caravan on the cliffs east of Watchet and she had remained in the area when her marriage broke up. She now had a job and was buying a small house but she missed London and her artistic and interesting friends. She had nearly appeared with Tony Hancock in Australia and had done several seasons in a Scottish repertory theatre. She hoped eventually to return to the stage but there was little chance of that while her daughter was young.

She spoke loudly and confidently but seemed anxious to make a good impression. She chain-smoked and drank successive of glasses of red wine but remained tense and slightly distracted and I got the feeling that she had problems which were far from resolved. When she asked me back for coffee I felt it would be unkind to refuse, and in any event I had nothing else to do. I followed her car for a few miles without knowing where I was going, and parked in a dark lane. The house was in a small Victorian terrace. It was cold and sparsely furnished. Her daughter was staying the night with friends. We had coffee in her bedroom which had a gas fire. She asked me which of the few pieces of furniture in the room had any value and I picked out a shabby replica Chippendale armchair, wondering if I was expected to make an offer for it. Instead, I seemed to have passed some sort of test of social suitability.

In the morning I realised for the first time that I was in a house high above the railway line in Watchet and from the skylight window I could see the sea. I never went back to my sister's. Three days later I drove a van to Cornwall with my good friend Martin and brought back half the contents of Farm Cottage to help furnish the narrow dark house. Martin still maintains that I never warned him of the possible perils of the expedition. My sister was very cross that I hadn't taken the flat. 'Don't come running back to me when it all goes wrong – as it will,' she said. And so it did, but by then I had lived in Watchet for over thirteen years.

The terrace was built not of local sandstone but of strange brittle flint, said to have been the ballast of ships sailing from Wales. The twenty houses, erected by a church charity, were built into a hillside and had small backyards which were below ground level. Some were rented to elderly people who had lived there all their lives. A few houses had been bought by incomers who like me seemed to have arrived largely by accident, including a local newspaper editor, two artists and the victim of a mysterious disease caught from cows.

My arrival in the terrace had passed apparently without comment, largely, it seemed, because the residents had become used to transient visitors at number 18, but when I started decorating the house and digging the back garden to plant a few rows of early potatoes, it seemed I might be there for a while and worth getting to know. An elderly partially blind nurse helped me plant a blackberry bush. Despite her disability she regularly went on day excursions organised by a local coach company. 'The only ones I don't like are those mystery tours,' she said. 'You don't know where you're going.'

The man in the next-door garden kindly helped me erect a small greenhouse and advised me what grew best on the bleak and windswept plots. Derek became a good friend and a valuable ally. He had lived all his life in the terrace and had never been abroad. He had briefly worked in Wales but didn't like it. Derek knew everything about Watchet and helped to run its small museum. He told me that the bane of the town's gardeners was a rank and fast-growing weed accidentally imported in the cargo of a Russian grain ship in the 1880s. A relative of dog's mercury, it had spread to surrounding villages, where it was known as the Bloody Watchet Weed. It was unknown in other parts of Britain.

Three neighbours kept small yachts on drying moorings in the harbour but, still believing that my stay in Watchet was temporary, I said nothing of my interest in boats and hid my oilskins in the garden shed. One of the boat owners had been a portrait photographer in London; another, Tom, a former UNESCO official in the Sudan, had taken early retirement and shared a yellow-painted cruiser with a good-natured sheep farmer from near the Quantock Hills. People who had crewed with them said that it was an interesting psychological experience. Tom sailed cautiously with minimum canvas. When he went below, either to cook or to check the chart for the next real or imaginary peril, his co-owner, Mervyn, a former dinghy-racer, would usually shake out the reefs, harden the sheets and 'get the old girl going.' Alerted by the increased heel and the unaccustomed thunder of water around the bow, Tom would reappear on deck and replace the reefs. The ritual would be repeated throughout the cruise without the slightest hint of acrimony, and the two remained the best of friends.

The third boat belonged to a small dark-skinned man who looked somewhat like a South American dissident but who in fact was a carpenter and joiner who had moved to Watchet from Southend. Terry and his wife Chrissie resembled the two figures in a Victorian weather-house. When one was in and the other was out, the weather was relatively predictable but when they were both either in or out who knew what would happen? Most of their arguments centred around the fact that neither consulted the other about their domestic arrangements. For instance, Terry, an insomniac, would cook a fried breakfast at 5 am and return to bed when his wife was getting up and had arranged for them to go out. Chrissie asked friends in for a drink and Terry might set up his workbench and began to reconstruct the lounge ceiling.

A neighbour claimed to remember the legendary occasion when Terry, sent to buy a packet of cigarettes from the town's late-night Spar shop, failed to return and instead made a two-year detour to Saudi Arabia. According to the neighbour, when Terry finally came home with no apparent explanation, Chrissie's first words were 'Have you got the fags, then?' When I once asked Chrissie if that was true, she replied, 'I said a bit more than that.'

The truth was that I couldn't have joined the terrace's boat owners even had I wanted to because by now most of the money from the sale of *Swift* had been spent buying the Actress's daughter a horse and on refurbishing the house, which successive owners had allowed to sink into bizarre neglect. In the bathroom, tiles loosened by steam fell on you in the bath and at night slugs emerged from the kitchen walls and scaled the breadbin. Wet and dry rot battled for supremacy in the sitting room and upstairs water dripped through light fittings and hissed on flickering bulbs. As the bills mounted it was necessary to increase the mortgage, which was still in the Actress's name and which made her worry that she wouldn't be able to afford the payments if and when I moved on. She suggested a joint mortgage and, as the building society offered preferential rates for married couples, we married the following week.

The local register office was closed for redecoration so the ceremony took place in an adjoining room used by driving examiners. Guests at a modest meal in a nearby restaurant included my mother, who had travelled from Derbyshire on a pensioner's return, and a man who the previous day had fallen from a roof and dislocated both shoulders. My mother gave me £20 and said, 'Let's hope you can make a go of it this time. Thank goodness she's too old to have children.' That night a late frost killed most of my early lettuces.

The Actress gave up work and settled back into an approximation of theatrical life but without the acting. She was intelligent, had a university degree and could be very kind but she had a restless wilfulness which could be very wearying and was destined to eventually scupper our relationship for good. She would rise late, read, play the piano and make telephone calls. In early evening she set out on a round of social visits which could last until the early hours. Returning home and reluctant to go to bed, she might make telephone calls to friends and relations in Australia or America, or dance alone to classical music wreathed in scented smoke. She was asleep when I awoke and went to work in my office in the spare room.

Fortunately, finding something to occupy me in the evenings was rarely a problem. Watchet was busier than ever with commercial shipping and the sight of a freighter anchored off the town waiting for a pilot would send me hurrying through the narrow streets to stand by the small cast-iron lighthouse at the end of the west pier as the ship, usually heavily loaded with timber, squeezed through the narrow entrance and was warped through 180 degrees onto the east quay. Within weeks of arriving in Watchet I had become a cargo-ship groupie, discussing with bystanders the merits of containers versus sheltered deck cargo and the viability of exporting waste paper to Turkey.

Sometimes late at night when the house was still empty I would be alone on the pier head standing in the wind below the lighthouse's green glow as a ship approached, a black bulk lit only by three tiny lights, muffled figures on its bow with heaving lines ready to throw to men waiting on the quay. I would wait until the ship was moored and its lighting generator echoed across the dock. Then I would go home. The *Celtic Endeavour*, Captain Sully, had docked safely from Portugal with 900 tons of timber and cork.

I became fascinated by the life of a working port and by the people who were doing for a living what I had been pretending to do as a hobby. I discovered an unspoken but rigid hierarchy which extended from the dockmaster down through the foremen, crane-drivers and stevedores to the dock labourers and to the old men who painted the bollards and complained that things had changed since the old days. On the periphery were other charismatic figures who were dependent on, yet essential to, the port. These included the Trinity House pilot and his coxswain, a customs officer known to enjoy a drink and who lived in a house called Dead End next to a cemetery, and a good-natured coastguard who gave VHF radio lessons.

Equally essential to the smooth running of the port were some half-dozen women, mostly of rather rugged appearance, who attended to the physical needs of visiting sailors, shouting their prices from the end of the pier as a ship came in. The authorities had apparently decided to turn a blind eye, allowing them to wander on and off ships when all other visitors had to report to the dock office. In charge of Watchet's sexual services was an extremely large and powerful woman who was claimed to have the proverbial heart of gold, to write poetry and be kind to dogs.

A generation of Watchet children claimed to have received rudimentary sex education by watching a line of men shuffling towards the stacks of waste-paper bales in which Big Alice had made a temporary boudoir and hearing shouts from within of 'Have your money ready, lads. I haven't got all day.' After a night on board ship, Big Alice would cook a fried breakfast for the entire crew. She said that was all part of the service. She apparently charged foreign clients an extra fee which she said was VAT. A docker remembered meeting Big Alice on a gangway as he was going aboard to start unloading a ship early one morning. She told him: 'I've earned more last night than you buggers will get in a week.' As Watchet shipping declined, Big Alice would take a party by minibus to the still-busy Welsh ports of Cardiff, Swansea and Barry. There is a photograph of Big Alice climbing a rope ladder up the side of a collier in Barry docks wearing a pale pink anorak and leg-warmers the size of small sheep.

Years later after delivering a tug to the Tunisian port of Sousse we tied up alongside the small shabby freighter, *Lady Rhoda*, once a regular visitor to Watchet. A man leaned down and asked where we were from. His face lit up. 'Ah, Watchet! Give my love to Alice. I look forward to seeing her again.' He never did. Shortly afterwards the *Lady Rhoda* foundered in a gale in the Bay of Biscay and was lost with all hands.

CHAPTER 11

# Dropping the pilot

A harbour-side phenomenon of particular interest to me
was a group of middle-aged and elderly men, mostly from
ancient families, who were known as the Watchet hobblers.
Hobblers had for centuries been responsible for the
movement and berthing of ships in Watchet harbour. In
the days of sail they rowed out to meet vessels and towed
or warped them in. The boats were owned by different
families and competed against each other, often racing to
be first aboard and to negotiate the handling charge,
known as a hobble. Sometimes there were fights between
competing crews, resulting in the formation in 1863 of the
Watchet United Sailors' Society, later the Watchet
Hobblers' Association, which co-owned the hobble-boats
and regulated ship movements and hobbling fees.

In 1890 a watch-tower was built on the west pier in which the hobblers waited for ships. It was also used for paying out the hobble and for meetings. Hobbling was highly sought after and prospective hobblers were voted on by members throwing black and white beans into a bucket. Those with the most white beans got the job. By the time I arrived in Watchet the hobble-boats were long gone and the watch-tower was part of a holiday cottage but the hobblers still had the monopoly on berthing ships although there were now barely half a dozen on the active list, including a retired merchant navy officer and geography teacher, and Ben Norman, a noted figure in the town, author and publisher of the definitive *Tales of Watchet Harbour*, and curator of the town museum.

Nylon ropes and VHF radio had long since taken the effort and uncertainty out of hobbling and the job now involved little more than throwing a heaving line, hauling hawsers ashore and looping them over bollards. But even in these days of unions and Dock and Harbour Board regulations, it was work no one else was allowed to do and the hobblers enjoyed a status which enabled them to wait for ships in the warmth of the dockmaster's office and wander onto prohibited areas of the docks. Suddenly pleasure-boating seemed to have lost its appeal and it occurred to me that the best way to get into Watchet's maritime inner circle with minimum effort was to persuade someone to let me become a hobbler.

Ben Norman, to whom I had been briefly introduced, seemed the obvious target. Now shameless in my ambition, I bought a copy of his book, knocked on the door of his cottage near the quay and asked if he would sign it. He said he would be pleased to, and as he hunted for a pen I admired the oil paintings of coastal ketches and schooners on the walls of his sitting room. He said the best were painted by Captain Thomas Chidgey, born in Watchet in 1855 into a family with a long tradition in the coasting trade. As a boy he would draw ships in Watchet harbour and later taught himself to paint. Sailors admired his skill and technical accuracy and hundreds of pictures were commissioned. He took his paints to sea and his greatest joy was to paint a ship in full sail.

Ben said that at one time many Watchet families had Chidgey pictures hanging over the fireplace, but sold them when they became valuable. He said that Captain Chidgey didn't make much out of his paintings but produced so many because he enjoyed it. He died in 1926 leaving a wonderful record of the last days of sail. We spoke of Watchet. I said I enjoyed living in the town and wondered if it was possible to become a hobbler. Ben smiled and said it was a jealously guarded tradition and some families had been hobblers for 300 years. He said it would be difficult for a newcomer to be accepted and that I should come and ask him again in another twenty years.

I was disappointed but by no means downhearted, for soon afterwards I heard of an even more glittering opportunity. It was rumoured that the man who drove the Trinity House pilot cutter was retiring through ill health and that the pilot, Captain Nigel Stokes, was looking for a replacement. The job involved putting the pilot on board ships waiting to enter port and removing him from vessels he had taken out. It was done at all hours and in all weathers and in the five years he had been doing the job Nigel had never failed to complete an assignment although the cutter, a small former Admiralty supply vessel, had several times been nearly capsized and swamped as it skittered alongside some rolling freighter in the blackness of a winter gale.

Nigel Stokes was still only in his late thirties, and had the blond good looks of a doomed war poet which concealed a steely and single-minded resolve. During a childhood spent in Burnham-on-Sea, a dozen miles up-channel, Nigel watched pilots boarding small freighters bound up the muddy River Parrett to the port of Bridgwater and as a small boy decided to become a Trinity House pilot in the Bristol Channel. Despite an education at a fashionable public school and the discovery that he suffered from chronic seasickness, he never deviated from that somewhat perverse ambition and, after sailing the world as a master mariner, was appointed Watchet pilot in 1978. He was married and lived in a hamlet in the Quantock Hills.

When I contacted him, Nigel was very friendly. He had in fact appointed a new pilot-boat coxswain that very afternoon but it was always good to have someone in reserve. I felt it wise to admit that I had no pilot-boat experience but I had delivered a dredger to Goole, steered a tug through the Straits of Hormuz and helped navigate a large motor-cruiser backwards under several London bridges. Nigel thought that would do nicely.

Two days later he phoned to say that his new driver had broken his nose in a fight in a pub and would I take him out to a ship the following evening? The pilot cutter was a dumpy black and white craft of 26 feet with a wheelhouse in the bow. This, Nigel explained, was against normal pilotage practice because it meant that it was hard or even impossible for the helmsman to see when the pilot had left or boarded the cutter because he was doing so behind the helmsman's back. Most cutters had aft wheelhouses which gave the helmsman a good view of what was happening, and stout rails on the foredeck to which the pilot clung as he prepared to join a ship by leaping up a dangling rope ladder. Even so, the number of injuries or even fatalities in the pilot service was high. The main danger, Nigel said, was falling between the cutter and ship and being sucked into the propeller.

It was nearly high water at 10 pm on a moonless March night when Nigel took the cutter out through the harbour entrance and I stood nonchalantly in the wheelhouse door, rolling easily with the swell, glancing casually at the sky as a small boy waved from the roundhead and a dog barked into the wind. I wondered whether to mention that not only was it my first time on a pilot cutter but that I had never even been out on the Bristol Channel before, but decided that Nigel, in smart blue jersey and white pumps, probably had enough on his mind. Away from the harbour Nigel turned west down-channel and handed over the wheel. The breeze was a light westerly but the waves were surprisingly steep and short and I realised that most of the Bristol Channel was shoaling water, exposed to all wind and weather, fiercely tidal and quite unlike anything I had sailed on before. As we rumbled in the vague direction of Minehead there was nothing between us and America.

Like everything else in the channel, pilotage was ruled by the tide, and Nigel said that ideally he liked to dock a ship during slack water just before the start of the ebb-stream which could be particularly vicious around the pier head. He had planned this for tonight but there was as yet no sign of our ship, the *Celtic Voyager*, 900 tons, due from Portugal. As we motored westward she radioed that she was at Hurlstone Point, some ten miles away, and that it could be another hour before she reached Watchet. By the time we saw her lights off Blue Anchor beach, three miles from Watchet, the ebb was gathering pace and, more importantly, the height of water in the harbour entrance had already fallen about three feet and was dropping fast.

All this, Nigel implied, would probably make my debut as a pilot-boat coxswain even more interesting, and so it proved. Normally, when picking up a pilot, a freighter slowed to walking-pace and turned broadside across the wind, making a lee to protect the pilot, who then boarded from a ladder on the sheltered side of the ship. But on this night the *Celtic Voyager*, churning through the black water at near maximum speed, had no intention of slowing down. A small spotlight illuminated a rope ladder as we turned to run alongside and the ship loomed above us like a rusty blue cliff. The bow wave of the freighter caught the pilot boat and soon we were pitching like a bucking horse. There was spray everywhere and engine fumes and noise and it was hard to gauge the cutter's speed in relation to the ship's. Nigel pushed past me and out into the darkness of the afterdeck. He was now wearing a smart red lifejacket. 'Keep her against the ladder and don't let her sag back,' he shouted and already I could feel the suction of the ship's propeller pulling the cutter into the stern.

We seemed to have been roaring alongside the *Celtic Voyager* for eternity, as in some modern version of Wagner's *Flying Dutchman*, but in reality it was probably less than a minute. Where was Nigel? As I turned in my seat to look out of the open door, I allowed the boat to veer away slightly and there was a shout from the darkness. Had I lost him over the side, to become another Trinity House statistic? Then I saw a flash of the red lifejacket as Nigel raced up the ladder and disappeared into the blackness above. Preoccupied by the drama, I was dropping back into the thrashing water around the freighter's stern until I came to my senses, applied full power and veered off, out of harm's way, rocking in the wash as the *Celtic Voyager* headed briskly towards the green glow of the Watchet lighthouse. Two men emptied a barrel of waste over the stern and seagulls swooped out of the night.

There was no further time for introspection. The cutter was required to be in the harbour first, ready to act as a tug if required, and I roared in a few hundred yards ahead, feeling as proud as I could ever remember, acknowledging the hobblers on the wall and loitering importantly until the ship had docked. Apparently when the *Celtic Voyager* finally came through the harbour entrance there was less than ten feet of water under the keel. Afterwards Nigel said he was pleased with my performance and paid me the statutory £7 fee in small change. It was nearly midnight when I walked home. I could hear the generator echoing up the empty street. The *Celtic Voyager*, Captain Rewe, had docked safely with a cargo of timber and cork, and maybe I could take a tiny share of the credit.

I was having a cup of tea when the Actress came home. She had been to someone's birthday party but had insisted on driving home. She had no wish to hear about my exploits in the pilot boat. She said that I was selfishly preoccupied with hobbies to the detriment of our marriage and left the room. She returned with what were apparently symbols of my extramarital interests, including my trombone mouthpiece, a model boat, my electric typewriter, a chart of the Bristol Channel, and a packet of carrot seeds, all of which she threw out of the front door. She then pushed me over. She went into the kitchen and was sick into the pressure-cooker.

It was some time before the coxswain's nose completely recovered and I enjoyed being his deputy. Outward trips were often the longest because some skippers would insist on offering hospitality to the pilot and the cutter might be tagging along behind a freighter for several miles before he finally climbed aboard clutching a clinking brown-paper parcel. Although Watchet had a relatively straightforward entry, captains, particularly strangers, usually preferred that the pilot personally conned their vessels into dock, which often meant Nigel steering a 2,000-ton freighter through the 28-yard entrance with a gadget resembling a TV channel-changer. Invariably the job was done with smooth efficiency but Nigel remembered a few difficult moments in the early days, including the time when a freighter drifted out of control against the garden wall of a harbour-side house and an irate woman wearing yellow Marigold washing-up gloves tried to fend off the unwelcome visitor with a broom.

For a quasi-government department, the Corporation of Trinity House, founded in the sixteenth century, gave its pilots a surprising amount of latitude and Nigel ran his boat without interference. He loved his job and the Trinity House traditions but by the mid-1980s Watchet's harbour trade was perceptibly declining and, as he was only paid for the ships he moved, so was Nigel's salary. Eventually he left to become a pilot in a still-busy Devon port. Later he moved to Dover where he became a dock manager and senior pilot. We still keep in touch.

Shortly after Nigel left, the local council took over the Watchet pilotage and there were no longer any opportunities for enthusiastic amateurs. A qualified coxswain was employed and the cutter was expensively rebuilt to conform to new draconian regulations. I went back to the lighthouse to watch the ships enter and leave. I had enjoyed my brief spell as a minor figure on the dockside scene and had even begun to warm to the bad behaviour of the Bristol Channel, but I had absolutely no intention of going through the traumas of buying another boat. I had recently joined a jazz band, which seemed altogether a safer and cheaper way of attracting attention. Only the previous day we had played on a hay-cart during the re-creation of the Battle of Gettysburg in a field outside Taunton ('General Lee, I think we have a problem'), and there were plenty of well-paid gigs around to keep us busy. Inevitably, soon afterwards I bought a boat that everyone warned me would cause serious problems.

Some time later a psychiatrist, vainly trying to save our crumbling marriage, inadvertently unearthed a clue as to why I continued to buy the wrong boats. Mesmerised by his pale-eyed gaze I recalled a childhood memory of owning a book of stories called, I believe, *Harry's Seaside Adventures*. In one, Harry, a snobbish child of about eight, took his expensive model yacht on holiday only to find that it wouldn't sail properly and eventually capsized while the humble craft of less privileged children bobbed happily on the waves. An old sailor, smoking his pipe nearby, rescued the boat and after explaining that it was hopelessly over-rigged and would never sail in that condition, took out his penknife and set about the mast and spars, quickly reducing the lofty schooner to a stumpy ill-proportioned ketch. 'There you are, young master,' he said, handing over the wreckage. 'Now she'll sail like a dream.' Harry was appalled and so was I. 'You've ruined my lovely boat,' he cried. 'You wait until my father sees what you've done!'

True, when Harry put the boat back in the water it sailed much better than before but that was of little consolation to the child who had enjoyed having a boat which looked so much better than everyone else's – and I knew exactly how he felt. To me, boats that excited comment by their appearance, regardless of performance, were always the ones to choose. I didn't pursue my childhood memories during the consultation as we had, in any event, exceeded our £17-worth of marital counselling and the psychiatrist, who looked very much like to the comedian Griff Rhys Jones, showed no interest in boats. Afterwards the Actress and I had a pleasant lunch and did some shopping. On the drive home I found myself returning to Harry's seaside adventures and their significance but it was by then a largely academic exercise. I already had a boat that would have kept the old sailor and his penknife busy for a lifetime.

The events leading to my buying the plastic half-decked yacht *Sophie* began on the morning of Prince Andrew and Sarah Ferguson's wedding in July 1986, when the Actress drank a private toast to the couple in home-made lettuce wine, followed by a bottle of Burgundy. When I objected that this seemed somewhat excessive at breakfast, and added unwisely that she seemed to be putting on weight, she smashed an antique moonstone ring I had given her with a hammer and threw it down the lavatory, broke a rather nice brass lamp and disappeared for four days. At the weekend, for want of anything else to do, I drove to

Exmouth in the rain. Edward Heath was on *Desert Island Discs*. The docks were empty of ships and there was talk that they might be closed and redeveloped as a marina. The beaches were wet and empty and the cafés loud with children. Outside Ron Lavis's yard a small red boat was for sale, laid up among the thistles. It looked familiar and I remembered that some years earlier I had been asked by the new owner to show him how to handle a gaffer. The boat was over-rigged, which made her lively and skittish. The owner was so alarmed by that initial sail that he rarely used her again, except to motor to a nearby beach for a picnic on windless days. Now he had her up for sale in Ron's yard for £1,500 and a sad sight she looked, half full of water and paint peeling.

Ron was in the office tidying up. His sailing trip had been cancelled because of the weather. The boat's papers showed her to be a gaff-rigged sloop, a fibreglass replica of a 19-foot half-decker built in 1920 for Essex police to patrol the oyster-layings off Brightlingsea. She was an unashamed inshore dayboat with a large non-draining cockpit, a massive 25-foot mast, a 10-foot bowsprit and a boom that extended three feet over the transom. The sail area of nearly 400 square feet would be generally regarded as too much for a shoal-draft boat of that size, but no one could deny it looked rakish and impressive. There were no cooking or toilet facilities, no winches or roller-reefing, no sleeping accommodation, no protection from the weather. It was a boat ideal for a Saturday afternoon jolly on the flat water of an Essex creek and home in time for tea. Anything less suitable for the short unruly seas of the Bristol Channel was hard to imagine. And yet…

Ron and I stood in the rain looking at the boat. A pile of rusty iron ballast lay nearby and the fibreglass of the hull was covered with what looked like red treacle. 'It should clean up all right,' Ron said, but he didn't sound convinced. We looked at the sails. There was a mainsail, topsail and an assortment of jibs in bags, all in need of a good wash. The running rigging was dirty but apparently sound. The shrouds and stays needed replacing. There would be a lot of work to do. The boat was called *Sophie* and that was my daughter's name. I remembered when the owner and I had sailed her back onto the mooring on the Exe just as the autumn sun was tipping the top of Haldon Hill and the sandbanks were in deep shadow. She had snubbed the mooring buoy very delicately and stopped obediently in the tide. As we rowed ashore in the dinghy I remember looking back and thinking what an unusually pretty boat she looked and that the scene had all the makings of a greetings card entitled 'Happy Birthday To A Dear Nephew.'

Ron was uneasy in the rain. 'I'll have her,' I said, 'but I'm not paying £1,500.'

'Give me £950,' Ron said. 'To be honest, I'll be glad to see the back of the thing.'

On the way home I gave a lift to a middle-aged man who was hitchhiking to London. He said he was a clairvoyant and psychic forecaster but had originally worked as a bath enameller in Hull. He had been visiting his aunt in Exeter hoping for a loan but had been disappointed. The premonition business was pretty poor at the moment. He said he had been sacked by a magazine for whom he had regularly written a prediction of the year ahead. 'I used to put in world calamities like the murder of the American president, and the one year I left it out, it happened.' He was now working for a London property developer doing what was known in the trade as 'death bedding', which involved visiting properties ripe for redevelopment while posing as a plumber and assessing how long elderly sitting tenants were likely to live. I told him I had just bought a boat and could he tell me whether I had made the right decision? 'Sorry mate,' he said, 'I don't do boats.' When I dropped him off at a service station on the M5 he said, 'I suppose I couldn't predict that

you'll lend me a tenner?' It was another of his less
successful prophesies: I only had two pounds fifty in small
change and I needed that for lunch.

With the boat arriving by road in three weeks' time, I
needed somewhere to carry out repairs and restoration,
which I knew would take several months. My neighbour
said that the Watchet Boat Owners' Association, of which
he was a member, had a large shed near the west quay
which would be ideal for the job, and if I liked he would
propose me for membership. He said that the association
was unlike any other boat club he had known in that it had
little interest in the sea, but only in owning boats, storing
them, and mooring them securely in the harbour. Most of
the members were middle-aged or elderly and the only
regular activity was a monthly meeting in the back room of
a pub which sometimes ended in bitter argument and on
one occasion a fight in the yard.

The association traced its history back to the 1870s
when Watchet sailors and fishermen organised regattas and
water sports in aid of the town's lifeboat. For nearly
seventy years, races and tug-of-war events held at low tide
in the deep harbour mud drew large crowds and helped to
keep the lifeboat financially self-supporting. Legendary
figures with such nicknames as Wacker Beans, Fearless Joe,
Teddy Slackass and Billy Go Deeper played football in the
mud, and became part of Watchet folklore. Mud sports
ended when the lifeboat station closed in 1944 but were
revived seven years later as part of the town's Festival of
Britain celebrations. Boat owners still descended into the
mud from time to time to lay mooring chains and there
were stories of men sinking to their shoulders and being
pulled out by dockside cranes.

I joined the Watchet Boat Owners' Association and for
six months worked on the boat in a shed made of timber
salvaged from wrecked ships. Few people visited and no
one offered to help but in fact no help was needed; the hull

and deck were glass-fibre and most of the work was largely cosmetic and I enjoyed doing it myself. Black Pete spliced new standing rigging and a local blacksmith forged replacement chainplates and rudder pintles. Varnished and painted in shamrock green, *Sophie* looked smart when she was launched into the harbour in the spring of 1987 and put on a mooring under the Esplanade. Three old men helped me raise the mast.

During a short trip the following day, the boat handled well in a light breeze, and as the only gaff-rigged boat in the harbour was admired by watchers on the shore, always a pleasant bonus. The log noted: 'Returning to the harbour, the petrol tank fell off the engine and disappeared. Sailed onto the mooring with difficulty. The nautical equation "a good time has to be paid for by a bad time multiplied by five" seems to be holding good.'

*******

A few weeks later, in company with two slightly larger yachts, my friend Tom's 26-foot *Moonraker* and Captain Stokes's 22-foot *Folkdancer*, *Sophie* made her first cross-channel trip to Barry. We left on the flood, early on a sunny morning on a broad reach in a light westerly, and completed the twelve-mile journey in little more than two hours. *Sophie* was first to arrive, bounding along under topsail and reaching jib in fine style. I was proud of my pretty little boat. She appeared to be the ideal single-hander, well-balanced, light on the helm and stable despite her large rig. By accident rather than design I seemed to have finally found a boat that was safe, sea-kindly and well within my capabilities. But the return trip that evening was a different story.

During the day, the westerly had backed south-south-west and by the time we left the shelter of Barry harbour it was heading us, and had increased to force five to six.

Wind against tide kicked up a nasty short sea which broke constantly over the bow as, close-hauled, we headed slowly for home. The English shore, which had looked so near in the sunshine, had now disappeared in the murk. It was soon apparent that going to windward *Sophie* was probably the wettest boat I had ever sailed. Water cascaded in on all sides and soon the floorboards were afloat. I steered with one hand and bailed with a bucket with the other. Reefed down, the boat had developed a vicious weather helm which screwed us continually into the wind, burying the bowsprit in the waves. The wind continued to increase, heading us up-channel and away from Watchet and home.

There was now over a foot of water in the cockpit. The boat had an ominous soggy feel. She was no longer lifting to the waves and there was always the possibility that she might broach and capsize. The problem was that I couldn't leave the tiller to properly bale her out. We were now in mid-channel and the tide was shoaling over Camber Sands, a long spit of shingle, which further stirred up the sea. There should be enough water over the sands at this state of the tide, but the chart had long since disappeared under the water which now surged across the cockpit. It was getting dark and at that precise moment there was only one thought in my mind: I could murder a bloody Kit-Kat.

Tom came alongside, motor-sailing with only a small jib set. He had taken almost no water aboard and was not even wearing an oilskin whereas I looked as though I had been standing under Niagara Falls. He said he would stay in close company until we got home. He later admitted that he thought he might be called upon to do somewhat more than that. *Sophie* was now pitching and rolling so violently that there was daylight under the hull. I shouted that I planned to stop and heave-to in order to bail the boat and sort things out.

*Heave-to: Backing the foresail by hauling it over to the windward side of the boat. Then by adjustment of mainsail and helm the vessel is held quiet and steady with very little forward movement. A very useful manoeuvre which is used less often than it might be* – Uncle Billy's Nicholl's Seamanship (and *viva voce*) Guide, 1922.

Most long-keeled gaff-rigged craft obediently heave-to, but I fully expected that *Sophie*, with her shallow bilge, would simply spin on her long narrow centreplate and charge off in any direction she chose. This time I was pleasantly surprised: turning into the wind, putting the helm down and backing the jib did indeed hold the vessel as quiet and steady as Uncle Billy's book had predicted and I was able to bail out the boat, put another reef in the mainsail, and to find the Kit-Kat which had remained dry and secure in a netting under the foredeck.

As we moved towards the lee of the land, the sea calmed slightly and things became a little more comfortable, and although water still came aboard I was able to contain it with the hand-pump. Tom was still reassuringly on the beam, but Captain Stokes was far ahead, emphasising just how much more efficiently an equally sized Bermudan rig sailed to windward. But by now there were more immediate problems: the tide was ebbing fast and it was a question of getting back while there was still water in the harbour. Luckily the wind veered slightly and we picked up enough speed to clear the harbour entrance with two feet of water under the centreplate. Ten minutes after reaching the mooring, the boat went aground and I walked ashore through the mud, tired, wet and fed up. It was 10 pm, pitch-dark and raining. It had taken five hours to sail just twelve miles. The final day's entry in the log read: 'Why do we do it? There will never be an answer to that.'

When I got home, the Actress was entertaining a male Danish folk-dancer she had met in a pub. They were eating gammon steaks and broad beans. The Actress said she would make me some toast. After we were introduced, the dancer said, 'I have never eaten beans like these before and if I don't like them I will spit them out. Why are you so wet and filthy with mud?' Later, too drunk to return to his bed and breakfast accommodation, he spent the night on a blow-up mattress in the kitchen. I went to bed but couldn't sleep. I was perturbed by the vulnerability of the boat and whether I would be so lucky next time. At one in the morning I realised that in my hurry to leave the boat I had forgotten to lift up the three-foot swinging steel centreplate and that, with the tide out, the boat's full weight on the plate could already be causing horrendous damage.

Sleep was obviously now out of the question. I got up, put on wellingtons and a raincoat over my pyjamas and left the house carrying a large rusty hammer. I hoped, with a bit of luck, to knock out the steel retaining pin, which would allow the centreplate to slide back into its case, assuming that it hadn't already been forced through the bottom of the boat. The town was empty as I walked through the rain onto the Esplanade. I climbed through the railings at the harbour's edge and descended a rusty ladder into the mud. *Sophie* was moored at the bottom of the wall and was still apparently upright. Leaning into the boat, I discovered my fears were groundless: I had removed the pin before leaving and the plate was safely in its case. It was, as Topsy Turner would have said, another one the Queen knew nothing about. I turned and climbed the ladder, wet and muddy and still carrying the sort of hammer used to hit people over the head in the *Beano*. As I emerged over the parapet I was aware of a figure standing at the top of the ladder. There was a long pause. 'Good morning, officer,' I said. 'Perhaps I should start at the beginning ...'

## CHAPTER 12

# Breakers on the side

The Actress was afraid of the sea. Although a fearless paraglider she had suffered a panic attack on a pedalo in a tranquil lagoon in Turkey. She had no interest in the boat and certainly no wish to go aboard but she did occasionally suggest possible crew from among the circle of acquaintances. One was a man I privately nicknamed the Professor, who had lectured at universities in Britain and America on the psychology of engineering. He was a willing and useful crewman but his thought processes were sometimes hard to fathom. Once, the Actress invited him to work in her garden but his progress was so slow that she was eventually forced to give the work to someone else. The Professor was appalled. 'You've got to let me finish the job,' he cried. 'I know where all the insects are.'

The Actress's main objection to my sailing activities centred on the basic uncertainty of the hobby. Where was I going and when would I be back? Would I be in for meals? Could I collect her from parties? Would I be able to pick up her daughter from school? In these far-off days before mobile telephones there seemed no answer until someone suggested CB radio. Several of the local fishing boats had these cheap 40-channel sets which they used to chat among themselves, free from the strictures of the government-regulated VHF radio. You were supposed to have a £15 licence but no one did and they were used mainly for mindless chat and the occasional sexual suggestion by people with time on their hands. By the mid-1980s when Citizens' Band had been legalised in the UK it was estimated that there were around half a million CB sets in regular use, mostly in lorries and cars but also in the houses of bored housewives, and people who liked to pretend they were secret agents or wireless operators on the *Titanic*.

It seemed that all I needed were a couple of second-hand portable sets for about £20 each, one in the house and one on the boat, for perfectly adequate ship-to-shore communication and the end of at least one cause of domestic misunderstanding. Apparently the best source of both equipment and information was the local newspaper's 75-year-old photographer, Randolph Priddy, known as Prid, who lived alone in a village in the hills. He had bought a huge collection of electronic gadgetry with a legacy from a relative, and much of it was now surplus to requirements. When I phoned, Prid said he had several CB sets he didn't want and invited me to visit. It was apparent he was a man who liked to talk.

Prid's cottage was so deeply submerged in a hillside it looked as though it was going down for the last time. The illusion was enhanced by radio masts and aerials which festooned the long yellow house like the rigging of a ship. Prid was a small white-bearded man who had the look of a nautical gnome. He was playing 'Abide With Me' on an expensive new portable electric organ next to the kitchen stove. When he opened the door a huge German Shepherd dog sprang out and immediately bit me in the groin. White-faced, I ran to the lavatory and found to my relief that although there were contusions and a nasty bruise, serious damage had been avoided by a mere quarter of an inch. 'She'll be fine now,' Prid said. 'She only bites people once.' He said that the dog had bitten nearly twenty people including the local doctor but he had persuaded them not to report it to the police. 'She's only trying to be friends,' he said.

The cottage was damp and untidy and smelled of stew. The sitting room was stacked with cameras, videos, cassette-players and CD systems, some still in their boxes. Prid said his children were trying to stop him frittering away his inheritance but they were wasting their time as his ambition was to die penniless. 'What makes life really worth living,' he said, 'is the knowledge that it's not going to last for ever.'

He plugged in a gadget the size of a car radio, fitted with a black plastic microphone, and gave me a lesson in CB technique. 'First, you've got to have a handle – that's a name they can talk to. You never use your real name,' he said. 'Any ideas?' 'What about Barnacle Bill?' I said. It was the first name that came to mind. Prid switched on the microphone and went into a curious sing-song routine: 'Breaker on the side, breaker on the side. Do you copy, do you copy ? Over.' The machine produced a sound like fat frying and after a few seconds a metallic Welsh voice replied: 'Breaker on the side. What's your handle, good buddy?'

'Barnacle Bill,' Prid said.

'Roger to that, Barnacle Bill. You're coming through clean and green, without pain without strain. Do you copy? This is Mike the Pipelayer in the chair, good buddy. Ten four. Anyone earwigging on the side who wants to come in for a ten-four with Bill? Put the hammer down and I'll patch you through.'

Before Prid could reply there was a muffled shout in the background and Mike's attention was obviously elsewhere. 'Bloody chip-pan's caught fire. Have to cut you loose, breaker. This is Mike the Pipelayer signing off. We're gone.' The set went dead. Prid turned it off. He said that was a pretty typical CB radio transmission. The jargon, although tiresome, was obligatory and was derived from American truckers who primarily used CB to warn each other of police patrols and speed traps. Local breakers were a different, and sadder, breed. 'There's hundreds like Mike the Pipelayer, specially in Wales,' he said. 'Most of them on the dole. Nothing to do and no one to talk to. Some of them sit half the night in their Ford Cortinas on the tops of mountains just desperate for a chat. Mike's on the rig every day, even over Christmas. They can't afford to go to pubs, you see.' Prid said that on the other hand he had personal experience that CB could have practical uses, as when he was trapped in his car in an Exmoor flash flood. The water was soon as high as the dashboard and climbing steadily. Prid used his CB radio to call for help; a woman in Watchet received his plea and alerted the emergency services, and Prid escaped with his life if not his expensive cameras.

I bought two CB radios from Prid and installed one in the boat and one in my office in the house, where it was tempting to flip through the channels when I had a spare minute and earwig on largely aimless conversations. It soon became apparent that breakers, though anxious to talk to anyone, were cautious about revealing their identities and whereabouts, which were known as 'personals' and 'home twenties', and so the personalities and stories behind such handles as Steve the Nickelby, Bob the Terrier, King Vidor, Sparkplug, Bald Eagle and Rainbow sadly had to remain a mystery. But there were occasional exceptions such as a conversation I overheard between three Welsh housewives on the Gower Peninsula.

First housewife: 'I can't stand broad beans. If you put a broad bean on a five-pound note I couldn't eat it and that's the truth.'

Second housewife: 'I have no problem with broad beans but you put a haricot bean on a fiver and see if I eat it and the honest answer is that I wouldn't. I just couldn't bring myself to consume it.'

Third housewife: 'All beans make me throw up but I'd take the five pounds.'

The Actress disliked my activities on the rig, particularly my eavesdropping on women when I was supposed to be working, but reluctantly agreed to a test transmission when I was out for a short evening sail. Returning to harbour and still about half a mile offshore, I put in a call.

Barnacle Bill: 'Home base, this is Barnacle Bill. Approaching harbour. Should be home for supper in half an hour. Do you copy? Roger.'

Home base (irritably): 'Don't you roger me.' Laughter and comment from unseen breakers.

The experiment was not a success. The two rigs were sold and we reverted to the previous system of blaming each other for burned meals and missed appointments. In fact, CB radio was already becoming a communications fossil, superseded by mobile phones and internet chatrooms. Today there are a few CB rigs installed in the shabby vans of men who read *Exchange and Mart* but the government can no longer even be bothered to collect the licence fees.

*******

I sailed *Sophie* in the Bristol Channel for seven summers. The log records some 150 voyages, mostly day-sails, but also many round trips of up to 100 miles to north Devon and Welsh ports, either alone or with one crew, sometimes the Professor, who claimed to enjoy minimalist sailing. In port or at an anchorage I would sleep in the coffin-shaped cupboard under the foredeck and the crew would beg a berth on some nearby yacht. There was no shelter from the weather in the tiny boat. We couldn't cook or wash and the lavatory was a bucket. There was a small battery for the echo-sounder and navigation lights. On fine summer nights when sailing alone I would put a hurricane lamp up the forestay when anchored in some deserted bay and lie in the cockpit among the ropes and anchors, to be rocked asleep under the stars. But these were rare occasions; most summers in the late eighties and early nineties were wet and grey, with prevailing strong north-westerlies and tumbling brown seas. One August Bank Holiday we were dripping wet and shivering for two days on a trip westward along the Welsh coast, drinking orangeade and eating Marmite sandwiches. I could have killed for a cup of tea.

Other days were remembered for different reasons. One July morning it was nearly eighty degrees before breakfast as we drifted down-channel for a weekend in Ilfracombe, some thirty miles away in Devon. The sails hung like washing but we were making four knots with the tide and anchored in the outer harbour in time for tea. It had been idyllic if slow progress past high Wagnerian cliffs from Porlock to the Foreland lighthouse, and goats looked down like sentries from the crags of the Valley of the Rocks. Chris had spent most of the time asleep or smoking on the foredeck in the narrow shadows of the sails. The sea was flat and shiny as silver-foil and when he put his hand over the side there were no ripples because the tide was moving as fast as the boat. 'Sod me, that's interesting,' Chris said. 'I could go for this sailing.' 'It's not often like this,' I said. 'In fact you'll probably never see it like this again.' As it turned out, he never did.

I had often offered to take Chris out in the boat but he

had never managed to make it until now. He was in his mid-forties, tall and bald with the twinkling eyes of a rogue in a Restoration comedy. He had a reputation in the district for being feckless, irresponsible with money, unfaithful to women, lazy and good fun. I was very fond of him and wanted him to have a nice time on the boat. I had never known Chris do what could be termed a proper job, although he occasionally played drums in a rock band and did a little antique dealing for cash. He also had brief spells as a gravedigger, as an attendant in a mental hospital and as an operative in a crematorium. 'When we came in first thing, we'd put our tins of Fray Bentos meat pies on top of the furnace and they'd be cooked by lunchtime.'

Now as the scenery slipped slowly by, I heard a little more about him. In circumstances he chose not to elaborate, he had met and married the beautiful daughter of a peer of the realm. Described in the *Daily Mail* as an 'import–export whiz-kid', he shipped dodgy batteries and light-bulbs from Eastern Europe, labelled them as expensive brands and sold them at vast profit. 'The batteries would last about an hour if you were lucky,' Chris said. 'But the bulbs would often explode when you turned them on.' There was not the slightest hint of remorse.

Soon Chris was driving a BMW and earning £1,000 a week in cash. 'I thought money was supposed to make you happy but it turned me into an absolutely horrible person,' he said. 'Snapping my fingers at waiters and sending perfectly good food back in restaurants. That sort of thing. I was quite glad when the business went bust and I lost it all.' By then he had also lost his wife by running off with the wife of a friend. Declared bankrupt, he could no longer pay the mortgage on what had been the family home. He moved out and posted the keys through the building-society office door, but not before he had removed and sold a spiral staircase and other expensive fittings.

At Ilfracombe we rowed ashore. The town was hot,

noisy and cheerful and we had excellent lamb chops at the yacht club. That night we slept side by side in the cockpit wrapped in sails. In the early hours I was awoken by a short sharp shower but Chris remained asleep, the rain glistening on his peaceful face. In the morning we went ashore for breakfast and caught the first of the flood home, winging back on a broad reach. The log records: 'A really happy cruise. Excellent sailing and company.' Back on the mooring in Watchet, we prepared to go ashore and Chris lowered himself into the dinghy. The boat instantly capsized and he disappeared underneath. A few moments later he reappeared, apparently unshaken by the experience, but later told a friend that he didn't think much of my immediate reaction. 'He just stood there saying "Oh my God. Oh, my God." I thought captains were supposed to rescue people.'

Chris said he really enjoyed his trip and would like to come again, but he never did. Not long afterwards he was diagnosed with a brain tumour and died a few months later. When I spoke a few words at his funeral I was wearing a pair of Chris's smart black trousers.

A few weeks later the dinghy overturned again in Watchet harbour, tipping the Actress and Nigel, a doctor friend, into the muddy water. They had been to visit the boat on the mooring and had shared a bottle of wine. Returning to a wall-ladder, they both unwisely stood up at the same time, promptly capsizing the boat. Such was the reputation of the harbour's sewage-laden water that the doctor hurried to his nearby surgery to inoculate himself against every known disease. The Actress went straight to the nearest pub.

*Sophie*'s accommodation, though limited, was useful in times of domestic crisis when I would leave home, usually in the early hours, vowing never to return and then realising that I had nowhere to go. Once I tried sleeping in a deckchair in the garden shed but left after a rat walked over my stomach. Other temporary accommodation included a church porch and a telephone box. *Sophie* was much better. Rowing out to the boat with a torch and a sleeping bag, I found the tiny forepeak cosy and well away from recriminations, and spent several peaceful nights as the boat rocked gently in the silent harbour. By the time I returned home in the morning, whatever had caused the argument had usually been forgotten.

It didn't always work out like that. Once I woke to find that I had misread the tides, the boat was aground, and I was stranded aboard until lunchtime, a perfect target for the Actress, this time in unforgiving mood. She appeared at the Esplanade railings to deliver a loud monologue about my shortcomings to passers-by. I made sure that in future I had an up-to-date tide-table aboard.

I became very fond of *Sophie*, for all her wilful ways, and she did my reputation as a sailor the world of good. We won a silver cup for seamanship in the absence of any other contenders and she was the fastest and prettiest sailing craft of her size in the harbour, although in reality that didn't say much. Her rig still needed careful handling, but roller-reefing on the jib and a couple of sheet winches had brought welcome docility in a blow, and higher sides on the cockpit now prevented some of the heavier seas coming aboard. I even had plans for a canvas spray-hood and a little methylated-spirit cooker, perhaps even a folding chart table. It seemed that there was a real possibility that *Harry's Seaside Adventure* would have a happy ending. Then, on Saturday 25 June 1994, something happened which spoiled it all.

It was a sunny morning with a warm south-westerly breeze and the Professor and I had planned to sail to Swansea for the weekend, a round trip of around eighty miles allowing for the tide, which was one of the largest of the year. We were in company with *Pendle*, a slightly larger yacht crewed by our friends Steve and Andrea, who had been known to sail alongside and thoughtfully hand over mugs of coffee and sausage rolls. We had sailed only about six miles north-west of Watchet, a few cables apart, when the wind increased, veered and began to head us. Immediately *Sophie* started to buck and to bury her bowsprit in the waves. It would be a long boring slog to Swansea. More sensible surely to put the wind on the beam and make for Barry, where there was water at all states of the tide and which was now only some nine miles to the north-east? It was a dismal place smelling of dog-turds but there was a good Indian restaurant. We would have a foul tide for some of the trip, but there was no particular hurry.

So the scene was set. About five miles ahead and glinting in the sunshine was one of the largest and most conspicuous seamarks in the Bristol Channel – the Breaksea LANBY (large automatic navigational buoy), some four miles south-east of Breaksea Point. Once it was a manned lightship. Now it was vast red buoy some 30 feet high on which ships converged to pick up pilots. An hour later we were about to leave it safely to starboard, allowing for the tide-set, when I inexplicably did something which has disturbed me ever since. I suddenly changed course from 20 degrees to about 60, which meant *Sophie* would leave the buoy to port at probably less than 100 yards distance. It was a stupid and pointless move: nothing would be gained in terms of time saved and the tide, now running westward at around three knots, would push us straight towards the buoy. Had I subconsciously worked out a triangle of velocities and decided that the boat speed would counteract the tide and allow us to squeeze safely past the buoy?

If so I don't remember. More likely I was showing off *Sophie*'s speed and agility to the Pendles, who were now coming up astern. What I do remember is that everything went into slow motion as boat and buoy were inextricably drawn together. I remember the Professor's anxious face. I remember trying vainly to bear away, but the boat suddenly seemed to be sailing in treacle and wouldn't respond. We could hear the rush of water around the buoy as it leaned away from the tide. Then, as we got ever closer, we lost the wind and from then on there was no escape. With a melodramatic crash, *Sophie* was sucked broadside into the Breaksea buoy. It was like driving a car into a small gasometer.

There was no time to do anything. The Professor and I watched in helpless fascination as the bowsprit snapped off at the stem, bringing down the jib and topsail. The boat ground against the rusty metal, ripping off woodwork and cracking fibreglass at waterline level. A backstay was torn out and the outboard bracket twisted until the engine was out of the water. Still the tide held *Sophie* locked fast to the buoy and the noise of wreckage was all around. What was happening was outside the Professor's experience and he was obviously so alarmed that he asked, 'Do you think we are going to die?' 'Oh yes,' I said, 'but hopefully not today.'

Eventually, using all our strength, we managed to lever the boat away from the buoy and *Pendle* took us in tow while we sorted ourselves out. *Sophie* was a sorry sight. We rigged a foresail from the stem-head and continued to Barry, the damaged side to windward and so out of the water. We goose-winged into the harbour and as a vessel in distress were allowed to tie up against the big black Barry pilot cutter.

As we sat among the wreckage I felt simultaneously depressed, shaken and ashamed to have done something so abysmally stupid. On a sunny day with perfect visibility I had managed to hit the biggest bright red obstacle in a sea area of about 300 square miles. We had a drink in Barry Yacht Club and then had a careful look at the boat, but it was hard to assess just how serious the hull damage was and whether it would withstand the return trip to Watchet. Understandably, the Professor had already decided to jump ship. Apparently, according to the philosophy of engineering, we had already had our share of good luck – but the decision was made for us when the wind increased from the west, which meant that the port side would be constantly submerged throughout the passage home. We had an Indian meal that evening and returned in *Pendle* the following morning, leaving *Sophie* on a mooring in the care of the yacht club. We motored back in a dead calm on a flat sea and could almost certainly have got *Sophie* back without mishap.

On a rainy afternoon a week later I had a kind offer out of the blue from my friend Steve Yeandle, skipper of a powerful local charter fishing boat. 'I've heard about *Sophie*,' he said, 'and I've got the evening free. Do you want to go and bring her back?' We were in Barry two hours later and returned at twelve knots with *Sophie* surfing in the wake. The sea was flat and sinister. As we approached the Somerset shore, a huge double rainbow framed Watchet like a Victorian religious embroidery. I thought: If this isn't some sort of omen, what is? A week later, after a paint job, a new bowsprit and an artful bit of fibreglassing, I sold *Sophie* to a man from Dartmouth for £2,000 and threw in the dinghy and the Old Gaffers Association flag. Loaded on the trailer she looked small and vulnerable. When there was no one about I wished her all the best and said I was sorry for what had happened. I told her she had done all I had ever asked and that she would be happier in the Dart and having picnics under the trees. Then she was towed away and I never saw her again. I didn't own another boat for nearly two years.

*******

I had just decided to replace sailing with serious organic gardening when I heard from one of the lads. Phil was now working as a property developer and freelance boat-builder in Brixham and asked if I would help him bring back a yacht from Spain. I travelled on the ferry from Plymouth to Santander with two other members of the crew, a fierce silent girl and a man who taught computer skills to murderers. Phil met us on the quayside. He was now sturdier and balding. He looked after the boat for two hotel proprietors and had skippered it for them to Spain, where they had a villa. They had now had enough of sailing for a while and wanted the boat, a posh 34-foot Roberts, returned to her home port of Brixham.

As there was no hurry, Phil decided to gather a few friends and port-hop up the French coast rather than take the direct route home. It would also be cheaper than employing a delivery crew, a point not lost on the co-owner, who spoke like the comedian Max Wall and had vetoed the purchase of a new chart as an unnecessary expense. To his chagrin, his partner insisted that they take the crew for a £300 farewell lunch at the city yacht club.

To show my appreciation, I dutifully ate what looked to be a small aquarium of marine corpses and immediately regretted it. I was sick for the next two days, during which the boat bashed into a persistent northerly wind and a tumbling sea. A small secret log written on the back of a cereal packet reads: 'Sick most of the night. Banging through the grey wastes has long lost its appeal. What's it all about? Good hobby, eh?' The crew, particularly the fierce silent girl, were unsympathetic. Phil had obviously sold me as his charismatic ex-skipper and mentor and here was some old chap lying down below, groaning and avoiding standing his watch.

On the third day, things looked up a bit; the sea calmed down, the wind veered and blew steadily from the land. In my new Helly Hansen jacket, I redeemed myself by standing a double watch. Late that night, under Phil's unerring pilotage, we sailed into La Rochelle through a mass of rocks and confusing lights to find the city in festival mood.

Once ashore, we threaded our way through stilt-dancers, ice-carvers, glass-blowers, jugglers and puppeteers to find a café still serving meals as dawn rose over the cathedral. Next day we sailed to the fishing port of Concarneau before taking a hammering through the aptly named Channel de la Helle, where a northerly force eight against a spring tide had the boat submerged in heavy seas and swamped the radar and other electronic gadgets. Two hours later, as we left Ushant to port, the sea was flat and windless and we were sunbathing again.

Phil's boat-handling and navigation were immaculate. He had made an excellent skipper. After more than 600 miles of sailing, the Start Point lighthouse appeared on cue at 11.45 the following morning and we were back in Brixham for lunch. The sea had worked its customary social magic: we had all become friends and were sorry to part. On the pontoon, as we left, Phil thanked me for coming. 'It was a really good trip. It was like sailing with my dad.' I wasn't sure if that was a compliment but I took it as one. It was a pity that when we warmly shook hands, a very expensive bottle of wine I'd bought for the Actress in Concarneau slipped out of the pocket of my Helly Hansen jacket and disappeared to the bottom of Brixham Bay.

CHAPTER 13

# A bucketful of jollop

Sir Robin Knox-Johnston sat in the stern of the boat bailing hard with a bucket. The water was already around the bottoms of his rather elegant trousers. Sir Robin was in Watchet filming an episode of a television series he was making on West Country harbours and the vessel in which he was being rowed was a 19-foot double-ended flat-bottomed fishing boat known as a Bristol Channel flatner, familiarly called a flattie. The last of its type, the flattie had recently emerged after many years of exile in the Somerset County Museum store in Glastonbury and arrived in Watchet on a trailer in the spring on 1996 as part of a publicity campaign for a possible community-run marina in the town, after the closure of the commercial docks three years earlier had put the harbour into near-dereliction.

Apparently there had been flatties in the harbour for centuries, used for sprat-fishing, tending the foreshore stake-nets and even bringing small quantities of coal from Wales, until after the First World War when, like the Ancient Mariner's albatross, they ran into bad luck and mysterious extinction. It was hoped that the reappearance of one, even though it had originated in the River Parrett some twenty miles away, might encourage more local people to take up affordable pleasure-boating, particularly as there was a chance that part of the harbour might eventually be converted into a marina.

The boat that my neighbour Bruce, chairman of an embryo community marina association, had borrowed was, in museum parlance, 'stuffed and mounted' – regarded as far beyond its useful life and of value only as a fishing-net-draped exhibit. It had been built by some unknown craftsman in the 1920s for use in the lower reaches of the Parrett and in Bridgwater Bay and was discovered and restored in the 1960s by the late Harold Kimber, a well-known local boat-builder. He had then sailed it to Bristol and presented it to the City Museum, which offloaded it on the county museum. They in turn put it into store alongside a horse-drawn hearse and a replica of a Roman sewer-pipe. It was there that Bruce, a well-known snapper-up of trifles, found it many years later while at the Glastonbury museum for some other purpose. They said they would be glad to be rid of it as they needed the space, and there were two similar boats available should he ever have need of them.

When the boat arrived it was hardly what we expected. It looked like something hauled up on a north African beach. It had no keel and the hull, with its piratical sheer and boldly angled stem and stern posts, was shaped like a slice of melon. It was painted duck-egg blue with red thwarts and gunwales. The inside was custard-coloured and the bottom-boards were black The oars were square-sided and used with thole-pins. The rudder was six feet long and little more than a foot wide, and a ridiculously long hinged tiller reached almost amidships. I had never seen a less English-looking craft.

Indeed, as we stood looking at it in silence on the dockside, almost everything about the boat seemed deliberately perverse, including the rig, a rectangular mainsail on a sprit (like a tiny Thames barge). There was an unstayed mast with a small jib set on a pitchfork-shaped spar which was tied to a ring-bolt on the stem. The mainsheet led to a block situated under the helmsman's knees. It was observed that when going about, the helmsman would need to lift his legs high over the mainsheet while passing the hinged tiller over his head, a manoeuvre which would probably require the attention of a qualified osteopath. 'No wonder the bloody things became obsolete,' someone said. 'They probably crippled the entire population.'

It occurred to me that what we were looking at was basically a dory of immense strength. The bottom was dished rather than flat and made of nine-inch-wide two-inch-thick oak planks secured to the sides with massive grown oak knees. A faded note accompanying the boat said that it had originally had elm sides, but these had rotted and Harold Kimber replaced them with marine plywood. Weight was vital to safety and performance and the boat had originally weighed over a ton. Flatties, according to our informant, had taken centuries to evolve and might have been the ancestors of the American dory, possibly taken as flat-pack deck cargo on Cabot's *Matthew* in 1497 to establish the Newfoundland inshore fisheries. Although essentially home-built, Bristol Channel flatties had the reputation of being excellent sea-boats, surprisingly fast, stiff and dry. Whoever wrote all that had obviously never been in one.

\*\*\*\*\*\*\*

We put the flattie under cover in the now-derelict cargo shed on the docks and wondered exactly what we should do next. She was thick with dirt and the years ashore had shrunk the timbers until there was daylight along the chine where the sides met the bottom. She was a sad old thing but there was still a jaunty elegance which interested and impressed me. As we stood looking at the boat, Bruce said, 'I wonder if we could get her to float.' We had been warned that the boat was still a museum exhibit and should not be tampered with, but there seemed little harm in constructing what looked like an enormous paddling pool out of plastic sheets and floating the flattie in the hope that her timbers would miraculously take up. When after a week the boat remained stubbornly on the bottom, stronger measures were obviously necessary and we consulted Graham Coggins, a local carpenter who wore a white apron and owned a beautifully maintained wooden fishing boat. Graham implied that painting the deckchairs on the *Titanic* came to mind, but suggested screwing on some discreet wedges to support the planks and then covering the bottom with what he called 'a good bucketful of jollop', a concoction he supplied, which looked like black treacle and smelled like an embrocation called Fiery Jack which my grandfather used for his lumbago.

To say it did the trick would be an overstatement, but when we launched the boat in the harbour the following week it took almost half an hour to sink and we felt this was acceptable as we didn't intend to go anywhere. When Sir Robin Knox-Johnston arrived in the town with his film crew and heard about the flattie, Graham agreed to row him and a cameraman across the harbour on the understanding that Sir Robin would do the bailing. When they returned, wet but otherwise unharmed, Sir Robin apparently remarked that at no time during his epic non-stop single-handed circumnavigation in his yacht *Suhaili* in 1968 had he felt so close to sinking as he had in the flattie in Watchet harbour.

We persevered with the jollop and when we could eventually keep the boat afloat with regular bailing, Bruce suggested we took it as an exhibit to the national Festival of the Sea in Bristol in May 1996. David Dawson, the Somerset museum officer, surprisingly agreed and encouraged us to launch it from its trailer near Portishead at the junction of the Severn and Avon rivers, and sail on the tide the six miles up-river into Bristol through the dramatic Avon Gorge and under the Clifton Suspension Bridge.

On a grey Monday evening, the day before the festival opened, Bruce, my son Tim and I climbed aboard the boat and sledged down the steep muddy bank of the Avon to meet the first of the flood tide. Immediately there was a torrential downpour, accompanied by a stiff breeze blowing down the river from Bristol. David Dawson arrived to photograph the beginning of the voyage, which took over two hours and involved over eighty tacks, some, as the river grew narrower, of less than fifty yards. It was soon apparent that the jib was far too small and that the mainsail set badly. On nearly every tack the boat swung into the wind and stopped, but the tide, now setting strongly, helped pushed the bow round.

The rain increased and the boat filled with water from above and below. We bailed to keep warm as we sailed deep into the Gorge past derelict Gothic houses and decaying terraces black with damp. We were almost certainly the first flattie ever to sail under the Clifton Suspension Bridge and David Dawson, driving on the riverside road, appeared from time to time from behind walls to photograph our progress. Despite the dismal surroundings we were surprisingly cheery as we locked into the docks in company with a huge Romanian brig and a gig crewed by men in bobble hats pretending to be eighteenth-century sailors. After we had taken up the mooring we would occupy for the next three days, an official asked where we were from and assuming we had actually sailed from Watchet, took another look at the boat and remarked, 'F-ing hell. Come and have some soup.'

There was surprising interest in the flattie, mainly because it sank each night and had to be hauled to the surface by helpful sea-scouts. A short sail Bruce and I made across the harbour was filmed by local television. Several old men told us that their families had owned flatties and that they were really farmers' boats. One man said that his father had built one in a week. He bent the bottom planks by covering them with wet sacks and loading them with heavy stones. Another way was to load the planks with 40-gallon drums of water and leave them for a year. Those boats were rough and ready but could take any punishment. 'When I was a lad I once got lost in the fog and drifted down the Parrett into Bridgwater Bay off Burnham. It was two days before I was found. The boat looked after me. I didn't come to no harm. At least not until my dad got me home.'

Without very much effort on anyone's part, an unexpected situation began to evolve when the flattie returned to Watchet. David Dawson suggested that the boat, and any other flatties still in existence, might form the basis of a collection of Bristol Channel coastal craft run by local volunteers under the patronage of the museum service. A stone-built Victorian goods shed which had lain derelict since the demise of the docks was commandeered to become what was soon being referred to with a straight face as the World Flattie Centre. Two more boats – once used for carrying reeds and peat on the Somerset Levels – arrived from the museum store-rooms. Graham Coggins lent a few spratting nets. A couple of other boats were discovered locally in varying states of decay – one was rescued from a town rubbish tip – and brought in to swell the numbers. David Dawson provided green baize boards for photographs and a notice reading 'An Exhibition of Traditional Bristol Channel Boats' to hang outside the door, and we were in business. In July 1996 we formed the Friends of the Flattie Association. Bruce was treasurer, I was chairman and my good friend John Nash, a former soldier with a serious dislike of the sea, became curator. We had no other members.

On weekend afternoons we put out our sign and sat with our tiny collection in the sooty gloom of the huge windowless building waiting to explain the magic of the Bristol Channel flattie to visitors, but only rarely did anyone come in, and then usually to inquire about the times of trains on the nearby preserved steam railway. When it rained, water dripped into buckets and on one occasion a gale lifted the roof several inches before slamming it down again. We had one electric plug and no water for tea. What the World Flattie Centre needed to make it even remotely interesting to outsiders was what David Dawson called 'hands-on activity', and one wet Sunday a Scandinavian family sheltering in the goods shed from the rain unwittingly supplied the answer. 'These boats of yours are all so old,' the husband said. 'Why don't you build some new ones?' To tell the truth, I said, that was something which had vaguely occurred to me almost from the first time I saw the Harold Kimber flattie, but I had dismissed it as impracticable, expensive and fraught with problems.

I had none of my father's carpentry skills and no knowledge of boat-building. Even creating some modest production-line kit-built dinghy from scratch would surely be traumatic enough without trying to bring some extinct species back from the dead. There were no plans, no complete specifications. There was no one alive who knew how to build or handle a flattie. There was no guarantee that it would be safe to sail. That night, as the Actress went out on her social rounds, which culminated in gatecrashing a select dinner party and insulting each guest in turn before falling down on the lawn, I stayed at home and began to make a small model flattie out of a cardboard box.

It came together almost magically as though following some unknown geometric rules: first a teardrop-shaped bottom, then matchsticks glued on both pointed ends at thirty-five degrees to form stem- and sternposts. The top edges of the sides were straight, but as they were bent from bow to stern to fit the line of the bottom they automatically curved to form the rakish sheer of the original and fitted snugly to the stem and stern. The cardboard frames and gunwale stringers were fitted later. It was an exact reversal of normal boat-building practice in which keel, frames and bulkheads came first and the outer planking was put on last. Building a flatner would be more like building a wardrobe, and I had done that several times in various domestic situations.

I made paper sails and fixed them to a knitting-needle mast. I sat and looked at the boat for a long time. It had the simplicity of child's toy and yet it was heavy with mysterious promise. The Actress returned in the early hours and sat down to write a letter to the host of the dinner party she had wrecked saying that she was withdrawing an earlier offer to knit him a jumper. But by then, my mind was already elsewhere. I would construct the first fully operational Bristol Channel sailing flatner to be built for a hundred years and the World Flattie Centre, in dire need of hands-on activity, was the obvious place to do it.

Building a flattie was far beyond me but I hoped that if I made the project sound interesting and looked helpless enough, someone would probably come to my rescue. And so it proved. Derek Vivian, a former Rolls Royce engineer, had retired early through ill health. He moved to Watchet from the Midlands and bought a boat which he sailed with his wife and son. By the mid-1990s his decreasing mobility meant he rarely used his boat, but his enthusiasm was undiminished, particularly for flat-bottomed craft, which he felt had never achieved the popularity in Britain that they deserved. He knew about flatners, and had some years earlier made a scale model of one for Ben Norman's museum. When I asked Derek if he would like to become technical director of the Watchet flattie construction project he readily agreed.

We set up a workshop in the corner of the goods shed next to what was now known as Kim's boat and waited for serendipity to dictate what happened next. Sure enough, a complete stranger appeared with the lines and detailed measurements of a derelict sailing flatner found many years earlier in the mud of a creek at Stretcholt on the River Parrett and annotated by some long-dead enthusiast. 'My father had these,' the man said. 'I read in the paper you had a flattie in Watchet. I thought they might be useful.' Although we had been told that the old flatner builders never used plans and built entirely by eye, the dimensions of Kim's boat and the one from Stretcholt were virtually identical. Derek's blueprints were an amalgam of the two boats but made provision for a slightly larger rig: our journey up the Avon had shown that when sailing to windward a small jib was worse than useless.

We bought our wood from a local Crown Estate timber yard and picked out planks with the fewest knot-holes. 'You won't get it perfect. It's only cheap deal,' the foreman said. I suddenly felt a surprisingly painful regret that my father, who had known all about deal, was not there. He would have enjoyed selecting the wood. We chose unseasoned red pine rather than expensive hardwood because the whole boat was to be encapsulated in epoxy resin making it impervious to water. That was a concession to technology which had been hotly debated in the shed. I did concede to tradition by buying two lumps of seasoned oak for the stem and stern posts from an ancient tree from near where my sister lived. These cost more than the rest of the timber put together.

We knew that the saucer-shaped bottom had to be made first and the rest of the boat built on it, but bending the five massive planks was a daunting prospect and we hadn't the time or the inclination to load them with stones or barrels of water. We visited a villainous pub on the Somerset Levels and bought cider for old men who all told us something different about building flatners, often changing their stories in mid-flow when they thought of something better. One man said his father put the planks on the cow-house floor where the cattle lay on them and bent them to the required curve. Another man said his father built his boats in a low shed, bending the planks with props from the roof. Another alternative was apparently to heat one side of the wood while dousing the other with cold water.

One man said he had been brought up on a smallholding on the river near Berrow Mump and they pulled a flatner along the ditches to collect withies and peat. 'My father always took his gun with him and shot everything he saw. I remember one time this short-toed lark come down on the marshes, first one for a hundred year. Birdwatchers come from all over England, lying in the withies with their binoculars. My father said the fuss over one tiny little bird was all damn nonsense. He went out with his gun next morning and shot it dead.' When they eventually lapsed into silence, we bought another round and left. The barman came to the door and said, 'You don't want to take no notice of they. That one that told about the bird, he used to drive a bus down Bridgwater.'

Eventually we dismissed all the folktales and decided to make a scaffolding frame 20 feet long and 3 feet high and build the boat on top of it, pulling down the bottom planks to the required bend with nuts and bolts. It was hardly ethnic but it worked. The flatner remained in tension on the frame until all major building was complete although the strain imposed by the wood was so great that it twisted the scaffolding several inches and we were always adjusting it to keep the correct bend. The only expensive pieces of wood I bought, apart from the oak, were two strips of kiln-dried Colombian pine which formed the top edge of the boat and provided its bold highly distinguished sheerline. These were carefully bent around from bow to stern, guided by a series of plywood frames. They broke three times while being fitted, despite being immersed for a week in the stream in Ben Norman's garden. One snapped with a sound like a gunshot, and made hole in the shed roof. Eventually they were replaced by pieces of cheap white pine, which bent perfectly without any problems

It took about six months to complete the basic structure and fit the plywood sides and laminated knees. Derek did most of the serious carpentry while I did the tedious sawing, planing and sanding. Kim's boat, standing nearby, was an invaluable guide and reference and a comforting reminder that what we were trying to do was actually achievable. By the early spring of 1997, the boat was nearly ready to be removed from its jig and sanded, coated with epoxy resin and painted. Spars were complete and sails and rigging were ordered. By now Derek's health had further deteriorated to the point where he found it painful to climb into the boat, but he never complained and had no intention of taking time off. Now there was hands-on activity in abundance: we often stayed in the shed until late, working on the boat in a theatrical pool of floodlight. We sawed, hammered and planed, watched by birds perched high in the roof.

One Sunday afternoon in March we finally unbolted the flattie from its scaffolding and slid it onto blocks on the floor. The boat looked surprisingly large and powerful and Derek's pleasure and relief were plain to see. I assumed this was because he was as pleased with our achievement as I was. In fact, he had just learned he was due in hospital the following week for serious surgery and had been afraid that he would have to leave me with some of the major construction. 'There's only the painting and decorating to do now,' he said. 'I can't imagine that even you could make a cock-up of that.' It wasn't for want of trying. Over the next three months I would return home semi-delirious with the fumes of epoxy resin, half-blind with filler dust and my fingers welded together with fibreglass. I went to my step-daughter's school prize-giving with one side of my face painted dark blue. White spirit temporarily affected my sense of smell and sandpaper wore away my fingerprints and turned typing into agony. The Actress said that she hoped this boat, whatever it was, would be worth all the time and effort, and wished she had married someone who read more books.

As David Dawson predicted, building the town's first flattie for a century did wonders for the World Flattie Centre's street cred, but sometimes I worried that things might be getting out of hand. Pieces appeared in the papers and on local radio and television, attracting visitors and people offering help. We got grants to improve the shed, now known as Watchet Boat Museum and officially opened by the local MP, Tom King. More boats arrived and were renovated before the admiring gaze of visitors. John Nash was asked to speak to local academics. There was talk of establishing links with a dory museum in Nova Scotia. Schoolchildren came on educational visits and old men appeared with marine artefacts in Tesco carrier-bags. And while I didn't object to being pointed out in the street as 'the flattie man' or getting a free lunch as guest speaker at Minehead Inner Wheel, I could see problems ahead. The truth was that none of us actually knew very much about flatties or about the days when, according to legend, Bristol Channel fishermen went to sea in their hundreds. I was worried that some day soon our bluff would be called. We needed our own consultant guru, and we found one in Bob Thorne.

******

No one answered the bell of the large stone cottage in the village of Pawlett, some three miles from the mouth of the River Parrett, but the kitchen door was open and a kettle was hissing somewhere inside. When no one responded to our calls, John and I walked into a large kitchen garden as immaculate and ordered as Mr McGregor's in the Peter Rabbit stories, but there was no one there either, although a spade, hoe and rake were propped against a wheelbarrow reminiscent of a woodcut in a Victorian gardening manual. We turned to leave when we noticed a tall thin man with a white beard watching us from behind a hedge. 'What do you buggers want?' he said.

Bob Thorne was not renowned for making strangers feel at home. 'He'll either tell you to sod off or he'll never stop talking,' said the man at the National Rivers Authority who had arranged the visit. 'It depends how you catch him.' Then in his mid-sixties, Bob lived alone in the cottage he had inherited from two aunts. We had obviously caught him on a good day. He invited us in for tea. The sixteenth-century house was below river level and had been flooded so regularly that Bob no longer bothered to furnish the ground floor. He slept and cooked in a small room above the waterline and used the large flag-stoned living room as a workshop. Apart from six years' war service, Bob had spent his life on the river. Over the field was Black Rock, a gaunt promontory from which the Thorne family had fished for centuries. Bob had two flatners on the bank which he had used for dip-netting for salmon. They were rowing boats made of fibreglassed plywood and adapted to carry outboard motors. You couldn't mess about with the river, Bob said. There were eight-knot tides at springs and unpredictable squalls which had laid over a 100-ton schooner.

He said that Captain Marchant, a Parrett pilot at the turn of last century, should have known better than to put a hitch on the mainsheet of his sailing flatner while he tended his pipe on a blustery March morning. A capsize followed an unexpected squall. They never found the captain's body or his flatner. The place where he was lost is now known as Marchant's Reach. A lot of flatner-men stuck to rowing after that, Bob Thorne said. Or they'd stick up their coats on an oar and be blown home when it was really quiet.

Bob said he rarely went dip-netting any more. You needed two people, one to row and the other to sit in the bow with a six-foot-wide dip-net shaped like an enormous catapult. Salmon were chased up-river and caught as they surfaced. Sometimes two flatners were lashed side-by-side and anchored broadside in the river, streaming 30-foot-wide salmon nets. This was called pitching. An axe was carried to cut the anchor warps if the boats got into trouble. 'I'm too old for all that stuff,' he said. 'Nowadays I stick to the butts.'

He was the last fisherman in Somerset, or anywhere else for that matter, to catch salmon using traditionally made salmon-butts, or putches – six-foot-long wickerwork cones made of local withies and built into barriers stretching nearly halfway across the river. It was a laborious and not particularly efficient way of catching salmon. Bob took over the butts from his grandfather, his father and his Uncle Cecil, and was currently maintaining a wall of 200 butts, half his legal allowance. 'There's nowhere near the number of fish there was when I was young,' he said. 'For every salmon that swims up the Parrett there were a thousand when I was a boy. Pollution means fish haven't got a hope in hell nowadays. I can go a weeks without

234

catching a fish, but you've still got to go down to the butts twice a day.'

Bob still made seventy or eighty new butts every year from withies he grew himself, with such resounding names as Prince Albert, Levantine and Black Smock, and carried them across the fields. The wall of butts was supported by iron stakes driven into holes in the rock. He hadn't caught a salmon for over two weeks. 'If a youngster came along and was interested in taking over the fishing it would be wrong to encourage him,' Bob said. 'There's no future in it for anyone. I only do it because I've never done anything else.'

He obviously couldn't understand why anyone should wish to conserve flatties. To him they were expendable tools of his trade to which he had no sentimental attachment. Nor did he have any interest in visiting Watchet. 'No one wants to see all that old stuff. And anyway I get sick if I go in a car.' Then, after making sure that we were thoroughly discouraged, he took us into his orchard and gave us an exquisitely made clinker-built oak flatner which he had bought for £32 in 1948, his grandfather's nets and a variety of other artefacts which he gruffly dismissed as 'nobbut rubbish'. Brushing aside our thanks, he said 'Don't expect me to give you anything else,' and went back to his garden. Since then a steady stream of information, gifts and advice has issued from the Pawlett cottage and continues to this day.

A few years after our first meeting, the licence for 200 salmon-butts increased to £200. When Bob first started it had been £2. Enraged by what he regarded as an extortionate fee, he hauled his intricately made putches ashore and apart from one he donated to our museum, burned the lot on the riverbank. There is now no one butt-fishing on the Parrett in the traditional way. Hearing of the cremation, the river authorities wrote a letter of regret. They said that had they known that Bob wasn't happy with the new fees they could almost certainly have come to some arrangement.

We decided to find a patron after someone said it would look impressive on the notepaper. We would also be taken more seriously when it came to getting grants. We wrote to Dr Basil Greenhill, former Director of the Greenwich National Maritime Museum and the country's most distinguished maritime historian, wondering whether he could suggest anyone suitable. We hardly expected that at nearing 80 the great man would immediately volunteer for the job and drive up from Cornwall to see what we were up to.

He was a tall thin man with a penetrating look and there was something rather intimidating about him until he started talking about boats. He was the author of over thirty books on marine history and archaeology and however small and humble the craft the pleasure and fascination remained. He knew all about flatners and had written at length about them in seminal works on inshore craft. He said they were part of the great European flat-bottomed building tradition of boats for the shallows and were related indirectly to the Gotland flataska, the German kag and the Hanseatic cog. There was silence and someone suggested lunch. Over a shepherd's pie the conversation became more relaxed and Dr Greenhill said that he still enjoyed a 'gentle potter' on the Tamar river near his Cornish farmhouse with his wife Ann in one of his three boats: a clinker salmon boat, a locally built double-ender and a flat-bottomed Maine lobsterman's skiff. 'I've always had small working boats,' he said, adding somewhat predictably, 'We have never been yachtspeople. Nowadays, Ann and I usually row rather than sail. It's a sort of waterborne jogging.'

Basil Greenhill was not the easiest man to know and had the reputation of being a somewhat autocratic figure at Greenwich, where he was director from 1967 to 1983.

During his tenure the museum was transformed from a dusty shrine displaying Nelson's underwear to an institution of worldwide influence. In his later years he was more friendly and approachable and made occasional visits to Watchet to examine any new exhibits and provide information and advice. When he died in April 2003, aged 83, we were all very sorry.

*******

Soon afterwards I took a welcome break from flatner painting and decorating to help Tom and Mervyn bring their boat *Moonraker* back from Brittany. They had spent several months in small French harbours and marinas. Now in the ancient market town of Pontrieux far up the Trieux river beyond Lézardrieux, they needed extra crew for the return trip. I went on the ferry with Alistair, a young doctor. Tom, who previously lived in France, was thoroughly at home. He had been busy constructing a sewage holding-tank system out of plastic drums, rubber tubes, old plumbing fittings and lemonade bottles. The result, looking like a colonic irrigation system for elephants, was finally completed the day before we sailed for England.

A gale delayed our departure by twenty-four hours and we were reefed down in a strong north-east breeze when we finally set a course for Falmouth, some thirty hours away. The home-made holding-tank system had worked well since leaving Pontrieux because we simply used the lavatory and flushed it with water from the lemonade bottles, but in the tubes and drums under the floor things were stirring and Tom had a thoughtful look. The wind increased, things were getting decidedly uncomfortable, Mervyn was on the helm, and Alistair and I were tucking in another reef. Tom was somewhere down below. It seemed a strange moment to pump out the holding tanks but captains move in mysterious ways. As we returned to the cockpit a long tube appeared from a porthole and the pumping-out process began. The pumping reached a crescendo and abruptly stopped. There was a muffled explosion and moments later Tom appeared looking not unlike the monster from the black lagoon. 'I have a feeling that it's back to the drawing-board,' he said. For the rest of the voyage it was bucket and chuck-it.

*Moonraker* was still operating her dual-captain system. As we motored towards Land's End in a dead calm, Tom was advocating taking the long way round the Longships Channel while Mervyn preferred to halve the distance by heading north along a narrow channel flanked by vicious rocks. While the captains conferred below, Alistair, on the helm, followed a large trawler which appeared to know where it was going and we emerged safely round-the-land while the matter was still being discussed over the chart table.

As we sailed homeward-bound into the Bristol Channel, the waves grew short and sharp and the wind inevitably swung north-east and increased. The full force of wind and tide was now against us and for three hours we made hardly any progress despite motor-sailing at nearly six knots. Tom decided to change course by ninety degrees to avoid the fierce tidal rip around Trevose Head, which had the effect of sending us even further backwards. It was now midnight. Mervyn suggested a reciprocal course back towards Trevose Head and into Padstow, a port none of us had previously entered. As we searched with torches for a route through the rocks and crab-pots into the unlit and notoriously treacherous River Camel, Tom was heard to wonder whether going into Padstow was a really a very good idea. Shortly afterwards further discussion became irrelevant when we found ourselves aground in a sheltered sandy cove. We made tea, had a short game of Scrabble and slept soundly until morning. We later found that we had missed the river's legendary Doom Bar, graveyard of over six hundred ships, by less than the length of a cricket pitch. The boat arrived in Watchet two days later without further incident. Despite the somewhat unusual command structure, a cruise on *Moonraker* was always a delight. Tom and Mervyn later sold *Moonraker* but they remained close friends. Mervyn now cruises the Midlands canals in a narrow-boat. Tom has a small yacht of which he is sole captain. When I think of Tom and Mervyn sailing *Moonraker* I'm reminded of the lines in Macaulay's poem about Horatius on the bridge which run, if I remember, 'Those behind cried forward, while those in front cried back.' It is one of my favourite poems and always makes me smile.

CHAPTER 14

# Yankee Jack sails again

By early summer the flattie was completed. When painting
the boat I rejected Watchet blue – said to be the colour King
Charles the First wore at his execution – on the grounds that
no one really knew what shade it was. The hull was a deep
navy with a red gunwale and the inside was varnished. The
top of the mast and tips of the spars were painted white,
fishing-boat style. The sails were tanned. On his return from
hospital Derek made several visits to the shed and sat in a
chair by the boat to make sure I did things properly. His
hip operation had not been the hoped-for success and there
was little chance of him sailing the boat in the foreseeable
future, but his enthusiasm was undiminished. He was
already planning to build a flattie twice the size of mine,
with a junk rig, and had done the preliminary drawings.

Standing in the shed on its trailer surrounded by its decaying ancestors, the flattie seemed to me to be eager to leave the past behind. All it now needed was a name. All boats are traditionally feminine. This one became an instant hermaphrodite by being named *Yankee Jack*, after John Short, a Victorian seaman and the closest Watchet had to a folk-hero. His nearest rival was probably St Decuman, a Celtic monk who was supposed to have sailed to Watchet from Wales on a hurdle accompanied by a cow. On arrival he was promptly decapitated, which showed that not a lot had changed in Watchet in nearly three thousand years. Being a saint, he was able to replace his head after washing it in a nearby well. The church which bears his name was the one the Ancient Mariner was supposed to have left behind when he sailed away to do a spot of birdwatching.

John Short was born in Watchet in 1839. At fourteen he joined his father, the skipper of a coastal smack trading with the Bristol Channel ports, but soon yearned for blue-water adventure. In 1857 John and two other Watchet youngsters signed as deck-hands on the Bristol brig *Promise*, bound for Quebec, via Cadiz.

*Was you ever in Quebec*
*Stowing timber on the deck?*

Ben Norman could remember hearing Short as a very old man singing those lines from the shanty 'Stormalong John', recalling the tough days of the Canadian timber trade. It was the start of a deep-sea career which took John Short to every major port from the South Seas to Arctic Russia. In the 1860s he earned his lasting soubriquet by serving on American ships running the Civil War blockade and had began to collect the shanties which would turn him into a folksong legend and make him the only merchant seaman to have an obituary in *The Times*.

He assiduously learned shanties from each new ship and eventually had total recall of over a hundred songs. He took the job of shantyman very seriously, remarking that sailors coordinated by the right shanty could do a job in half the time. Yankee Jack finally came ashore at seventy-five to look after his sick wife and became Watchet town crier and captain of the fire brigade. He still occasionally worked as a hobbler on the docks and used his skills in decorative ropework to make sennet doormats, but it was in the summer of 1914 that his past caught up with him in a fairy-tale manner. Two visitors called at the harbour-side cottage where Yankee Jack was nursing his wife, Anne-Marie. One was a local clergyman. The other was Cecil Sharp, friend of Vaughan Williams and Gustav Holst, and the world's most distinguished folksong collector.

For three days the following week, Yankee Jack sang over sixty shanties, patiently repeating some half-a-dozen times for the benefit of Sharp's secretary, who transcribed the words and music in those distant days before tape-recording. A total of forty-two subsequently appeared in Sharp's volume of *English Folk Chanteys*, including what have become the standard versions of such classics as 'Rio Grande', 'A-Rovin', 'Spanish Ladies', 'Shenandoa' and 'The Watchet Sailor'. It was the culmination of fifty years in sailing ships, singing the solo parts of the work-songs which were an essential part of seamanship under sail. Cecil Sharp readily acknowledged that Yankee Jack had saved dozens of long-forgotten sea-songs from extinction. He wrote, 'He has a voice which would excite the envy of many a professional vocalist. He has, although I am sure he does not know it, a great musical ability of the uncultivated unconscious order. I count myself particularly fortunate to have made his acquaintance.'

Now a musical celebrity, Yankee Jack's cottage became a place of pilgrimage for folksong enthusiasts until his death in 1933 at the age of 94. Yankee Jack was buried in St Decuman's churchyard to a reading of Tennyson's 'Crossing The Bar' and with a red ensign on the coffin, but exactly where remains a mystery. Strangely, there was no headstone for Yankee Jack and no memorial to him in the town, but at least there would now be a little boat in the harbour which bore his name.

The launching, in the middle of July, originally intended as a modest affair for a few friends and helpers, quickly escalated out of control. I put on a smart grey shirt I had ironed myself in circumstances which will be explained. It was the hottest Saturday of the year. The shed was crowded with noisy well-wishers and passers-by attracted by the free drinks. Ben Norman spoke of his last meeting with Yankee Jack when at, well over 90, he appeared at a local concert to sing shanties in a still-powerful voice. Songs and toasts continued until the booze ran out. Eventually, hours behind schedule, and led by the Watchet town crier and a platoon of sea-scouts, the flag-decked flattie moved erratically down the main street towards the harbour through crowds of holiday-makers who must have wondered what on earth was going on. Musicians and singers had climbed into the boat, which was now being pulled by anyone who could still stand up, and local radio and television recorded the scene. It was all I could have wished for in terms of personal glory and yet I was sober and apprehensive as I walked behind the boat. Would the launching trolley bear all that weight? Would the boat actually float?

But the real cause of my morbid apprehension that summer afternoon had nothing to do with boats. I had finally fled from the Actress some three weeks earlier after deciding that the relationship had become unworkable to the point where one partner might well eventually kill the other. Since then, I had been hiding in the homes of friends and working on a laptop in the car. A confrontation seemed inevitable and the flattie launch, with its captive audience, would be perfect for a public announcement of my many shortcomings as a husband and a human being.

As it happened, the Actress had decided to have a small drinks party at home. She did not appear as a spectre at the feast and the flattie was launched uneventfully after a blessing, inexplicably in Celtic, by the local vicar. Derek and his wife then officially named the boat by pouring a bottle of Cripplecock cider over the bow and I feared for the varnish. In fact, the Actress had decided to reserve her vengeance for the subsequent divorce proceedings, from which she got almost the entire assets of the marriage apart from a rocking chair and a vase of dried flowers. Shortly afterwards her daughter became the beneficiary of a huge legacy from a distant relative.

*******

Although the flattie bobbed alarmingly on its mooring like something in a child's bath, it felt surprisingly stable when I sailed out of the harbour on the next day's early-morning tide, intending to be out for an hour or so to discover how the boat performed. There were no leaks and most of the rigging was in the right place. A friend who was watching from the Esplanade reported that as I hoisted the sails and dropped the mooring, a bystander said, 'He's never going to sea in that? He should be taking the owl and the pussycat with him.' There was only a light offshore breeze and the sea was a pale silver bobble but we were soon making around five knots on a broad reach with the centreplate half down. It was a curious sensation to sail a boat you had built yourself, particularly as it behaved in an unexpected manner, sliding along the surface of the water with almost no bow-wave or wake. Close-hauled, it was hard to make it heel. The rig was small, but with only four inches of draught, it drove the boat well. I had never sailed a boat which needed so little wind to move it.

But it still needed some, and when the wind dropped completely and the ebb tide picked up, Yankee Jack drifted sideways towards America at a steady four knots. Within five minutes I was a quarter of a mile downstream from the harbour and there seemed little prospect of returning until the tide turned in four hours' time. By then, *Yankee Jack* would be in Porlock Bay some twelve miles distant, and I was supposed to be having lunch with my mother.

The boat's alternative power was a pair of eight-foot oars, but it soon became apparent that rowing a half-ton boat against the second highest tide in the world was a pretty pointless exercise. In ten minutes I managed to row less than a hundred yards. By then I was dripping with sweat and cross-eyed with the unaccustomed exertion. I was also getting a pretty good idea of why there were no longer any flatties in Watchet harbour. Eventually I gave up the struggle, lowered the sails, dropped anchor in about forty feet of brown water and sat in the boat for two hours waiting for the tide to slacken. I could see men fishing on the pier and boys hoisting up small crabs in nets attached to bicycle wheels. No boats came by. I felt as isolated and alone as the man in the moon. To add a surrealistic touch, someone in a harbour-side house was playing the bagpipes.

When the tide began to turn, I rowed slowly towards the harbour and anchored for another hour until there was enough water to pass through the entrance. I had not expected *Yankee Jack*'s maiden voyage to be like this and I was irritable and extremely hungry. The pier roundhead, with its red lighthouse, looked deserted. Now all that was needed was to row through the entrance and pick up the mooring that I could already see at the far end of the harbour. It had hardly been the most auspicious of voyages but at least no harm had been done. But although the tide was surging in through the harbour entrance, all was not as it seemed. Nigel Stokes, the pilot, had mentioned the problems he had with an eddy which swirled clockwise between the entrance piers and now I experienced it as first hand: the flood tide pushed the boat through the entrance and immediately pulled it out again. The boat spun sideways and collided heavily against the stone roundhead, trapping the starboard oar, which immediately snapped off at the rowlock. The 20-foot wall had no handholds apart from a large growth of bladderwrack sprouting from a crack in the rock and onto which I clung as the boat surged madly in the eddy.

> *Bladderwrack (*Fucus visiculosus*): common seaweed. Leather straplike branching fronds arise from a circular rootlike anchor (holdfast) Grows tenaciously in rocks* — Encyclopaedia of Marine Biology.

How long *Fucus visiculosus* would tenaciously support a large man and a 19-foot boat before it gave way and sent them scudding off towards Bristol I didn't know but I tended to look on the black side. There were steps on the harbour side of the roundhead and posts, to which I could moor the boat while I worked out a way of getting back to the mooring, but how could I get there? As I clung to the seaweed I looked up and saw, hanging from the railings surrounding the lighthouse, a lifebuoy and a coil of rope. They were at that moment as inaccessible as the planet Mars.

There were footsteps from the direction of the lighthouse. I couldn't bring myself to shout the word 'Help' and instead called, 'I say. Excuse me. Have got a minute?' A small man in a baseball cap leaned over the rail. 'Could you lower that lifebelt and pull me round to the steps? I'm having a bit of trouble.

'Sorry mate. I don't live here.'

'That doesn't matter. Just chuck the thing down. I don't know how much longer I can hang on to this bloody seaweed.'

A pause. 'I'm just a visitor. You need someone who's authorised. I'll see if I can find someone. Sorry mate.' He disappeared. Moments later he was replaced by a fisherman in a bright red hat who had caught nothing all day and welcomed the chance to participate in a minor marine drama. He lowered the lifebuoy on the rope and hauled me round to the steps. Once safely ashore, I borrowed an oar from some passing sea-scouts and rowed the boat back to the mooring.

Thinking over the day's events that night in a sleeping bag on a friend's sofa, it was blindingly obvious that in its present form the flattie was unsafe for serious sailing in the Bristol Channel. For a start there was no method of reefing the mainsail or even hauling it down. It was permanently lashed to the mast like an enormous flag and the only way to stop sailing was to pull the mast out of its hole in the thwart and throw it, and the sails, into the bottom of the boat. Having to lift the tiller over your head was clumsy and inefficient and, more important, made the helmsman look ridiculous. The long tiller also made it uncomfortable to steer from the stern seat.

But the biggest problem was auxiliary power. Oars were clearly inadequate, so why didn't I just stick a small outboard motor on the back – and problem solved? Because then the boat would no longer have been an historic rarity, or a subject for discussion by maritime historians, and I would no longer be the only man in the land who skippered a Bristol Channel flatner under oar and sail. Surely that was worth a little inconvenience?

So I left the boat as it was and, sure enough, it was soon making good copy. There was a half-page picture in *The Times*. There was a two-page feature in *Sailing Today* magazine under the heading 'Flat-out Flattie', a historical assessment in *Traditional Boat*, and articles in half-a-dozen other magazines and newspapers. I was also asked to do a local radio chat-show as a last-minute deputy for a shoe-shop manager who had died that morning. There were long pauses. When the female presenter, who originally thought flatties were some sort of sandals, asked what I liked about being a sailor, my mind went completely blank and the conversation petered out, to be replaced by a Frankie Vaughan record.

I had more success talking to yacht clubs and bluffing my way through discussions on marine adhesives. I had dawn telephone calls from men seemingly unaware of the time differences, who had bought plans from the flattie museum and were now attempting to build their own vessels as far away as Germany, Cyprus and New York harbour. One man planned to sail the Atlantic in a flattie but his family persuaded him to seek psychiatric help before the project got beyond the planning stage. I was now the undisputed authority on sailing flatties. No one ever thought to question my advice on stropped blocks and spider-bands, delivered in what I hoped was a slight accent of the Somerset wetlands. In the meantime I continued to venture out in a boat with a performance ranging from poor to dangerous and calamity was never far away.

A few weeks after the launch there was a significant development: I finally persuaded someone to come out with me in *Yankee Jack*. Weeks earlier an entry in my diary read 'Met a narrow woman. Very nice.' Her name was Vivienne but I have always called her Myrtle, and compared with most of my previous wives and girlfriends, she was very narrow indeed. Myrtle had studied politics at university but latterly she worked in her father's building firm. She had been a junior county tennis champion and was still slender and attractive although she took no exercise and tried to avoid walking whenever possible in case she damaged her immaculate shoes. Myrtle was unmarried and regarded in the district as something of an enigma. She was caring, sympathetic and sociable. Everyone liked her and enjoyed her quirky humour. She was also intensely private and few people were encouraged to visit her home in a nearby village – a bungalow surrounded by a high hedge.

People told her secrets knowing that she would take

them to the grave, but her own secrets remained largely unshared and her past, and those who figured in it, were rarely mentioned. She loved gardening and poetry and football and constantly worried about her family. She hated tomatoes, except in soup, and understood all the finer points of snooker. She refused to eat blue Smarties. She was unlike any woman I had ever met. Against the advice of all her friends, and her own better judgement, she became the love of my life and still is. Every day with her is a delight.

Myrtle had never sailed but had seen the boat on launch-day and had liked the look of it because it was small enough to reach down and put your hands in the water. She arrived with her long dark hair in a plait and carrying a large heavy handbag which she insisted on keeping at her side. She was instantly at ease in the boat and spoke to it warmly like a dog. When she took the tiller she knew instinctively what to do although the theory of sailing was a mystery to her, and remains so.

My hopes of impressing Myrtle quickly took a tumble soon after leaving the harbour when we appeared to be under artillery fire from the east quay. Later we learned that the commotion was caused by a firm of specialist undertakers firing the ashes of a former coastguard into the sea in canisters attached to ten large distress rockets. Myrtle seemed unconcerned, but it was hardly the start I had hoped for, and from then on, things only got worse. A strong easterly wind and an ebb tide sent us scudding to the westward and I enjoyed showing off *Yankee Jack*'s rollicking style, but when we turned for home in a flurry of foam the boat was unable to make the slightest progress against wind and tide and there seemed no way we could get back while there was still water in the harbour.

Once again I was rowing vainly against the current when Steve Yeandle's powerful charter fishing boat, *Scooby-Doo*, which had previously rescued *Sophie* from Barry, appeared astern, returning to harbour with a party of anglers after a day's fishing down-channel. Steve shouted from his wheelhouse offering a tow which I accepted after the obligatory protestations. Steve came alongside and after dropping the mast and sails we climbed aboard, Myrtle tightly holding her handbag. The anglers, mostly large men with tattoos and baseball caps, were too busy disembowelling their catch and wrapping it in supermarket bags to take much interest in the new arrivals although one did warn Myrtle to avoid a large conger-eel thrashing in the corner of the boat.

By the time *Yankee Jack* was secured on a towing-line astern, wind and sea had increased and we were still over a mile from Watchet. Steve was anxious to get back while there was still enough water to disembark his passengers but, as soon as he started the tow, Yankee Jack rolled and plunged in the wake, shipping solid water over the bow and filling up before our eyes. Steve slowed down, which inexplicably made things worse. As we watched in disbelief, the tiller, rudder, centreboard, oars and almost anything else that wasn't secured floated away over the stern. By now there was nothing left to lose, so we lashed the waterlogged hulk tightly to the side of the boat to prevent it sinking, and sped back to Watchet, leaving a collection of lovingly-created flotsam bobbing on the waves, never to be seen again. It was not one of my more successful voyages in *Yankee Jack*, but Myrtle did not seem disconcerted and afterwards we shared a large bag of chips. She said she would certainly like to come out sailing again.

It took a month to replace all the equipment we had lost, but I obstinately refused to learn from the experience and when the boat returned to its mooring nothing had been changed in order to make it more seaworthy. Soon afterwards we were asked to take part in the annual Brixham trawler festival and race in an event for small open fishing boats. With my friends Bob Eaglesfield and

Rick Pook as crew, we trailed the boat to Brixham through traffic-choked roads on a bank holiday. The weather on race-day was appalling: heavy rain and a strong easterly which turned Torbay into a lee shore with breaking rollers and the air thick with spray.

We were the smallest boat in the race and were assured there would be nothing dishonourable in withdrawing before the start as the weather appeared to be getting worse. Bob and Pookie said it was up to me and I said I wasn't sure. Three negatives mysteriously made a positive and we found ourselves in the middle of Torbay surfing down ten-foot waves and losing sight of the rest of the fleet as we disappeared into the troughs. The boat was soon half-full of water and we were left far behind but we completed two legs of the course before we decided that both crew and boat had had enough and made a course for the harbour without rounding the last buoy.

The return was almost a dead run, so we dropped the jib and continued on mainsail, rolling and pitching so violently that Myrtle, watching anxiously from the shore, was certain that every moment was our last. In one particularly violent gust the boat gybed and with no jib or forestay to restrict it, the sprit sail was free to swing round and round the mast, rolling itself up neatly like an umbrella. By then we had reached the harbour wall, and were thankfully out of what had become a full-blown gale. We rowed to a jetty and bailed out nearly thirty buckets of water.

When a bystander asked about the unusual furling system I said it had been developed in the eighteenth century by Bridgwater Bay sprat fishermen and was useful when short-handed in bad weather. We later learned that the race had actually been stopped on our last leg and that with our unusually generous handicap, had we rounded the buoy we would probably have come first and won a large silver cup. As it was, we had to be content with a small brass badge. Later that season we won another trophy in a local race run on a windless afternoon. It was awarded for taking an hour to drift sideways over the start line. On balance, I preferred the badge.

*******

It took me three years to agree to fit an outboard engine on the boat and that was mainly because after helping me row fifteen miles through a glassy calm Myrtle was threatening to leave me for ever. I also put on reefing gear and made other adjustments which made the boat safer and more seaworthy, although it was still a handful in anything more than a force four wind. There was now a portable VHF radio, flares, medical kit, two anchors, compass and safety equipment on board. There was general relief in the harbour that I had finally come to my senses, but as usual there was another and less laudable motive: I was planning what, to me at least, would be an absolutely spiffing adventure.

I had discovered that the original Yankee Jack had been persuaded by his wife Annie to return to the home trade in 1890 when he was fifty-one, subsequently serving for the next twenty years as mate on coastal ketches and schooners and making what he derisively called 'shopping trips' from Somerset and Devon ports to Bristol. He complained that it wasn't real sailoring and that he missed the great oceans but his skill and experience were appreciated by the 'down-homers'. Isaac Allen, master and owner of the ketch *Annie Christian*, one of Yankee Jack's last ships, provided a glowing, if idiosyncratic, reference which read:

> This is to certify that John Short of Watchet, as serve a Mate on bord thee Annie Christian for to years in a honest and faithfull SeamanLike manner, one cold be trusted.

So why shouldn't Yankee Jack sail again, rediscovering the Bristol Channel's forgotten ports and using chart, lead-line and compass to recreate John Short's coasting journeys? My friend Stephen Swann, editor of the magazine *Traditional Boats & Tall Ships*, liked the idea and for the next two years I wrote a regular account of our peregrinations under the title 'Sentimental Journey'. We started at Weston-super-Mare and worked gradually 100 miles westwards onto the iron coast of north Cornwall with a fetch all the way to America and where only lunatics would consider putting a port, let alone sailing into it without an engine. Whenever possible, we sailed the entire way to our destinations, but as the journeys grew longer and the coast more inhospitable, it seemed sensible to take the boat by road at least part of the way, particularly when we were duplicating passages we had made before. I also didn't want to frighten myself any more than necessary.

My companion was Wilberforce, a shadowy figure with whom I could share experiences and whom I could blame when things went wrong. Like popes and foxhounds, Wilberforce's identity might change but the name remained the same. In our recorded conversations he invariably had the best lines. He also sang from time to time in what was described as an unpleasant tenor. He was a good man to have in a tight corner. The voyages would not have been the same without him.

*Yankee Jack* sailed eastwards in the spring of 2003 to investigate the derelict harbours of Highbridge, Combwich and Bridgwater. Nowadays the wastes of Bridgwater Bay, where unmarked drying banks of sand and mud reach out five miles from low featureless shores, are something of a maritime no man's land. They are little used by commercial traffic and avoided by pleasure sailors in offshore winds. A leading mark into the River Parrett is provided by a wooden lighthouse on the beach standing on stilts like an enormous white henhouse. Before it was built in 1832, a fisherman put a candle in his window.

The first paragraph of the first piece unconsciously set the tone of 'Sentimental Journey':

> Anyone needing a sharp reminder of just how ephemeral life can be should take a trip to the muddy River Brue in the bottom right-hand corner of Somerset's Bridgwater Bay in search of the port of Highbridge. It simply isn't there. Or if it is, I'm damned if we could find it.

In fact the grandiose Victorian dream of a major Bristol Channel port now lay beneath twenty feet of blancmange-textured mud. There was virtually nothing to show that there had once been impressive granite quays berthing up to six ships on a tide or that you could once get a ship in Highbridge which would take you to Australia.

Bridgwater, a puzzling mixture of Georgian squares and drab terraces reminiscent of Burnley on a bad day, is fourteen miles up the River Parrett. The Parrett has a tidal range of 35 feet and is officially the muddiest river in Britain. It has drowned over a hundred people in the last century. Bridgwater was once second only to Bristol as the major channel port, handling half a million tons of cargo a year, but it isn't interested in ships any more. The docks have been concreted shut for twenty years, the slipways blocked off, and low bridges span the river. We scrambled ashore into a supermarket car park and were told off by a lady traffic warden for unauthorised mooring.

Back in Bridgwater Bay we anchored near Steart Island, an uninhabited sandy hump, and saw two camels looking out over a grassy dune. Wilberforce went ashore to check that we weren't hallucinating. He found a total of five single-humped dromedaries eating cattle-nuts. They were owned by an ex-poultry farmer named Neil McCallum who once crossed the English Channel in a septic tank and was now proprietor of the Bridgwater Camel Company. The camels, from Tenerife and with names like Telfet, Tazruk and Vera, were hired out for camel-trekking along the sands at £100 a day. At night the trekkers camped in a field next to the pub. Neil McCallum told Wilberforce he was booked up for the next year.

A few miles along the coast, in the shadow of the monolithic Hinkley Point nuclear power station, a man was seen out on the lonely mudflats half a mile from shore, pushing a wooden contraption somewhere between a sledge and an upturned kitchen table. He was wearing a costume resembling that of a courtier in a pantomime: blue woollen hat, blue shorts, a yellow ex-Post Office raincoat and what appeared to be women's stockings cut off at the knee. His name was Brendon Sellick and he was the world's last surviving mud-horse fisherman.

Twice a day he pushed his sledge, designed in the Middle Ages, across the bleak mudflats to empty and repair a mile-long line of stake-nets which had given his family a livelihood for almost 400 years. Now in his mid-fifties, Brendon had taken over the nets from his father. He put out twice the number of nets and caught a fraction of his father's catch. 'In my dad's day it was nothing to come back with two hundred pounds of shrimps and some lovely big fish. He'd be heartbroken to see what has happened to the fishing.' Brendon blamed the power station for sucking in millions of gallons of water every day to cool the reactors and killing marine life. 'I can't see anyone taking on this job after me,' he said.

His day's catch was about forty pounds of fish and half a bucket of shrimps. The fish included a hake, which Brendon said was lovely cooked in the oven with a drop of vinegar. 'I'll boil the shrimps when I get home,' he said. 'There's nothing like them with a nice bit of bread and butter.' Brendon said his was a hard but interesting life and he had never thought of doing anything else. 'When you've been out on the mud for as long as I have,' he said, 'it gets in your blood.'

Brendon wasn't the only one who blamed Hinkley Point for past and future misfortunes. In a remote wooden bungalow down the coast, built without planning permission and surrounded by a huge meticulously kept kitchen garden, Ted Bosley, a reclusive retired builder in his eighties, was making plans for the day, inevitable in his mind, when the power station blew up and slaughtered the population. 'It's the plumbing,' he said. 'They don't have the sense to scrap it when it's worn out and one day soon it will break and everyone will be done for. Everyone, that is, except me.'

His optimism was due to the fact that he had built his own nuclear fall-out shelter deep under his house, moving a thousand tons of earth single-handed and wheelbarrowing in a thousand tons of stones to make a labyrinth of tunnels and chambers resembling an Egyptian burial vault. It was almost impossible to believe it was the work of one old man. Ted said he could live underground for a month. 'It will happen, you can be sure of that,' he said. 'In the meantime it's a very useful place to store my potatoes.' If at some distant date Hinkley Point does explode like some vast Roman candle, both Wilberforce and I felt that, secure in his underground vault, Ted Bosley's main emotion would be a frustration that there was no one left to admit that he had been right all along.

Sailing westwards to Minehead from this grim and bleak place, we found a much jollier old man leaning over the harbour wall, but even he had a doleful tale to tell. Stan Rawle was over eighty and a former Minehead harbourmaster. He said it was fifty years almost to the day since he had left the harbour with his father and uncle in the Emma Louise, a pretty 75-foot ketch and the last Bristol Channel sailing coaster, for a final journey to Appledore in north Devon, where she was to be laid up. 'We had kept her going since the war by only taking £2 a week wages,' Stan said. 'But now the motor-ships were getting all the cargoes. I'm not ashamed to say I cried when we took her on that last trip. She was a lovely old ship and had looked after us so well. We painted her up to look her best. It was the least we could do. My father had her for twenty years and I think losing her broke his heart. They put her on the mud down the river from Bideford and that's where she stayed. There's not much left of her now. You can see her from the new bridge over the Torridge and she's a sorry sight. It's a pity things have to end like that, but it's what they call progress, I suppose.'

We surfed into Porlock Weir along a channel marked by two bean-sticks, looking vainly for a Porlock oyster. At Lynmouth we inspected the spot where Mary and Percy Shelley launched fleets of bottles containing his revolutionary poems. We had lunch at the pub where R.D. Blackmore sketched out *Lorna Doone*. Ghosting along amid the catspaws on a gentle summer evening, the scent of Ilfracombe's thirty-one fish and chip shops and cafés (I counted them) sent us into a frenzy. Once Ilfracombe was the herring capital of the channel but there wasn't a silver darling to be had, not even in Damien Hurst's new restaurant, and Wilberforce had to settle for a pair of Icelandic kippers. At the private fishing village of Clovelly, which hung perilously on a steep cliff, Wilberforce refused to go ashore because of vertigo.

At Bideford, going under the low medieval bridge into the tranquil River Torridge, Wilberforce claimed someone on the bank shot him with an airgun. At Hartland Quay, where a substantial harbour vanished under 80-foot waves one night in 1887, we chickened out and sailed on to Bude. Behind us lay Lundy Island like a half-submerged crocodile and in front were the iron-bound ribs of the 100-foot Warren headland. It was no place for heroics in a 19-foot open boat. In Bude we found boats with wheels which once carried sand along a canal. Wilberforce thought wheels on *Yankee Jack* would be a definite improvement.

Stephen Swann, an east-coast man brought up in the Brightlingsea mud, visited north Devon and was horrified by the violence of the sea and the hostility of the coast. In the issue of his magazine containing my piece on Hartland Quay, Stephen wrote in his Editor's Letter, 'The skippers and crews who sailed their schooners and ketches into places like Porlock Weir, Lynmouth or Hartland must have been men-mountains, or mad, or, more likely, both.' Comparing them with the relative sanity of east-coast sailors, Stephen remembered crewing a charter barge into the upper Stour estuary in the 1960s:

> We had a party of yachtsmen aboard and as we approached Mistley one of them asked the old skipper at the wheel if there was much water off the quay. 'Yes, mate,' came the reply. 'But 'us spread out awful thin.'

CHAPTER 15

# The stuffed weasel and the price of fish

My father had liked a nice blazer. He wore it with dark slacks and highly polished shoes. With it he wore a selection of his vast wardrobe of ties including guards regiments, Oxford colleges and exclusive golf clubs, none of which he had the right to wear, but he bought them because he liked the colours. I, on the other hand, hated blazers mainly because they reminded me of the miseries of school, where they were compulsory wear. They were dark maroon. On the pocket was the school crest: a bad-tempered bullock sitting in what looked like a metal basket, and the motto 'I Bide My Time'. That was probably the most useful thing I learned in six years at that school. The colour was supposed to commemorate the death in the fifteenth century of the Duke of Clarence who was said to

259

have drowned in a butt of malmsey wine. One of the first jokes boys heard at the school was, 'Why did the Duke take three days to drown in the barrel?' Answer: 'He had to keep getting out to go to the gents.'

When I left school I burned my blazer on a bonfire in the garden. Now, some fifty years later, I was persuaded by Myrtle to buy another from Marks and Spencer. I had become, through lack of any other contenders, chairman of the Watchet Boat Owners' Association and blazers were what chairmen wore. My friend Tom Head, commodore of the club, wore a very smart blazer. He was a retired boat-builder whose family had run passenger steamers on the River Severn and who now lived in a house overlooking Watchet harbour. It was his mother who had objected to having a freighter against her garden wall. Hearing that I was in need of a new office, Tom Head told me that another association member, a chiropodist known as Tom Foot, was giving up his surgery in a former sail-loft on the Esplanade in an ancient building owned by the Watchet Conservative Men's Snooker Club. Tom Head said the first-floor room overlooked the harbour and would probably do me very nicely. As he was a trustee of the snooker club he kindly put in a word for me.

For a very reasonable rent I took possession of the world's best office and I have it still. It is long and low and on dark nights, when I'm working late, the light of Nash Point on the corner of Swansea Bay flashes twice every ten seconds into the port side of my window and the Flatholm lighthouse twice every fifteen seconds to starboard. From the desk I see every boat in the harbour, including my own, and no one passes along the Esplanade without my knowing. There are pictures, photographs, cases of knots and charts on every wall and sailing books and model ships on every shelf. There is a compass in case I become disorientated in old age, and a pair of dividers and a set of Captain Fields' parallel rulers next to the kettle ready for use if Watchet floats out to sea as a result of global warming. A tidal clock ticks next to the tea-caddy so the tide can never catch me unawares if I nod off after lunch. Recently a man visiting for the first time asked whether I was by any chance interested in boats. He had a painful corn and had come hoping to see the chiropodist.

*******

The snooker room across the landing from the office is a quaint fifties time-warp in faded pink and pale green. It could be a set from the television classic *The Last of the Summer Wine*. The massive table, shrouded in sheets, is used mainly by elderly men. I joined the snooker club so that I could use their lavatory. There is a portrait of Winston Churchill as a middle-aged man above the lavatory door, and trophies on a nearby shelf include, inexplicably, a stuffed weasel. The walls are hung with stern warnings: DO NOT SMOKE OVER THE TABLE, PLEASE DO NOT SPIN COINS ON TO THE CLOTH OR CUSHIONS and DO NOT SIT ON THE HEATERS. When, shortly after moving in, I asked about fire-drill procedure, I was told, 'There's a good long rope. You can tie it to the leg of the snooker table and throw yourself out the window. You'll never move that bugger – he weighs nearly two ton.'

My blazer was dark blue and had black buttons embossed with the sort of vague crests found on pickle-jars and sauce bottles. Whenever I wore it I seemed to get invited to more meetings of organisations in the town and I found to my surprise that I came to quite enjoy taking it out of the wardrobe and releasing it from its transparent plastic cocoon.

I wore the blazer to numerous meetings about the harbour in the late 1990s. The docks had closed abruptly in 1993 and for the next seven years controversy raged over what best to do with the harbour and its three quays. A succession of unlikely schemes, including a hovercraft service to Wales and a whelk-boiling factory, came and went. A plan to build the Watchet Star – a hotel in the shape of a huge concrete liner – foundered under a tidal wave of incomprehension. Efforts to encourage other shipping lines to use the port came to nothing: small coasters using drying harbours were now virtually an extinct species. No one carried scrap iron and esparto grass, bicycles and wastepaper, hen food and skirting boards around the British coasts by sea any more.

By the mid-1990s, Watchet was a ghost port. Weeds grew on the empty quays and vandals were busy dismantling the warehouse. Only members of the boat owners' association and charter fishermen now used the harbour. All dredging and pilotage had long ceased but until the harbour was stripped of its official port status by act of parliament it was required to be manned by qualified staff. The harbourmaster and his assistant sat in their office day after day like Chekhov figures who were victims of forces beyond their control. The radio was silent, the phone rarely rang and ships sailed past to other destinations.

Meanwhile, the tide inexorably added an estimated forty tons a day to the hillocks of glistening slime. However, it was not until 1995 that the local council began to formulate its own plans for a 300-berth marina taking up half the harbour and retaining two metres of water at low tide. The marina would be accessed by a lock set in a massive wall stretching across the harbour from north to south.

The job of designing the project was given to a council official whose usual work involved drains and footpaths The scale of the scheme steadily diminished as promised grants turned out to be unavailable and one morning, at a meeting at which the drainage engineer's proposals were unveiled, we were told that some drastic economies had

had to be made. For instance the marina walls would not be built to full height but would actually disappear at high tide.

The general view was that it was an excellent job for a very reasonable price and the meeting was about to end when, as in the case of the late Major Ferchbind, I suddenly realised that something important needed to be said and no one else was going to say it. Still holding a coffee cup and two digestive biscuits, I said that I thought the council should be ashamed of itself.

I said that I had nothing personally against the drainage engineer and thought it unfair that he had been given a job for which he was the first to admit he was inexperienced, but I felt that if the present scheme went ahead future generations would curse us as the people who gave Watchet the marina equivalent of the *Titanic*. Leaving three hundred boats on pontoons largely unprotected from the winds and tides, which could turn the harbour into a maelstrom, was surely a recipe for disaster.

The plan was referred to a subcommittee for further discussion and those responsible for it were to be sent on a day excursion to Cardiff in order to see a marina in action. I went back to the office relieved that major folly had at least been temporarily averted. Shortly afterwards the engineer rang and harangued me for making 'silly statements'. I said that I thought that complaining about spending millions on a protective wall which would disappear when it was most needed was hardly silly, and hung up.

An hour later I left the office briefly to buy an orange in a small greengrocer's and general store run by a nice woman called Edna. I enjoyed shopping there: goods were displayed in the windows on paper doilies and once, when buying a quarter of ham for lunch, I overheard two elderly women discussing the death of an acquaintance.

'I didn't even know she was poorly. What did she die

of?' said one woman. 'Oh, it was nothing serious,' said the other.

As I emerged from the shop with my orange, a small car drew up and the engineer got out. He said he had been looking for me all over the town. He was obviously still extremely cross. He threw off his coat and placed it on a nearby wall. I felt it appropriate to point out that I was a man in late middle age with high blood pressure and that any unpleasantness might result in some sort of seizure.

By this time, several customers had left Edna's and were watching with interest from the pavement. A woman with a carrier bag of leeks spoke on my behalf, saying, 'I know this gentleman and his dog is friends with our dog.' Faced with such spirited opposition, the engineer seemed to lose interest in further discussion and drove away.

A few more drawings were produced but inevitably the scheme was eventually taken over by big business and a large private developer put in an impressive full-height impounding wall and marina costing £5.1 million in subsidies and grants. In due course the drainage engineer took early retirement. Later we shook hands over a drink and agreed to differ, although I think we both privately thought we had been right. He became a full-time artist and could be seen painting marina scenes on the Esplanade on fine days. I felt there was an irony there somewhere but I could never quite define it.

While the marina was being built, boats were removed from all the Watchet moorings and *Yankee Jack* spent the 2001 season six miles away in Minehead harbour, snugly protected from all but north-easterly winds by a wooded cliff and high walls. To the west there were coves and inlets to explore on sunny evenings, sometimes with Bob Eaglesfield, who lived in the town. Bob was about my age but was an active runner and motorcylist. He rode a 1960s-design Royal Enfield he had bought in India. We rarely saw another boat along a coastal landscape broken by rocky ridges and falling away to precipitous cliffs. Only five miles from Minehead at Hurlestone Point is a small beach on which the French schooner *La Mouette* went ashore in fog in 1913. Before a tug could reach her from Cardiff she broke her back on the rocks. Locals stripped the ship of anything worth taking. They said the bell and barometer found their way onto the wall of a local pub.

Some ten miles further to the west, Woody Bay has been called the finest piece of coastal scenery in Britain. The singer Elkie Brooks lived in a house perched almost vertically above the bay and huge oaks sweep down the cliffs like wooden waterfalls. The Victorians decided to build a jetty to bring steamers to this beautiful but sepulchral place only to find, when it was built, that there wasn't enough water to bring ships alongside. Bob and I once had an idyllic sail to Woody Bay: an easterly wafted us there, dropped while we ate our sandwiches and obligingly turned west for the run back. I had a feeling we would have to pay for such rare perfection and we did. A violent squall sent us scurrying back into Minehead bay where we dropped the sails and attempted to start the motor. As neither of us had brought our reading glasses we couldn't tell whether the fuel was turned on or off. Eventually the outboard started and with a convulsive jerk threw itself off the stern and disappeared. We had hit a submerged fishing stake. We rowed back to the mooring and recovered the engine at low tide. It seemed none the worse for its ordeal. Bob wondered whether we were perhaps getting a bit old to be allowed out sailing on our own. Soon afterwards he left the Bristol Channel and moved to the tranquillity of the River Dart.

*Yankee Jack* returned to Watchet that July for the official opening of the marina, an event which coincided with the annual carnival and brought thousands of visitors to the town. The day was hot and sunny and Watchet was in festive mood. Eight years after the docks had closed, the marina was finished at last. It was jammed with visiting boats rafted up three or four deep and cheerful with flags and bunting. Watchet was back in business. That night every pub in the town ran out of beer and fireworks made daylight of the sky.

The plan was that Sir Robin Knox-Johnston, back in the town, would officially open the marina by motoring out through the lock in an inshore lifeboat. *Yankee Jack*, dressed overall and with Bob Eaglesfield and me in bright red shirts and straw hats, would lead a procession of local boats which would follow him into the outer harbour. At least that was the intention, but as *Yankee Jack* motored forward to follow Sir Robin into the lock, the outboard abruptly seized solid, screwing the flattie round into the path of the dozen following boats. After three minor collisions, Bob seized the oars and we laboriously rowed through the lock, far behind the rest of the procession, which by then was on a lap of honour past the lighthouse.

We never did catch up. By the time we finally returned to the pontoons, people were getting drunk and jumping naked into the marina and we had missed most of the official lunch. The rowing debacle got two seconds of coverage on local television. Later, when I asked Sir Robin if he would like a trip in a flatner without getting his feet wet this time, he said that sadly he had to return to London but would certainly like to do it on some future occasion.

The marina has prospered and so has Watchet. House prices have more than doubled in the past five years and there are middle-class accents in the shops and pubs. Visitors come to look at the boats and the town has evolved to accommodate them. There are two museums and a fine-art gallery, four restaurants with tablecloths, and the milk bar is now a shop selling objects made from recycled timber. The electrical shop is an estate agent, the butcher's is now a boutique, and one of the banks is a centre for Celtic crafts. Miss Hibbert, an elderly *Guardian* reader, retired from selling sweets and bicycle parts. Her shop is now an up-market coffee house and delicatessen. A life-sized bronze statue of the Ancient Mariner, with crossbow and albatross, has been erected near my office and is frequently photographed by tourists. The Bristol Channel still delivers forty tons of mud per tide to the harbour but, with the retained water, no one can see it.

*******

'Tell us, Mr James,' said Mr Justice Broomfield, 'what exactly are your nautical qualifications?' I was standing in the witness box of Court 27 in London's Royal Courts of Justice on a hot Thursday afternoon, once more wearing my blazer, and appearing as an 'expert witness' in an insurance claim. In the silence of the oak-panelled courtroom they sounded quite impressive when noted down by the judge with a golden pen. Neither he nor the two QCs in the case further questioned my credentials. After all, everything I had said was basically true – or more precisely it was not basically untrue – but I could not help feeling slightly concerned that Mr Justice Broomfield was not perhaps getting the complete picture, and that there was still plenty of time for him to suss me out.

The case had begun several years earlier when a handsome young ornamental blacksmith named Dominic was driving his van home from work one evening along a country lane when he was confronted by a Dutch holiday-maker driving a hired car on the wrong side of the road. In the collision, Dominic suffered head injuries and spent some time in hospital. Afterwards he complained that he could no longer concentrate on his work and was suffering from a variety of nervous disorders ranging from anxiety to panic attacks. The Dutchman had immediately accepted liability for the accident but what had remained unresolved through long and bitter litigation was the exact extent of Dominic's suffering and how much it was worth in compensation.

The Dutchman's insurers, presumably convinced that Dominic was trying it on, had hired a private detective to spy on him and had him assessed by a Harley Street psychiatrist. For some time before the accident Dominic had been building a boat. It was a large and beautifully constructed steel gaff cutter, designed by his brother, in which he intended to cruise the world with his family. Already the traditional boat magazines had shown interest and Dominic hoped there would be enough commercial potential for him to produce a limited number for sale. The boat, looking somewhat like a transom-sterned pilot cutter, had been launched at Falmouth and had created a good deal of local interest. She was called *Rosebud*.

I had sailed on her the previous summer and found her surprisingly responsive for a big heavy boat, although, like *Shamrock*, she needed a high-activity crew. *Rosebud* was now ashore for fitting out, but Dominic claimed that since the accident he had neither the ability nor the enthusiasm to complete the boat and to construct others. Surely he should be compensated for this loss of potential income? Early in the claim negotiations, Dominic's solicitors had asked me to write a letter assessing the sales potential of the boat and whether I thought that Dominic in his present state was able to complete the project. There was absolutely no doubt, said the solicitors, that the case would be settled out of court. As another of Dominic's brothers was a close friend, I agreed to help.

I wrote a short letter saying that the boat was well designed and constructed and should appeal to a specialist market. From what I had seen of Dominic since the accident his mental and physical condition had dramatically declined. 'He certainly appears,' I wrote, 'to be a shadow of his former self.' I heard nothing and forgot all about it. Then a month later came a subpoena to appear before the High Court and a day-return railway ticket to London.

Arriving at the Royal Courts of Justice in the Strand on the third day of the hearing, I joined a small group of Somerset witnesses who were preparing to testify to Dominic's deteriorating condition. They seemed uneasy in the cathedral-like surroundings and most wore T-shirts and heavy boots. Apart from a middle-aged blacksmith who was making his first trip to London, I was the only one wearing a tie.

When witnesses' evidence was delayed by legal submissions, the Somerset party moved to a pub across the road from the court for several hours. When they did finally appear, they had little to contribute to the proceedings. My own evidence took less than five minutes and also appeared to have little bearing on the case. When counsel for the defendants asked what I meant by 'a shadow of his former self', I replied that I did not feel qualified to elaborate. The judge said that was a responsible answer and, even better, it was a short one. When Dominic's counsel asked whether all the Somerset witnesses could be dealt with in time for them to catch their late afternoon train from Paddington, the judge replied that as far as he was concerned he had heard quite enough already. At that point a man in a crumpled Taunton Cider T-shirt who had fallen asleep in the pub finally appeared in the court doorway, prompting the judge to cry, 'Hold the train – here's another one!'

The case dragged on for another week, and several years later had still not been resolved. Dominic, like a participant in Dickens' Jarndyce v. Jarndyce case, waits daily for a settlement, and meanwhile *Rosebud*, still unfinished, remains in the corner of a Mylor boat-park. Dominic now has a new partner and a small child and no longer talks about sailing around the world.

The day after I returned from London, I planned a short sail in *Yankee Jack*. With the newly acquired confidence of a legally acknowledged expert, I reversed briskly from the marina pontoon and straight into a passing yacht. The collision, loud enough to bring out several old men from the nearby snooker club, tore off the flattie's rudder, snapped the tiller and ripped the outboard from its bracket. The engine flew backwards into the water and disappeared into at least ten feet of mud. There was silence. Barry Humphries, a sailing friend, stood speechless at the tiller of his expensive yacht. He had bought the immaculate 34-footer only a few weeks earlier and was about to sail it to Spain. I tied the wreckage of *Yankee Jack* onto a nearby pontoon and hurried to inspect Barry's damage. What had I done? What would it cost? Together we examined the yacht's gleaming white side. Incredibly all we could find was a small blue mark which was removed with a rub of cutting paste. Once he had got over the shock and seen there was no harm done, Barry took the incident very calmly. Today when we meet he graciously never mentions it.

It took a month to repair the flatner and from time to time I took a dinghy out into the marina and poked about in the mud with a long stick but couldn't locate the engine. Brian Rich, sometimes known as Brian The Hat, who ran the local club boatyard, took me out several times in his fishing boat to the approximate site of the collision, where we unsuccessfully searched the harbour bed with an assortment of grapnel anchors. Brian said that if we didn't find it by the following week it would be too late: a suction dredger was arriving to clear the marina, and 40,000 tons of mud, and anything it contained, would be blown over the harbour wall.

Brian said he would have another look. Meanwhile, I returned to London with Myrtle, leaving behind yet another debacle that the Queen knew nothing about. More to the point, nor did her daughter, because Myrtle and I were on our way to meet the Princess Royal and I was anxious to make a good impression. We met the Princess at an RYA reception for provincial sailing clubs in the Commonwealth Institute. Myrtle looked very glamorous in a mauve suit borrowed from her sister. We stood in lines as the Princess, a small brisk woman, patrolled the room asking people where they came from. In front of her walked a man who whispered instructions on how to behave. We should address the Princess for the first time as 'Your Royal Highness' and subsequently as 'Mam', not 'Ma'am'. She would take the initiative when shaking hands.

The Princess had a very small hand in a soft blue glove. 'Where are you from?' she asked. 'Watchet, a small town in Somerset, Your Royal Highness. I shouldn't think you've heard of it,' I said. 'I think I passed by it once,' she replied. 'Most people do, Mam,' I said. The Princess smiled grimly and moved on. That evening Myrtle and I had supper in a restaurant in Kensington Church Street. At the next table two very fat men were boasting about publishing deals. I had a piece of fish the size of a Swan Vestas matchbox surrounded by strips of carrot looking like orange pencils. It cost £19. That night, lying in bed in a hotel Myrtle had booked in Hammersmith, listening to the traffic and thinking about the day, the cost of the fish remained the most persistent memory.

We returned to Watchet to find dredging had started the previous day. I was told by one of the old men who loitered on the Esplanade that at one point the dredger had encountered something in the mud which it had finally regurgitated over the wall with a sound apparently similar to that of an elephant being sick. I walked along the beach below the sea wall at low tide and found a fragment of the plastic casing of a Mariner outboard motor wedged in the rocks next to half a propeller. Reporting the accidental loss of a virtually new outboard engine to my insurance agent, I found I had forgotten to add it to the insurance policy.

Meanwhile *Yankee Jack*, now repaired, needed an engine and another brand-new Mariner was supplied by Terry, a local agent, who delivered the engine and told me to read the instruction book. I threw the book into a drawer. There wasn't much anyone could tell me about outboards. That evening I fixed the engine to the boat. It wouldn't start. I rang Terry and said that I couldn't help but feel let down, to which he replied that he would drive over the minute he had finished his supper. It was a forty-mile round trip, but luckily the problem was quickly found and easily rectified. There was no fuel in the tank. I gave Terry a tenner for his trouble – a small price to pay for a reminder of a timeless truth: in a sailor's life there's always something to learn.

CHAPTER 16

# Reflections on the sea

The following year I stopped sailing *Yankee Jack*, mainly because I was fed up with having to bail it out every time it rained. The flat bottom was divided into watertight sections. Each needed bailing with a plastic dustpan and there seemed no way of fitting an efficient bilge-pump. *Yankee Jack* is currently a main exhibit in the Watchet Boat Museum, standing on the spot where it was built, safe and sound and surrounded by its press cuttings. I will never sell the boat and like to think that in a few minutes it could be ready for sea. That's the theory, anyway. There are no immediate plans for any further sailing but there's fuel in the tank. At least I think there is.

Strange how quickly your attitude can change towards boats you no longer sail, and not always for the better. Phil rang me recently with news that *Shamrock*, now owned by another committee of well-wishers, was lying ashore in Lowestoft in a piteous state and was up for sale. 'I wonder if we should get the old gang together and buy her,' Phil said. A terrible weariness came over me. 'Done all that,' I said. 'Yes, maybe you're right,' Phil said. 'See you.' Like holiday romances, some things are best left as happy memories.

Recently I bought *Kittiwake*, a red GRP four-berth Bermudan-rigged fin-keeler, from my good friend Chris Webb, and for the first time in thirty years I have a sensible boat which can be sailed easily and safely. It takes some getting used to. Myrtle comes out when the weather's fine. We don't seem to make long trips any more, mainly because Chris has never got around to unearthing the boat's cooker from the depths of his garden shed, and you can't go far without a cup of tea.

Funny business, sailing. I've been doing it for fifty years and yet I still forget how to tie a rolling hitch if anyone's watching. I took up sailing for reasons that escaped me and they escape me still. I have been more frightened and humiliated by sailing than by any other human activity except perhaps riding a horse and getting married.

Note in diary, July 2005:

> Went out for a short sail with friend Sue and her daughter Emma. Not much wind but gloriously hot – could have been the Caribbean. Magic. Emma said she wants to live on a boat for ever.

For those rare moments when it all goes well, when it's as good as it gets, I guess that's why we do it.

Now in their thirties, my children Tim and Sophie remember the *Shamrock* days largely as inexorable boredom punctuated by cameos of pleasure and pain. Sophie is a highly talented actor with a growing reputation: two seasons at the National Theatre, eight months in *Coronation Street* (wronged wife Justine Davenport) and some nice one-offs like *The Bill*. She told me recently that, to break the monotony of one long and slow Channel passage, she had pierced her ears with a rusty drawing-pin from the chart table. She was nine. I had wondered what happened to that pin.

'We just got accustomed to going on the boat at weekends because mum wanted a break from us,' she told me recently. 'We couldn't do much on *Shamrock* because everything was too big and heavy and the crew said we got in the way. Usually we stayed in the cabin and ate Smarties and read the *Beano* and waited until we got somewhere. When friends came with us we played cards. In France we would go off and buy cakes. In the Channel Islands we took the dinghy and fished for crabs in pools. I remember once when I fell full length in the mud you carried me back to the boat like a brown parcel. You didn't say anything but I knew you were very cross.'

Tim remembers when, to escape the tail-end of the Fastnet gale, we locked into the little north Brittany port of Paimpol, where *Shamrock* stayed for several days until the weather improved. Tim got to know three French boys of around the same age. 'They were called Dee-Jay, Jan and Frederic and they became my best friends. When we sailed away we vowed to keep in touch but of course we never did. When I got home I wrote a song about them.'

When Tim moved to London to join a pop group and no longer came sailing, I assumed he had lost interest, but apparently he would hire dinghies on lakes and reservoirs. He dreamed of a future at sea. 'Even as a kid I knew what sort of sailing I wanted to do when I could afford my own boat – nice day-sails in sunshine and gentle breezes and overnight stops in sheltered bays with a good meal and glass of wine and a swim. I would take my own family sailing but I wouldn't do long hauls like you did. I wouldn't inflict that on my own kids because I' remember how boring it is for a child.'

A very successful media composer, Tim now lives in
Falmouth with his partner Juliet and their three young
sons, Ben, Harvey and Oscar. He sails a top-of-the-range
35-foot Moody with central heating and en-suite bathroom
but, true to his dream, he rarely ventures far from Carrick
Roads. The boat is named *Devoran*, after a village up the
Fal. They use her a lot. Tim sails her well and so does
Juliet, who is an RYA day skipper. The boys like helming
when it's rough. Otherwise they go below and play with
electronic toys. There is no sign of the *Beano*. The boat is
so full of electronic gadgetry that it virtually sails itself.
Feeling utterly superfluous, I sit in the cockpit and tie
figure-of-eight knots into the ends of ropes. Oscar, six, sits
out of the wind snuggled up to his aunt Sophie. They are
playing a quiz game Sophie has invented to allow Oscar to
ask all the questions.

'Think of a number between one and ten,' Oscar says.

'Five,' Sophie says.

'You have chosen to answer questions on boats,' says
Oscar. 'This is the question. What is the name of the Lord
Jesus?'

Back on the mooring at Mylor it's starting to rain as we
tidy up the boat and put things away. Eventually the family
is crammed into the dinghy, anxious to get ashore, while
Tim, alone on board, makes the ritual final checks. 'Come
on, Dad, for God's sake,' Ben says. He is eleven and
spokesman for the younger generation. Eventually Tim
boards the dinghy, starts the outboard and makes a slow
circuit round the boat. Just to make sure. He takes a look
over his shoulder as we motor away.

'Funny business, sailing,' I say. 'I really don't know why
we do it,' Tim says. 'You feel guilty if you do it, because
you feel you should be doing something more useful with
the time, and you feel guilty if you don't, because you've
spent all that money and you can't justify the expense.' He
looks up bleakly at the sky. 'Welcome to Maritime

Neurotics Anonymous,' I tell him. 'I've just proposed you as a life member.'

'You always did all that fiddling about,' Tim says. 'And now I find I'm doing exactly the same, and the kids shout at me just like Sophie and I did when we were little. But you can't help wondering if you've turned everything off.'

The rain increases. The boys are talking about going to their friends for a sleepover when they get back. Tim looks preoccupied as he steers the dinghy through the crowded moorings towards the shore. I assume that he is still wondering whether he actually turned off the gas. Without a word, he and I simultaneously turn to look back once more, just to check, but by now the boat has vanished in the rain.

# TONY JAMES

Tony James is a freelance journalist and writer. Formerly he was a theatrical entrepreneur, magazine agony aunt, crime-writer, Fleet Street editor and education correspondent of the Jamaican *Daily Gleaner*. The author of over twenty books, he still writes regularly for thirty publications worldwide. For a ghosted autobiography of the football legend Pele he became the first British recipient of the Brazilian Government's *Fire Urn of Culture*. Sadly the trophy was lost in the post.

Tony lives with his partner Vivienne on the edge of Exmoor. When not at sea he plays jazz trombone and makes model boats. Over the last fifty years he has sailed the equivalent of twice around the world, stopping off as often as possible for chocolate cake. He still doesn't really know why he goes sailing.